UNDERSTANDING
ISLAMIC ARCHITECTURE

UNDERSTANDING ISLAMIC ARCHITECTURE

Edited by
Attilio Petruccioli and Khalil K. Pirani

with a foreword by
Oleg Grabar

RoutledgeCurzon
Taylor & Francis Group

First published 2002
by RoutledgeCurzon
11 New Fetter Lane, London EC4P 4EE

Simultaneously published in the USA and Canada
by RoutledgeCurzon
29 West 35th Street, New York, NY 10001

RoutledgeCurzon is an imprint of the Taylor & Francis Group

Printed and bound in Great Britain by
Biddles Ltd, Guildford and King's Lynn

British Library Cataloguing in Publication Data
A catalogue record of this book is available from the British Library

Library of Congress Cataloguing in Publication Data
A catalogue record for this book has been requested

ISBN 0–7007–1437–5 (Hbk)
ISBN 0–7007–1438–3 (Pbk)

In Search of Understanding Islamic Architecture

Table of Contents

Section I

Meaning from Faith

Section II

Meaning from History

Section III

Contemporary Trends

Preface

The contributions in this book represent an effort to clarify how the various disciplines of the design profession can be employed to build in the spirit of Islam. It is not the intent of the book to prescribe or identify a specific formula.

The aim of this book is to energize the debate in academia and among practitioners on the meaning of Islamic architecture, particularly among architects who seldom get to participate in these discussions. Very often seminars, lectures and conferences are limited to academicians. Practitioners—who are primarily responsible for designing buildings—do not get to participate in such discussions. This book is an attempt to or at least started with the intent to discuss this issue for the benefit of practicing architects and clients.

The rationale for inviting essays from various professionals was to bring diverse thought processes together in the debate. Each essay was peer reviewed and the author was provided the opportunity to respond. Given the complexity of the subject, combining article, comments, and responses elicited diverse viewpoints from architects, planners, academicians, and theoreticians.

Issues raised in this book can then be applied to architecture and living environment in the broadest possible terms for the betterment of all humanity in any culture, society and country.

Acknowledgements

We extend our greatest appreciation to all the authors for giving us the benefit of their knowledge, wisdom and insight on this complex subject. In addition, we convey our thanks to the reviewers who so painstakingly reviewed the articles and offered their comments and suggestions. Thanks to Professor Oleg Grabar for his suggestions and encouragements, and for writing the foreword for this book. Much of the work for this book was completed under the auspices of the Aga Khan Program for Islamic Architecture at MIT. We would like to acknowledge the assistance and support of the staff at the Program office particularly Alberto Balestrieri. We are also grateful to Margaret Sevcenko for helping edit the essays and to the Aga Khan Trust for Culture for allowing us to use images. Last, but not least, our deepest gratitude to the Barakaat Foundation for their generous grant to cover the manufacturing cost of the book.

Foreword

When, nearly half a century ago, I was taking the first steps toward becoming a historian of Islamic art and architecture, no one really worried much about what these terms actually meant. Matters, then, were quite simple: there was a geographical area with a history and a culture and our task was to tell, as intelligently and sensitively as possible, the story of that art, to explain the monuments, occasionally to elaborate on their context, perhaps to evaluate their quality and their impact on later times or on surrounding areas. Hardly anyone worried about the contemporary scene except as a possibly exotic backdrop to intellectual, scientific, and therefore presumably objective ambitions.

At some point, perhaps already in the sixties, certainly in the seventies and eighties, the contemporary world entered the ivory tower of the Orientalist scholar. It did so in three ways.

One way was the involvement of practicing architects, westerners called to build, plan, or design in Muslim lands or practitioners from Muslim lands often trained in and operating from non-Muslim centers. Psychological and ideological needs of new nations, practical problems created by demographic growth, and a newly acquires wealth in many Muslim countries led to massive building projects which required, if not a philosophy, at least a set of guidelines, a collection of formal and verbal slogans to justify, at times even to inspire designers and builders. Historians, it was thought, and even philosophers and theologians were seen as possible sources for such statements.

The second way could be defined as a mixture, not always successful, of new research in the social sciences (instead of the humanities which had prevailed earlier) and reactions against a paternalistic Orientalism. The former brought to the fore the anthropologist's or sociologist's involvement with an actually existing society, with its life, its behavior, its economic state, its hopes, its fears, and its traditions; it also adopted a vocabulary if reflection and of explanation derived from the works of brilliant European and American theorists. The latter questioned the motives behind so much concern with the Muslim world by non-Muslims and suggested, without doing much about it, that the terms by which a society's architecture is to be defined must come from the traditions of that society, a predominantly Muslim one. In many ways, the sharp debate between "modernism" and " post-modernism," so visible in the pages that follow, is an extension, with modifications of course, into contemporary criticism of the earlier critique of Orientalist writing by so many publicists since the mid seventies.

And the third way in which the contemporary world entered the foray is political and ideological. Social or governmental authority wanted to express its existence and its power through forms that would at the same time demonstrate the modernity of the nation-state or of society and exhibit its relationship to past traditions or to old ways. Some of these ideological pressures were national, in ways well known in Europe; some were regional, although regional definitions did not usually fare very well; but, for reasons which go much beyond the scope of this foreword, most of them were given the label "Islamic." Thus were united in the same bag very different areas and histories, like Morocco's or Indonesia's, and a series of learned seminars and books outlined what is, was, or should be "Islamic" in visual forms, especially in architecture.

All these contemporary approaches and concerns appear in the essays which follow. They are argued with some of the same documents and with many new ones. Ultimately, they probably come into conflict with what I would like to call a "new modernism." Most strikingly expressed in the concept of "typology" as developed by some of the writers, it implies a universality of procedures rather than of forms or techniques in understanding or explaining anything architectural. Only the superstructure, the appearance, of a building or of a new urban ensemble can or should be defined through terms like "Islamic" or "Tunisian" or "Bangladeshi," or even "European Islamic." Deep down, the infrastructure represents the needs and functions which are local and immediate, successfully treated or not, beautiful or unattractive. This is so even if the patron, the maker, and the user prefer to identify and define the work under consideration in culturally restricted terms.

The debate will continue. In fact, there never will be an answer to the correct way of designing within any one culture or to classify and evaluate whatever creation one contemplates. This is so, because man and his built environment are in a constant state of flux, even if man sometimes would like to stop and feel that all is good around him. In the meantime, essays such as the ones that follow, serve to sharpen the mind of the reader to understand the architecture of today, if not that of the past.

Oleg Grabar
Institute for Advanced Study

Introduction

The urban landscape of the Islamic city, both in developing countries blessed by petroleum such as Dubai or Oman and in economically depressed ones like Pakistan, is desolating. New urban development is the suffocating counterpart of mostly rundown colonial neighborhoods and old *medinas*, progressively abandoned for the new housing schemes. These new neighborhoods cannot even be blamed for the sterile urban decor that characterized previous ones: they are urban aggregates lacking any order and coherency, propped down in splendid isolation or mutual competition. Inspired on one hand by international design reviews, and on the other by western living models promoted by global media, their architecture has lost all reference to local tradition, and eclectically adapted to the ever-increasing standardization of cultural and architectural values. As mirrored in contemporary urban development, this loss of identity is the result of a two-fold crisis of architecture. The first is what we may define as "internationalism"—the illusion brought by the Modern Movement that different cultures could express themselves by using the same language. Paradoxically the International Style has devastated more the Islamic environments because of their eagerness for progress, identified tout court with the Western product. As a result all the airports of the world are the same, depriving the traveler of the pleasure of leaving and arriving; all the markets are the same, clean and odorless, depriving the buyer of the pleasure of the human contacts with the shopkeepers; but worstly all the residential quarters tend to be the same, depriving people of their identity.

The second is the rise of the figure of the "designer", leading to the self-referential statements of today's architectural star system as products of a consumer society. In general terms, this crisis is the outcome of a long-lived cultural involution of the Western world, the origin of which can be traced back to the Enlightenment. From the XIXth century the architectural discipline started to run after the artistic one, forgetting the deep differences from practice, objectives and even rituals. In fact a building first of all has to stand and work for the users, which is not required to the piece of painting or sculpture. Its ultimate result is the progressive fall of the common architectural know-how that had built cities for centuries: the lack of collective spontaneous conscience no longer plays an active role in the building of society. During the involution of architectural praxis, the Modern Movement, despite its 1930's research on social housing, represented its lowest point by its deliberate rupture from architectural heritage. The notion of historical discontinuity brought to a progressive alienation of contemporary urban peripheries and to the concept of architecture as creation ex-nihilo based on abstract, self-referenced design methods. Although their social and political structure didn't allow major transformations, most Islamic countries have indirectly suffered of this Western crisis during the colonial period. They have been indirectly intoxicated like an innocent fetus of an alcoholic mother. Furthermore, Islam went through its own cultural crisis at the end of the Caliph domination, which coincided with the fall of the territorial and political unity of Dar al-Islam. Ever since, progressively and continuously the cultural strength of Islam was first influenced then eroded by western capitalism, ultimately provoking a religious reaction that imposed a literal interpretation of the Koran in all aspects of political, economic and social life.

At this point we need to clarify what I mean by "crisis". It should not be intended as an irreversible catastrophe, but as a difficult transition period characterized by a lack of clear ideas and objectives. However, each crisis contains in itself the seed of a positive evolution. Once lost the spontaneous conscience of how to do, that was typical of the medieval artisan, it cannot be recovered. It could be reconstructed only a-posteriori by a critical conscience. A critical conscience and an objective analysis of the existent situation, i.e. the build landscape that everyone has inherited from the past in a given cultural area, are the necessary conditions to understand the causes and identify the appropriate solutions to overcome the crisis. However, it should be also clear that a disciplinary problem can be only solved from within - alternative approaches relying on economic, social or political sciences have rarely been able to help in practice, if not proved to be completely misguiding. The sum of all statistical data on a city would not, could not, and should not portray city form nor produce urban design.

The approach necessary to overcome such contemporary uncertainty consists of a courageous turn-around of today's architectural discourse, one capable to take the distance from ephemeral fashion, from the cult of the architectural object, from self-referenced debate through international architecture media, and from individualism and nihilism at once. This approach is one of a humble and honest research in order to retrieve objective data and design criteria—one that centers on the critical observation of the building landscape. In its view, the existent local architectural context is the only objective reference point. It also represents reality, thus the truth, for what has already happened cannot be false. The building landscape is seen as the layering of design ideas and rules over time evolved according to dynamic historical processes. This architectural layering is the collective memory of the society that produced it—a canvas containing all traces of its transformation in time. It is in this complex palimpsest that the Western and the Islamic worlds ought to search independently in order to find principles and rules for building the future.

The analysis of these historical processes cannot focus on each building, as exemplified by the scarce methodological utility of many studies on vernacular architecture. It is as if a biologist studied mosquitoes one by one. On the contrary, it is necessary to adopt a research method capable to group individual entities in structural categories. This is the concept of "type". We may define it as "the organic ensemble of the common characters of buildings in a defined cultural area and over a defined period of time." The second part of this definition represents the new aspect of this methodology, as opposed to the formalistic interpretation of type suggested by Aldo Rossi and Leon Krier in the 80's. It implies that type, and in particular the residential one, is based on local building features as expression of a precise culture settled in a territory—it is not shared nor exported to other cultures. Moreover, type changes in time: being one with the culture that produces it, it constantly evolves, following the evolution and involution phases of its society. In synthesis, the concept of "type" is a dynamic process, never a formal scheme. Understanding and evaluating the building landscape entails the analytical reconstruction of its evolution—the retrieval of its "typological process". This is a crucial operation in understanding one building as well as assessing an urban area or a landscape before any intervention. In the definition of type, the word "organic" is of an essential importance, for it excludes all positivist sciences based on strict classifications. Inspired by the Vitruvian notion of architecture as a combination of *firmitas* (load bearing structure), *utilitas* (distribution and use), and *venustas* (language, but also legibility), the adjective "organic" implies that type cannot be a simple scheme but a structure made of inseparable parts behaving according to a hierarchical order and collaborating one with the other. The typological process aims to synthesize its evolution throughout its history. Each process is the formalized expression of one or more cultural phenomena—their evolution, involution, overlapping, substitutions and transformations. It simultaneously mirrors and transposes in architecture the values and actions of its civilization, where religion and culture were once considered as one in the Islamic world. If we agree that an architecture project should be the continuation of this typological process in the future, its realization should be almost automatic, for it continues and reinterprets previous rules in a coherent manner.

In this case the problem of reintroducing the religious sentiment into the design is not an issue. Simply it is. In fact, all the great works of Islam in the past were realized by humble craftsmen who always worked in the name of God. Architecture was a social and religious task requiring great skills and responsibilities toward the community. It was the product of constant training and tireless repetition of the same exercise as many times as it took to reach perfection. Architectural principles retrieved through the typological process by a critical conscience will contain the religious sentiment in them. If, on the contrary, the project is seen as an artist's invention, Avant Gard style, then religious values, regardless if orthodox or symbolic, are detached from architecture and reduced to mystical criteria to justify unclear design choices. On the other hand, in those extreme cases of literal interpretation of the Koran, religion risks to become an easy alibi of poor design. In either case, the same mistakes will be repeated over and over again: arches and domes as formal decor (for they recall people of a generic and outdated Islamic imagery), and exaggerated, gratuitous expressionism often played on natural lighting as the personification of the Divine. The most eloquent example of the latter is the Banglanagar Capital mosque designed by Louis Kahn in Dhaka, where openings at the four corners of the roof over a simple cubic volume diffuse natural light on the interior concrete walls. Louis Kahn's mosque certainly is an admirable space—one capable to invite and inspire prayer. I am not sure if it is also an Islamic space. Le Corbusier at Ronchamp uses the same design approach with excessive contentment. The small openings characterizing the side facade were inspired by the small Bou Noura mosque in M'zab— a design choice exemplifying the acritical adoption and manipulation of design elements freely drawn from other cultures. In both cases we are witnessing the use of only one of the three Vitruvian elements: *venustas* has been used to the detriment of the other two. In other cases, in order to demonstrate the modern character of new Islamic architecture, technological components are often overdone or detached from plan layouts, functional distribution or structural organization, thus reducing technical innovation to mere decor (as for example in the photovoltaic veneer of the Institute du Monde Arabe in Paris). In the past, architecture has never refused innovative materials and techniques. However, it has adopted them when they represented a real improvement to the building as a whole. On the other hand, architecture has never let a material down until it had fully experimented all its possibilities. Great lessons for contemporary design— professionally and spiritually.

In conclusion I believe that far from aiming to re-sew architecture and religion together, and from sterile repropositions of vernacular canons, the crucial issue is the retrieval of the generative rules of design according to the principles history has left in the building landscape.

Attilio Petruccioli

Section I

MEANING FROM FAITH

Essays in this section attempt to draw meaning from the faith Islam. Concepts expressed by the authors do not necessarily reflect the ideas of the editors and are open to each reader interpretation. Regardless of the approach adopted by individual authors and proposals made, one theme that is common to all essays is that they all propose a built environment that is universally beneficial to all humanity.

Mohammed Arkoun shares his experiences from the 1995 Aga Khan Award Jury deliberations about two very different mosques. Using these as examples he discusses his understanding of the spirit of Islam. Nader Ardalan uses the example of the paradise garden and discusses Koranic terms and their meanings that an architect should embody in creating architecture. He supports his arguments by sharing projects from his recent practice. S. Gulzar Haider has mapped the faith of Islam in four distinct contexts and then cross-referred these concepts with different building types. Abdul Rehman extracts references from the Koran and attempts to create a connection between historical monuments of Islamic societies and the Faith. Khalil K. Pirani uses Koranic verses to put forth concepts that may provide directions for building in the spirit of Islam.

Spirituality and Architecture

Mohammed Arkoun

Architecture is "built" meaning. It fatefully expresses who we are.

Charles Jencks

[Harmonious proportions] arouse, deep within us and beyond our sense, a resonance, a sort of sounding board which begins to vibrate. An indefinable trace of the Absolute which lies in the depth of our being. This sounding board which vibrates in us is our criterion of harmony. This is indeed the axis on which man is organized in perfect accord with nature and probably with the universe.

Le Corbusier

They will ask you concerning the Spirit. Say to them, the Spirit (ruh) is from the Command of my Lord and of knowledge you have been vouchsafed but little.

Koran 17:85

The concept of spirituality is loaded with meanings and connotations. It is used loosely in contexts as varied as religion, architecture, music, painting, literature, philosophy, and alchemy, as well as in spiritualism, astrology, and esoteric knowledge, to mention a few. The passages just quoted refer to three of them. In the first, art and architectural criticism, it is supposed to make explicit in a rational, analytical discourse the "harmonic proportions" inherent in the work of artists and architects, which emerges in the form of a poem, a picture, a symphony, or a building. In the second, it is the lyrical-romantic expression of that which the artist/creator feels and projects into words whose connotations are more complex, abstract, and specula-tive than those the work of art can actually convey to the observer or receiver (for example, a building of Le Corbusier does not necessarily possess all the resonance expressed in his quotation). In the third, a religious discourse has been transformed by generations of believers into a source of spiritual experience projected onto the "revealed word of God."

In this essay, I shall not consider the visions, conceptions, practices, and discourses generated by spiritism, esotericism, astrology, theosophy and animism, although these psycho-cultural spheres of human manifestation interact in many ways with the undefined field of spirituality, which is more closely related to creative imagination, aesthetic works in different fields of the arts, and religious and transcendental values. Because these overlapping forces, notions, concepts, spheres, and fields converge in the meaning of the word spirituality, the efforts of art critics, philosophers, theologians, historians, anthropologists, and psychoanalysts are essential to achieve precision and coherence in a matter which, until now, has been continuously confused.

As a historian of Islamic thought, I agree with the architectural critic who raises such problems as "the power of a reigning paradigm" (although I would restrict the reigning paradigms to those in a given language and for each language to successive periods). There is also the problem of interpreting phrases such as "the creative use of new languages" stemming from "the developing story of cosmogenesis."[1] These problems are evidence of the profound cultural gap and historical differences that exist between Islamic and Western contexts when they confront spirituality and architecture.

I shall begin with the basic assumptions about spirituality that characterize the Islamic tradition, and then identify a number of unperceived and therefore unthought-out issues that are raised by so-called religious architecture and spiritual expressions in contemporary "Islamic" contexts.

Glimpses into Spirituality in the Islamic Tradition

In the series "World Spirituality," Seyyed Hossein Nasr edited two volumes devoted to Islamic spirituality entitled *Foundations* (1987) and *Manifestations* (1991). In these works, spirituality is presented as a purely religious quest originating with the Koran and the hadith; rites are described in terms of their "inner meaning" and Sufism is referred to as "the inner dimension of Islam." Reality itself is reinterpreted in the framework of this constructed spirituality; literature, thought, architecture, and the arts are also annexed to this spirituality, which is actually a complex combination of subjective desires, hopes, and representations embodied in rites and words, and projected onto spaces, places, time, cultural works, and so forth. God, the angels, the cosmos, and eschatological expectations are simultaneously both sources and objects of spiritual contemplation, the initiators and ultimate references of the systems of values and beliefs transmitted and reproduced with devotion in each spiritual tradition. All individuals born and trained in such a tradition spontaneously share the inherited values and psychological mechanisms of spiritualization, sacralization, transcendentalization of the profane, and the modest realities of their own environments.

It is crucial to make a clear distinction here between spirituality, sacredness, and transcendence as substantive values used in theology and classical metaphysics, and spiritualization, sacralization, and transcendentalization as the products of the agents of social, cultural, and historical activities. This difference will become clear with the following example of the "wrong" mosque.

Spirituality in all cultural traditions has not yet been analyzed and reinterpreted with the new conceptual tools that were elaborated in the neurosciences to map the spiritual functions of the brain. Thus, the history of spirituality has to be (re)written in light of this neuroscientific approach. Fundamentalist believers from all religions will immediately reject such a "positivist" explanation. It is true that intellectual modernity has generated two competitive psychological frames of mind: the spiritualist attitude sticks to the mythical, metaphorical, lyrical cognitive system taught by traditional religions (as described in the World Spirituality series); the empirical scientific attitude does not reject spirituality and its various manifestations but aims to elucidate and to differentiate between spirituality, spiritualism, phantasmagoria, subjective arbitrary representations, theosophic constructions, et cetera.

This critical approach to spirituality is absent in Islamic contexts today; political scientists and sociologists speak of the "return to religion," the "awakening of Islam," the struggle of an emotional, unthought-out spirituality opposed to "Western materialism and positivism." Within this confusing ideological discourse, which is disguised by religious claims and vocabulary, great architects are commissioned to revitalize, restore, and preserve "Islamic" cities; to design "Islamic" urban patterns, not only with select, often stereotypical "Islamic" features, but also with mosques juxtaposed to—or inserted in—airports, universities, banks, hospitals, palaces of justice, parliaments, factories, and so forth. Whether the architects themselves do or do not have an Islamic background is not important; what matters is the content and the functions they give to spirituality in the present cognitive, anthropological mutations that are imposed upon the human condition.

It is a well-documented fact that many leading architects who have tried to build mosques in "the spirit of Islam" have neither a critical historical understanding of what the spirit of Islam might be nor an anthropological approach to what I have called the "metamorphosis of the sacred."[2] Are the main components of the mosque—*mihrab*, *minbar*, minaret, courtyard, ablution fountain—intrinsically Islamic and therefore unchangeable, or are they arbitrary forms and signs made orthodox by theological definitions and made sacred by rituals established over centuries? Islamic thought itself has not changed intellectually, conceptually, politically, or culturally to any significant degree since the thirteenth or fourteenth century. Consider two striking verses from the Koran:

> And those who took a place of worship (*masjid*) out of opposition and disbelief, in order to generate dissent among the believers and to provide a place of ambush for those who warred against God and His messenger aforetime, they will surely swear: we purposed naught save good. God bears witness that they verily are liars.
> Never stand there [for prayer]! A place for worship founded for piety from the first day is more worthy that you stand in it. Therein are men

Mohammed Arkoun

Figure 1. View of the Grand National Assembly mosque, Ankara, Turkey. (Photo courtesy AKTC)

who love to purify themselves; God loves the purifiers. (9: 107-8)

These two verses clearly show how spiritual values, sacred places, and religious truths which are considered to be absolute, intangible and ultimate references, are historically contingent and dictated by a violent confrontation between social and political groups of believers still struggling for survival; the opposing group, called the "warriors against God," founded a place for worship to compete with the same semiological tools used by the believers. Potentially, at this point in the competition, either of the two groups could have won the confrontation and imposed its own semiological code as the transcendental, sacred, unalterable model for pious reproduction.

A Reappraisal of Religious Architecture
The 1995 Aga Khan Award master jury had long and fruitful deliberations on two mosques: the Great Mosque and the redevelopment of the old city center of Riyadh, and the mosque for the Grand National Assembly in Ankara. Rather than proposing a model to be followed, the Award has always aimed at encouraging debate on innovative solutions to changing situations and new challenges. In this case the jury felt that neither of the two mosques under consideration deserved an award purely for architectural merit, but both had raised important questions related to religious architecture in two very different ideological contexts. The solutions proposed for each were clearly dictated by two diametrically opposed attitudes toward Islam and secularism.

The Riyadh mosque conforms strictly to traditional models with all of the usual components; as in all heavily financed mosques throughout the world, including Europe, religion is celebrated in architecture with large volumes, ostentatious luxury, and sumptuous spaces, which suggest the will to power, material wealth, and physical comfort, rather than a concern for aesthetics, emotions, harmony and intimate peace, or the urge for spiritual contemplation.

The architect for the Riyadh mosque is a Muslim and certainly familiar with the ancient and recurrent opposition between *taqlid* (the strict repro-

Mohammed Arkoun

5

Figure 2. Interior view of the Grand National Assembly mosque, Ankara, Turkey. (Photo courtesy AKTC)

duction of orthodox teachings in one of the recognized theological-juridical schools) and *ijtihad* (the individual intellectual endeavor to seek new, original solutions for new situations). Facing the task of building a mosque in an urban setting largely shaped by modern city planning and pompous modern buildings is no different from searching for a new definition of "personal status" (*al-ahwal al-shakhsiyya*). No architect can change the expression of "orthodox" forms, features, and components of mosques just as no theologian-jurist can introduce any change in "personal status" which has been fixed by divine law.

How did the Turkish architect handle the problem? Turkey is a secular republic; the Grand National Assembly was created by Atatürk in 1923. As in its French Republican model, religious beliefs are private affairs, and control of public space is the monopoly of the state. That is why commissioning a mosque on parliament premises could not be done by the Turkish deputies until 1984. The challenge is unique in the contemporary Muslim world, and we

can easily imagine the enormous difficulties that the architect confronted when he set about building a mosque like a modest chapel, scaled down, and hidden underground. The triumphant minaret is suppressed, the mihrab opens onto a beautiful green garden; the main mosque components usually expected and demanded in a mosque are avoided or modified. Whether this *ijtihad* is a success or failure in architectural terms remains to be considered, but the posture of mind adopted by the architect to interpret in a modern context a venerable semiological legacy deserves attention and was the subject of an exceptional debate in the Aga Khan Award for Architecture, which, as an organization, is a unique space for free thinking, free expression, and free and constructive criticism which starts from and relies upon architecture, artistic creativity, and spirituality, not on abstract, dogmatic, militant ideologies.

It is obvious that the mosque in Riyadh aims to translate into an architectural vocabulary the orthodox theological statement that God's sovereignty supersedes any human claim to sovereignty, al-

Mohammed Arkoun

though the neo-traditional design of the mosque, its conservative style, and the lavish materials fail to deliver an authentic spiritual message. The mosque of the Grand National Assembly does the opposite: it affirms the priority—but not necessarily the primacy—of popular sovereignty and the privatization of religious belief or God's sovereignty in a secular, democratic republic.

The 1995 master jury did not favor either one of these competing statements, but there is an urgent need to provide more examples, more potential solutions that can enhance criticism and cultural debate in the still poorly explored field of architecture and urban fabric. The contention is that architects, more efficiently than intellectuals and scholars, can resist the devastating violence generated by the confrontation of religion, state and society (*din, dunya, dawla*, the three major concepts developed in classical Arabic thought) on a greater scale than all societies and cultures in history have achieved thus far. This means that all important architectural achievements contribute either to strengthening the dominant ideology in any given historical tradition and political order or to creating a breakthrough in the inherited, imposed system of values and beliefs. In contemporary Islamic contexts, the second possibility still meets with many obstacles; the historical, intellectual, and cultural gap that separates them from Western societies, where "the jumping universe" is explored, thought about, and expressed simultaneously in all fields of human existence. This gap is widening, and is likely to increase even more in the next few years.

If, like other artistic expressions, architecture translates the main trends of the dominating cognitive system and cultural representations in a given tradition, then we must recognize that the built environment in contemporary Muslim societies is under the influence of a generalized ideological bricolage, which can also be described as a semantic disorder.

High-tech images such as the Hajj airport terminal in Jedda, the IBM tower in Kuala Lumpur, and many other public buildings emerge among the more or less stereotypical "traditional" city centers with their conventional mosques in redundant, populist, or ostentatious styles and their monotonous social housing complexes and slums. The rift that has developed between the hard and the social sciences; between high technology and the quest for authenticity and identity; between the demands for modern, efficient economies and the dogmatic rigidity of moral, religious, and juridical authorities that delay the emergence of citizens, individuals, civil society, and patriarchal political systems that perpetuate in many cases predatory states must be analyzed in order to explain why the quest for meaning has such a long way to go in combating the will to power. My contention is that the field of "spirituality and architecture" is the richest, the most promising and most rewarding, where human desire for a better life and affective, aesthetic environments can best achieve pluralistic manifestations and optimal satisfaction.

Notes

1. Charles Jencks, *The Architecture of the Jumping Universe,* Academy Editions, London, 1995, p 153.

2. In *The Mosque*, edited by Martin Frishman and Hasan Uddin Khan, Thames and Hudson, London, 1994, p 268-72.

• • • • • • • • • • • • •

Comments
Oleg Grabar

I am not convinced that spirituality is a meaningful concept in architecture, because it cannot be an attribute of built forms as such. Spirituality can be applied to human behavior in architecture, but cannot be imposed by architecture. In other words, while I suppose it is conceivable that there is an architecture that makes spirituality impossible to achieve, I can-

Mohammed Arkoun

not imagine an architecture that compels it, unless the user is already spiritually inclined. I am also dubious about an abstract spirituality that seems to lack concrete cultural or religious references. A *mihrab* and a minaret are Muslim signs, they could be symbols, but they do not inspire a Muslim spirituality; they only signal the possibility for a Muslim to act out his spiritual yearnings. As to a broader universal spirituality, it can only come from men, not from buildings, although I may concede that some buildings or spaces are more inspiring than others. Shrines operate better than mosques, because their associations are exclusively with piety.

Response

I would agree fully with the terms used by my friend Oleg Grabar in his short comments on my text if he accepts the following additional remarks I did not make in my presentation, namely that "spirituality is a meaningful concept in architecture," nor did I claim that spirituality can ever be "imposed by architecture" only. I have the same approach to spirituality as I do to that other complex concept, currently used, but still debatable in its real content and functions--that is, the sacred. In my contribution to *The Mosque*, a book edited by my friend Hasan Uddin Khan, I wrote on the metamorphosis of the sacred, just as I suggested that spirituality is not a substantial, intangible, given value, but is subject to change in the conditions of its emergence, its genesis, its functions. Both spirituality and the sacred are experiences strongly related to religious experiences; that is why we are accustomed to interpreting them with the same theological, essentialist criteria applied to all major religious values; we think of these values and related teachings in the intellectual frame described, analyzed, criticized by Michel Foucault under the expression *thematique historico-transcendantale*. This thematic is still alive and influential in the current discourse as well as in the more elaborated academic thinking. It is certainly a decisive dimension of all inherited systems of thought, including, of course, the metaphysical systems commanding the philosophical tradition going back to Classical and Neoplatonic Greek thought. It is well known that Platonic spirituality and Islamic spirituality had many deep interferences; classical metaphysics and various theological elaborations in Jewish, Christian, and Islamic traditions have inspired many essays, teachings, and interpretations. The paper presented by Nader Ardalan is a clear illustration of this line of thinking. Ever since what is currently called the return or awakening of Islam, there has been a strong tendency to use Islamization as a counterweight to Westernization. All manifestations of modern life, knowledge, thought, art have to be given an Islamic character and definition opposing their "spiritual" inspiration to a materialist, secularized, irreligious one. When this opposition is systematically applied to all fields of human activity it becomes, of course, ideological: it is more political than intellectual or spiritual.

Mohammed Arkoun

"Simultaneous Perplexity": The Paradise Garden as the Quintessential Visual Paradigm of Islamic Architecture and Beyond

Nader Ardalan

The request of the editors to discuss what the fundamental concepts of Islamic architecture might be brought back memories of many such searches related to the architecture of various world cultures in which it has been my privilege to work over the past thirty-five years of architectural practice. Without hesitation, I considered that the answers had to deal with the themes of how we think about architecture; the important role that alchemy[1] has played in Islamic architecture and the visual paradigm of the paradise garden.[2]

This in turn brought to mind the observations of the late Professor Toshihiko Izutsu, the noted scholar of comparative world philosophies, who said, "At the high level of abstraction, human nature is the same the world over."[3] He sought a marked personal and cultural "coloring" in the key philosophic concepts of the different world cultures, however. Through a rigorous philological world survey, he found in the "lower realms of human existence and practical experience," the core of transcendent conceptual seeds that constantly links a particular key philosophic concept with the higher, universal realm of the Absolute. By seeking ever deeper into the concrete and immeasurable that differentiated cultures, he was led in his research to the archetypal and immutable truths that are common to the human condition.

In my own far less complete studies, I too was made conscious of the unity of cultures expressed in the diverse architectural traditions of the world. Yet, my specific exploration of such universal expressions has focused primarily on their manifestation in Islamic cultures and the unique coloring that distinguishes this architecture from others.

In this essay, I would like to give an example of this particular way of viewing Islamic architecture, as an outgrowth of both the measurable forces of the "lower realm" and the immeasurable forces of the "higher realm". This exploration will be placed within the general theme of the *wahdat-i wujud* (unity of existence), as conceived by the very original thinker of the twelfth century, Muhyid Din Ibn Arabi of Andalusia and brilliantly elucidated and explained by Professor Izutsu in many of his works.[4]

The specific theme selected is the concept of paradise, from its ancient conceptual beginnings in Mesopotamia and ancient Persia; its incorporation into the Ibrahimic faiths, with special reference to Islamic culture as a key idea within the Koran; and as manifested in the classical gardens, arts, carpets, and metaphoric poetry of diverse Islamic cultures. I will also consider how this theme, as an ever-vital design conception of place making, has been integrated into contemporary designs.

The Paradise Garden as a Visual Paradigm

A visual paradigm is a mental model with form. In alchemy, a paradigm is reached only at the culmination of a three-stage process of purification, transmutation, and crystallization. After the final stage, all the unessential surroundings of an idea have been cast aside. The slag has been shed, and only the pure incombustible ore remains. The idea of the paradise garden is one such visual paradigm of the alchemical process that existed in Islamic cultures,[5] where spirit and matter have reached perfect union in a visual model of great potency common to all Muslims.

In formal religious terms, this paradigm deals with the concept of a primal timeless unity at the mythic creation of humankind in the Garden of Eden and is the ultimate promised place of return for the righteous on Judgment Day. In the more general Ibrahimic context, it relates to over half of humanity today. Metaphorically, paradise is a place of the mind where a serene sense of seamless oneness exists between humanity and the universe. The specific Islamic visual paradigm of the paradise garden is well known and carefully described in over 120 passages in the Koran. It is a walled garden of orthogonal geometry in plan, containing water courses laid out in precise straight channels emanating out from a central fountainhead in the four cardinal directions, nourishing rows of fragrant flowers, shrubs, and trees beneath whose shadows are pavilions of everlasting bliss. Allegorically the Koranic *suras* describe even the promised images and elements, as in the following verse:

> "In it are rivers of water incorruptible; rivers of milk of which the taste never changes; rivers of wine, a joy to those who drink, and river of honey pure and clear . . ." (97:15).

The State of Simultaneous Perplexity
We have now briefly reviewed the theological dimensions of the paradise garden. In this view, paradise serves as one of the main fields or loci of a Muslim's referenial journey in life. It is the place from whence he was plucked and to which he yearns to return. But in this day and age of scientific inquiry into black holes, debates about the "Big Bang Theory" and the origins of the universe, what is the proper place of such speculation? In particular, how does it relate to a better understanding of Islamic architecture?

The utility of the paradise paradigm is as a symbol and a metaphor for sensing ultimate reality, while allowing ever fresh and innovative design expressions of this primary theme. How can we cultivate the ability of seeing things symbolically and not only literally? Ibn Arabi answered this difficult question in his classic work, the *Fusus*.[6] It is a way of discipline, a way of practice for cultivating what he called the "spiritual eyesight" (*ayn al-basira*). It is a way that renders possible the inner transformation of man and allows him the understanding of the "unity of existence." This unique theory of the essential interrelated oneness of all existence forms the cornerstone of Ibn Arabi's perception of reality and man's relationship with the Absolute.

The *wahdat-i wujud* concept is structured upon the simultaneous knowledge of two basic aspects of the Absolute, in His Transcendence (*tanzih*) and His Immanence (*tazhbih*). Various degrees of compre-

hension of this simultaneous knowledge of the Absolute are possible for us ordinary human beings, depending upon our spiritual training in the unveiling (*kashf*) of ultimate truth. *Tanzih* (transcendent knowledge) is comprehensible through the faculty of man's creative imagination (*khayal*) whose principle instrument is intuition. This faculty in an architect or artist should generally be well developed, but it needs to be combined with and elevated above a purely temporal aesthetic level to the higher spiritual realm as well.

The *tazhbih*, or measurable knowledge, is more easily accessible through man's five senses and his faculty of rational discourse, reason (*aghl*). Reason is needed to collaborate with the intuitive imagination to generate a complementary and organically balanced perception of ultimate reality. "Only by combining the two concept of *tazhbih* (reason) and *tanzih* (intuition) simultaneously does one generate a state or formula of simultaneous perplexity that truly captures the essence of the Absolute.[7] This "unique perplexity" consciousness lies at the root of the Islamic *shahada* or statement of faith: "There is no God, but God" (*la illaha il Allah*). Awakened by such a particular state of consciousness, the artist/ architect is ready for his new creations.

The Historic Application of the Visual Paradigm
The architectural application of the paradise garden concept relates to the "sense of place" (*makan*). The garden is viewed as a defined space encompassing within itself a total reflection of the cosmos. This concept, which seeks to foster order and harmony in the beholder, may be made manifest to the senses through the language of numbers, geometry, color, matter, and a positive space system of design. Two categories of garden exist: (1) *Bagh* (garden), a manifestation of the centrifugally oriented form of the microcosm, symbolizing the manifest (*al-zahir*) and *tazhbih* dimensions of the Absolute, and (2) *hayat* (courtyard), a manifestation of centripetally oriented form of the microcosm symbolizing the hidden (*al-batin*) and *tanzih* dimension. They may be viewed as mutually complementary and as completing the two aspects of Islamic place making.

Historically, the garden concept in Iran had already reached a high level of development by the Achaemenid period (500-300 B.C.). Gardens in this period were set out in precise compartments within overall symmetrical arrangements. The English word "paradise" is simply a transliteration of the old Persian word *pairidaeza*, referring to the walled gar-

Nader Ardalan

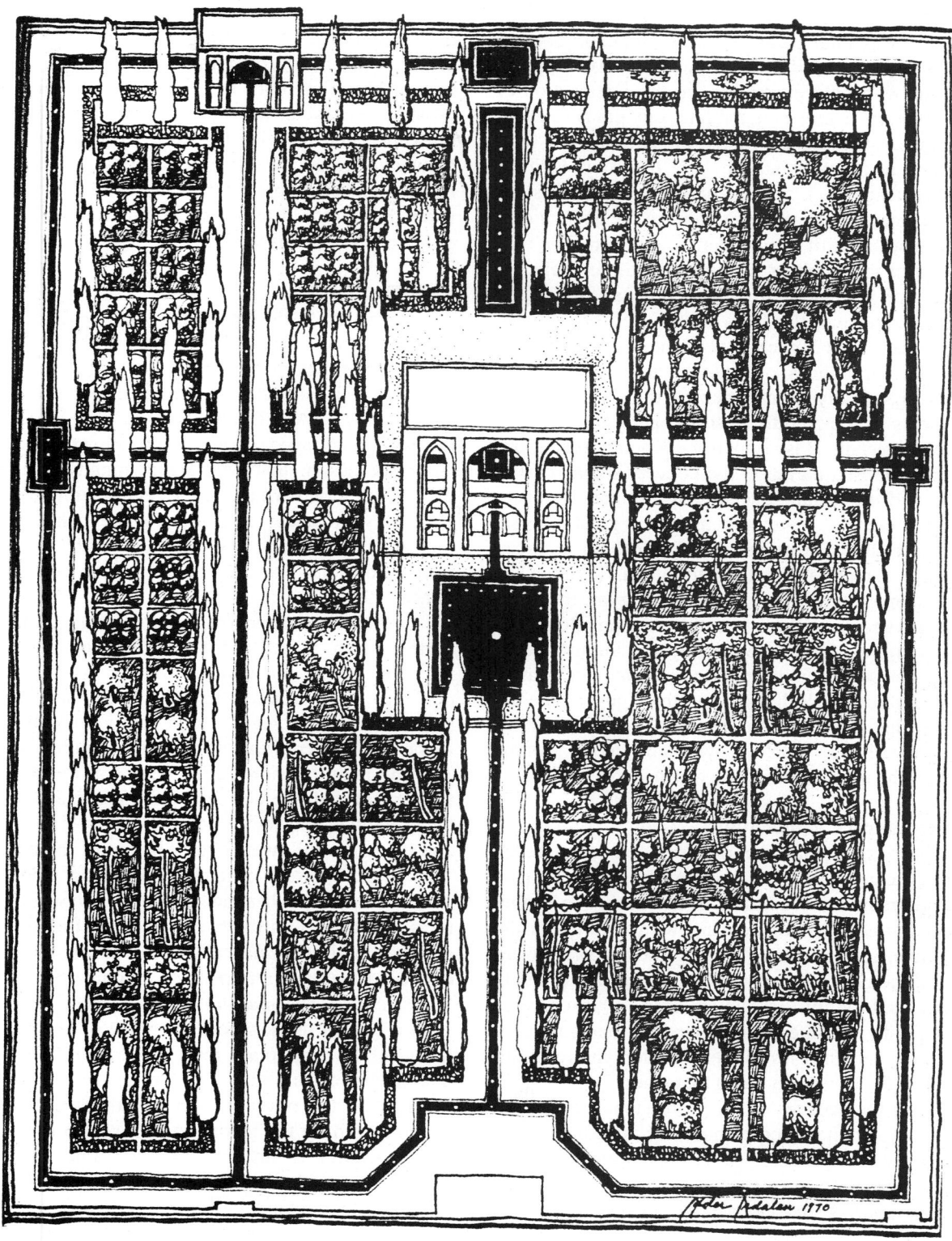

Figure 1. Kashan, Iran. The Bagh-i-Fin. 17th century. (Drawing by Nader Ardalan in Avery Library Archives, Columbia University, NY)

Nader Ardalan

dens of this ancient time.

The Sasanian paradise parks (A.D.200-600) of Iran created magnificent garden plans of mandala designs with palace pavilions at the intersection of four avenues. Here, as in the later city plans of Herat in Afghanistan, the Taj Mahal in Agra, the still later gardens of Safavid Isfahan, and the Bagh-i-Fin in Kashan (Figure 1), the use of *chahar bagh* designs and mandala forms merely extended the ancient cosmological ideas of Mesopotamia and Iran. The reiteration of the symbols of fertility and the cyclic rejuvenation of nature in such motifs as the sacred tree, sacred vine, the lotus motif, etc., perpetuated the overall idea of man's dependence upon nature.

The early ideas of walled gardens and courtyards organically complemented the hot arid environments of the Middle East and persisted after the advent of Islam. Based upon the Koranic recitations of the promised paradise, the concept spread east to India and the Asian subcontinent, ultimately reaching its height of development in the great Mughal garden tradition. Through the Timurid era it spread north to Samarqand and Central Asia. Through the Arab conquests of the Levant and Egypt, the paradise garden spread west to the Arabian Peninsula and on to the Maghrib, Sicily, Spain, and ultimately to France where it helped to generate the classic French gardens.[8] Still today, in the Court of the Lions in the Alhambra at Granada, a classic Persian garden with the fourfold symmetry of its cosmic plan, is the admiration of the world.

Contemporary Applications

We have seen that the enclosed paradise-garden theme has pervaded and inspired the most poignant metaphors in many cultures. It has served to further man's harmonious relationship with nature and the Absolute. In recent times, our growing comprehension of the *gaia*[9] concept of the earth as a total living interrelated entity, in which man is inseparably linked with the blue planet's survival, has generated ever new demands for the reformation and recapitulation of the paradise garden metaphor.

Over the decades of my professional career as a practicing architect and planner, it has been possible to re-create the paradise-garden paradigm in various scales related to a variety of project types. It has been reassuring to observe the sympathetic resonance that this theme has generated in clients and users in every walk of life and income level. I have chosen here to illustrate briefly two of the more recent applications that are now in various stages of

realization. They also represent a wide range of aesthetic approaches from a highly technological interpretation to a much more traditional rendering of the theme. This flexibility of design approach is only possible because of a firm foundation of archetypal thinking using the visual paradigms of a particular culture. A paradigm can be creatively expressed in mud or mirror or both. One only needs a sense of when the threshold of the paradigm violation or aberration has been reached.

An Office Tower

An international design competition was held in 1990 to select a concept for a state-of-the-art headquarters building to accommodate the office and support needs of 1,200 staff related to the oil and gas industry of Abu Dhabi. The site was located on the well-landscaped corniche; the client sought a landmark design that would functionally integrate the architectural heritage of the region with the contemporary advances available in the construction industry. Our entry[10] was selected as the winning submission, and construction work was completed in May 1997.

One of the outstanding features of the design is a great atrium placed at the very heart of the building. The atrium contains the "hidden, vertical garden" that brings filtered natural light, a view, and a symbolic sense of regeneration of a verdant garden to the very center of the office tower (Figures 2-3).

The main interior garden begins at the base of this atrium with the corniche palm grove and fountains moving into the building at lobby-floor level and rising the full twenty-story height of the atrium. This vertical garden resembles a classic paradise-garden carpet. Porches, niches, *mushrabiyyas*, and a transition garden on the twelfth floor at the level of a prayer hall (*musalla*) allows the stress-relieving quality of the garden to pervade a contemporary office building. The *musalla* is placed at a crescent-shaped garden level, where the place of prayer, nature, and the work place meet in a tranquil, innovative integration of tradition and technology.

Just as the interior (*al-batin*) of the tower is characterized by the garden theme, so too the exterior (*al-zahir*) is inspired by the same unifying theme; it is clad in light-hued granite panels. A studied use of thermal and polished finishes on the granite panels has added a subtle, rich pattern to the exterior facade. The pattern theme and system design are based on the "Tree of Life." Conceived at three metamorphic levels, the Tree of Life motif inte-

Nader Ardalan

Figure 2. Abu Dhabi. ADMA-OPCO and ADGAS headquarters with view of vertical paradise garden. (Drawing by L. Bancescu).

grates the ancient historic roots of the Mesopotamian cultures of the Gulf, the Islamic paradise-garden theme, and the idea that petroleum and gas products, which generated the need for the new building, were the product of the vegetative, organic groves that once covered this land.

A Sea Palace
On the Gulf Coast of Abu Dhabi, on a six-hectare flat site surrounded on the three sides by high walls, we received a commission to design a palace and

garden complex by the Sea[11]. From the very first sketches, it was proposed and accepted that the enclosed paradise-garden theme becomes the generating design paradigm (Figure 4).

The setting out of the geometric plan created a series of gardens related to different functions and to a progression from the landside to the seaside. The outer garden, square in spaces, is approached through a main gateway place accommodating guard quarters and service space. The visitor traverses a date palm grove through an avenue of tall

Nader Ardalan

13

Figure 3. Abu Dhabi. ADMA-OPCO headquarters. Computer rendering of the interior garden atrium looking north. (CADD perspective by T. Johnson).

fan palms to the inner garden. The inner or main garden is set out as a golden rectangle in proportion of 150x250 meters. The actual palace is located exactly on the central axis and at the center of an imaginary square held by four fountains. The Sea Palace is designed as a *"Hasht Bihist"* or "eight paradise" concept. This ancient design motif has historical origin in the region and has spread west to Morocco and Spain, while eastwardly it has influenced the Mughal architecture of the sub-continent.

The special feature of the design has already been described in the previous section. In summary, it is mandala plan. The form provides an outward movement through the octagonal plan of the palace into the great surrounding garden of the orchards and flowers. The central fountain wet within the atrium of the palace generates an inward movement. Finally, an upward movement from there is served through the ontological, vertical section of the naturally illuminated atrium.

The essence of the main garden is the creation of the world of shadows, of quiet cooling reflecting

Nader Ardalan

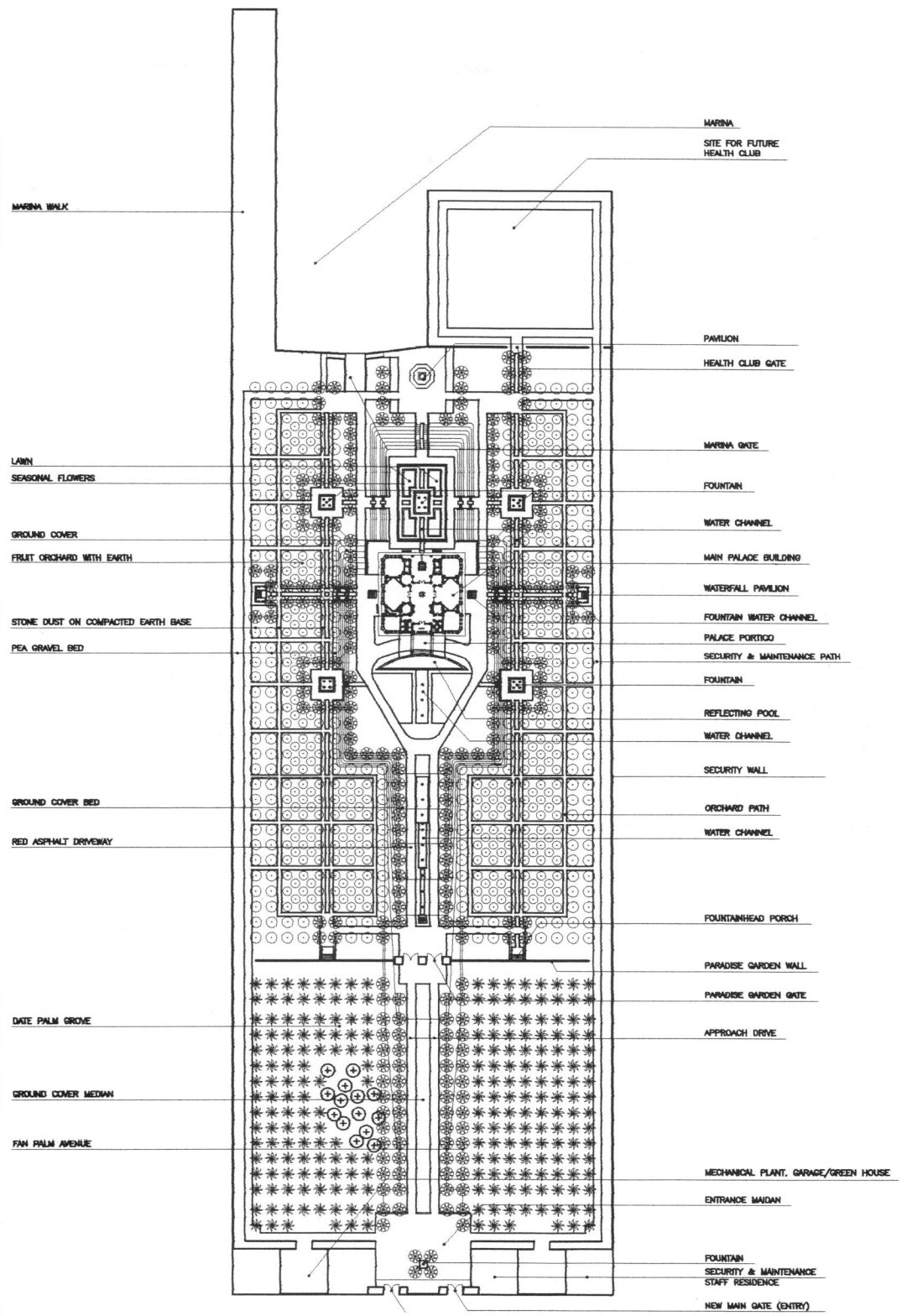

MARINA
SITE FOR FUTURE HEALTH CLUB
MARINA WALK
PAVILION
HEALTH CLUB GATE
LAWN
SEASONAL FLOWERS
MARINA GATE
FOUNTAIN
GROUND COVER
WATER CHANNEL
FRUIT ORCHARD WITH EARTH
MAIN PALACE BUILDING
WATERFALL PAVILION
STONE DUST ON COMPACTED EARTH BASE
FOUNTAIN WATER CHANNEL
PEA GRAVEL BED
PALACE PORTICO
SECURITY & MAINTENANCE PATH
FOUNTAIN
REFLECTING POOL
WATER CHANNEL
SECURITY WALL
GROUND COVER BED
ORCHARD PATH
RED ASPHALT DRIVEWAY
WATER CHANNEL
FOUNTAINHEAD PORCH
PARADISE GARDEN WALL
PARADISE GARDEN GATE
DATE PALM GROVE
APPROACH DRIVE
GROUND COVER MEDIAN
FAN PALM AVENUE
MECHANICAL PLANT, GARAGE/GREEN HOUSE
ENTRANCE MAIDAN
FOUNTAIN
SECURITY & MAINTENANCE STAFF RESIDENCE
NEW MAIN GATE (ENTRY)

Figure 4. Abu Dhabi. The Sea Palace Paradise Garden plan.

Nader Ardalan

15

pool, of regeneration and fertility, and ultimately of a sense of inner tranquility and equanimity.

Epilogue

A contemporary, popular painter named Thomas McKnight, whose work I admire, wrote of his art: "I suppose every life has a leitmotif—a guiding vision. Mine has been a search for paradise, a nostalgia for an earthly Eden that possessed me, even as a child."[12] McKnight's statement resonates deeply with me, for it parallels my own life's leitmotif and reminds me of the even broader and more universal dimension of the Paradise paradigm. Today, at the threshold of the new millennium, with the dynamics of "globalization" transforming our world population and the critical environmental crises that *gaia* must contend with, the basic problems facing us must deal with nothing less than humankind's ultimate relationship to the Absolute. Humanity at the more unified, transcendent level of homo sapiens archetypes, beyond cultural and historical limitations, needs to be the focus of our concern. Similarly, at the antipode, the Absolute, in its purest, undifferentiated state beyond the names and attributes given by any particular culture, needs to be made more conscious. Here in this state of *Mundus imaginalis* of the collective consciousness of all humanity, we may become aware of the mythic paradigms, gestures, memories, and signs that resonate with all of humankind.

How can a very materialistically defined paradise garden of finite sensual delights lead to a transcendent spiritual awareness that is beyond materiality? The answer lies in the *coincidence oppositorium* or metaphysical perplexity as a state of consciousness. The earthly garden of happiness provides the sensual "perfume" that kindles two levels of awareness. The first is awareness of the delicate beauty of multiplicity inherent in this temporal world and the need for the preservation of this fragile planet. In particular, the paradise garden as a visual paradigm provides the cultural sign that activates this awareness in the Muslim. The second is awareness of the unity within the multiplicity that the Absolute is the locus of all phenomenality. This at-oneness is the ultimate experience of the paradise garden. The paradise garden may well be one of the quintessential paradigms that is universal to most of humanity and one that can simultaneously serve to provide culturally specific identity to the architecture and place making of Islamic lands.

Notes

1. Although from the European Renaissance to the present, alchemy as a science has been debunked as the primitive precursor of modern chemistry, this should not detract from its continuing pervasiveness in the artisanal crafts of most world cultures and the especially profound wisdom that it can shed on Islamic aesthetics. On the contrary, the method of alchemy, with its outward metallurgical symbolism, also deals with an inward process whose goal is the ripening, transmutation, and revelation of the true nature of the soul of the architect/artisan, the beholder, and the matter transformed.

2. Thomas Kuhn's *Structure of Scientific Revolution* brought the term "paradigm" into common usage in the 1960s.

3. Toshihiko Izutsu, *Ethico-religious Concepts in the Quran* (Montreal: McGill University Press, 1966).

4. For a detailed discussion of Ibn Arabi's conceptions of the *wahdat-i wujud*, see Toshihiko Izutsu, *Sufism and Taoism* (Berkeley, Calif.: University of California Press, 1983).

5. The very ancient art of alchemy entered into the spiritual world of Islam very naturally, as Islam at its origins was genuinely ready in principle to recognize any pre-Islamic art that appeared under the aspect of "wisdom" *(hikma)* of the earlier prophets. In the Islamic perspective, the mythic founder of alchemy, Hermes Trismegistos, came to be known as Enoch (Idris) in the Koran. The basic belief of alchemy in the oneness of existence *(wahdat-i-wujud)* reinforced the Islamic confession of faith. The major surviving documents on the ancient art of alchemy in the West are to be found in Arabic and Latin texts. See Titus Burckhardt, *Alchemy* (1967).

6. R. W. J. Austin, *Ibn al-Arabi: The Bezels of Wisdom* (*Fusus al-Hakim*) (New Jersey: Paulist Press, 1980).

7. Toshihiko Izutsu, *Sufism and Taosim* (Berkeley: University of California Press, 1983).

8. Elizabeth Moynihan, *Paradise as a Garden in Persia and Mughal India* (New York: George Braziller, 1979).

9. James Lovelock, *The Ages of Gaia* (New York: Bantam Book, 1990).

10. I was partner-in-charge of design of the joint ven-

ture, Jung/Brannen Associates and Ove Arup Partnership, who were commissioned by Abu Dhabi National Oil Company to design the Abu Dhabi Marine Operating Co. (ADMA-OPCO) and Abu Dhabi Gas Liquification Co. (ADGAS) headquarters in Abu Dhabi.

11. The Sea Palace in Abu Dhabi for private client by KEO International Architects, with Nader Ardalan as

the director of design. Construction completed in 1997.

12. Thomas McKnight, *Thomas Mcknight's World: A Vision of Earthly Happiness* (New York: Abbeville Press, 1997).

• • • • • • • • • • • • •

Comments
Mohammed Arkoun

Nader Ardalan confesses that he shares with the popular painter Thomas McKnight the same "search for Paradise, a nostalgia for an early Eden that possessed me, even as a child." A rich, strong experience can be translated through poetry, painting, sculpture, music, dance, and architecture to the level of artistic experience. But the receptions of these artistic expressions are not necessarily on a level with what the author intended to communicate. When Ardalan refers to Ibn 'Arabi's visions and its interpretation by Toshihiko Izutsu, "the important role that alchemy has played in Islamic architecture, and the visual paradigm of the Paradise Garden," he refers to a line of thinking, imagining, writing, performing which had and still has many supporters, disciples, devoted defenders. Scholars are endeavoring to find the relevant interpretation of the type of spirituality represented by this trend that has parallels in other religious traditions. It has to do with Gnosticism, alchemy, Neoplatonism, theosophy, illuminative philosophy, mysticism, revelatory discourses, popular beliefs. . . . Interpreting all these complex traditions of esoteric knowledge, imaginal creativity, psychological experiences, cultural practices with the postulates, the logical and rhetoric paradigms of Aristotelian reason, or our Modern, secularized rationality is, of course, unacceptable. But it is also very dangerous and questionable to use these references which are still obscure and confusing to support the disputed notion of an Islamic architecture, or to claim a direct impact, or link between what is called arbitrary Islamic spirituality and an architecture which does not necessarily convey in the mind of all observers or users the

"spiritual" representations aimed by architects inspired by very subjective (I mean difficult to share) paradigms. Only a sociological survey combined with historical criticism would assess the exact content of the paradigms used by the architect and the concrete impact of his buildings on several categories of interpreters. We know that creation (the author side) and reception (the user, or reader, or interpreter side) are two related dimensions of criticism; but this type of criticism is not applied often enough to what I prefer to call architecture in Islamic contexts. There is more to say about all these issues.

Response
Apparently Professor Arkoun has structured his comments based upon a belief in "modern, secularized rationality." Of course, this Western modernist view has its more recent historical roots in seventeenth-century Cartesian thinking and a linear, deterministic clockwork world. The goal of this so-called modern view was to explain all phenomena as essentially simple variants of rational behavior. Some of the results were that the Behaviorist B. F. Skinner brought up his daughter in a "Skinner box" and the Bauhaus architects helped to create "Machines for Living," where rows upon rows of monotonous housing complexes now blight all modern cities, including many in Islamic lands.

However, over the past thirty years, due to breakthrough information about man and the Universe on subatomic and macrocosmic levels, some leading scientists and philosophers began to realize that the cosmos had more non-linearity in it than predictable linear thinking could explain. Since then, a revolution in thinking has been underway opposing the still dominant modern rational world view with a post-modern science based upon complexity, approximations, and chaos theory, where the dichotomy of the measurable versus the immeasurable is overcome by a unity of their simultaneous coexistence.

Naturally, this perception of reality has many similarities to those of traditional wisdom systems encompassing such philosophies as Islamic Sufism, Zen Buddhism, Christian metaphysics, and others that are based upon the union of complex rational and intuitive knowledge and the important role of imaginal creativity. These traditional systems give cause for their very vital reevaluation and selective incorporation into our current overall advanced perceptions about ultimate reality. Especially the rich, Islamic heritage of metaphysical thinking and traditional craftsmanship can be combined today with advances in science to generate new, significant creations in the field of art and architecture for Islamic societies around the world.

The paradise paradigm, as both an Islamic visual model and a mythic image of mankind, combines both a material impression of beauty and a non-material allusion to the essential order inherent in chaos. As such, it is an excellent example of the kind of simultaneous perplexity thinking that will be necessary before we can convincingly deal with the real world after the straitjacket of the modernist, secular rationalist mind set has been cast aside, allowing the dawn of a dynamic and illuminated information age of the new millennium to begin.

Nader Ardalan

On What Makes Architecture Islamic:
Some Reflections and a Proposal

S. Gulzar Haider

In my years of wandering in pursuit of the "Islamic" in architecture four encounters are particularly unforgettable. First, after I had made a presentation at a prestigious school in the Islamic Republic of Pakistan, a young woman instructor, quite visibly uncomfortable with General Zia ul-Haq's Islamization program, looked straight at me and asked: "Have you come all the way from Canada to convert our bricks and beams to Islam?" Second, after a lecture on the Alhambra at a Malaysian university a visibly pious professor challenged me: "How can you call the pleasure palaces of kings, who violated Shari'a and the Sunna[1] of the Prophet examples of Islamic architecture?" Third, again during discussions after a lecture, this time in the United States, a white American convert to Islam wearing a green pill-box cap and a long white robe over his blue jeans suggested: "Since Islam is for the good of all mankind, don't you think that all good architecture can be claimed as Islamic?" And fourth, when I sought the guidance of a respected theologian of Islam permanently residing in the United Kingdom, I received an hour-long lecture on the "architecture of a believer's heart," but no specific answers to my questions. The cumulative memory of these and other such incidents has made me feel like a traveler through a bazaar where religious illusions can be touted as scientific reality and academic objectivity can mask ideological prejudice. In my own writings and encounters with academics at North American universities I have continuously struggled to see or conjecture correspondences between Islam as a worldview and its manifestation through architecture. I have often ended up on the wrong side of serious "forensic"[2] historians, ideology-driven claimants[3] of Islam's achievements, and hardened secular modernists[4] who doubt any crea-

tive impulse coming from Islam as a faith. What follows is an attempt at clarifying these marginalized, oppositional stances on about a thousand years of architectural production that defies any monolithic definition.

First I have tried to map Islam in the sense that it is understood in four different and distinct contexts—cosmology, power, law, and spirituality. I have then identified another four intentions and imperatives in terms of which we can discuss the nature of any architectural work. Third, by crossing the first two, one dealing with ways of looking at Islam and the other aimed at understanding architecture, one can arrive at a manifold[5] definition which can be used to identify a whole spectrum of Islamic architectures or discuss the Islamicity of any particular structure.

Islam in Four Perspectives

Words like Islam or Islamic uttered in the presence of a non-Muslim can lead to diverse images ranging from bearded horsemen with drawn swords, a sumptuous palace with an obese sultan surrounded by his harem, the Taj Mahal, whirling dervishes, or a historical landscape full of treasures still to be discovered and written about. A Muslim, on the other hand, may construct a world of spiritual perfection and civilized glory and lament the misreading of it by others. Such a vast gap between the understanding of Islam from within and without has led to rather ruptured, occasionally oppositional views of Islam's architectural production.

To grasp the challenge of understanding Islam less prejudiciously, we can look at four distinct perspectives within which it is often discussed:

I1. *Cosmology.* This perspective encompasses God-man-nature relationships within the grand scheme of time and history. A belief system ties the creation of the universe, that of Adam and Eve, their mission on earth, God's guidance through revelation, mankind's diabolic enemy and the detractor of revelation, the code of morality and ethics, willful actions, life, death, and return to God and finally the Day of Judgment leading to paradise or its opposite, hell. This view locates man as the creature with free will, responsible for himself and for his fellow man, a trustee of nature, and ultimately answerable for all his actions to his creator and master, the God.[6]

I2. *Power*. Within this perspective Islam is seen as an unfolding political and imperial phenomenon fueled by its universal religious mission. It becomes synonymous with its history as sequential and later parallel dynasties covering vast geographies. Settled power and desire for dynastic expression turn into patronage of architecture. Expressing the glory of God through mosques and foundations, the protection and pleasure of the king through his citadel and palace, and the benevolence towards the populace through civil works all go hand in hand as the expression of Islam's power.[7]

I3. *Law*. Islam also involves a complex system of strictures on human conduct in all spheres of life. The purpose of Islam's way (Shari'a) is to affirm the beneficial by identifying it as *halal* (permissible) and to warn us against the harmful by identifying it as *haram* (forbidden). Between the permissible and the forbidden are numerous shades of desirable and distasteful. In this sense the expressions of Muslim civilization, architectural and others, can be judged as in or out of the domain of jurisprudential Islam. In many revivalist movements in the last two centuries it is the legalist view of Islam that dominates and becomes the medium of its assertion. For example, the heightened emphasis on gender separation in religious spaces like mosques, or women's dress codes in markets, and safeguards against violation of domestic privacy by neighbors are treated as fundamental issues in contemporary Muslim societies that decide to adopt Islam as the renewed basis of its affairs.[8]

I4. *Spirituality*: This is the perspective of Sufi philosophers, sages, poets, and spiritual masters of guilds and brotherhoods. While there is no denial of the religious law and the exoteric manifestation of Islam, this path seeks the irreducible essence of things through pursuit of knowledge as cognizance of God, reflections on reality of nature beyond appearance, disciplined prayer, remembrance of God and those Whom He loves. While there is much dis-cipline, hierarchy, and protocol here, the focus is on spirit rather than matter, on content rather than the form, on evocation rather than sensation, on journey rather the destination, and on divine love rather than desire in pursuit of consummation. It is this perspective that makes the non-functional constituents of architecture like the light-filled void and the calligraphy of the revelation, for example, to take their honored place with formal, functional, and structural aspects.[9]

The Fourfold Phenomenon of Architecture
Architecture is a complex phenomenon and any attempt at compressing it into single definitions only marginalizes it. The following presents it as a four-fold phenomenon of societal imperatives:

A1. *Dwelling imperative*. There is a deep-seated desire in humans to assert their collective being through sedentary location as opposed to nomadic wandering. This choice is the fundamental architectural act of marking one's permanent bearings in nature, of dwelling, against the horizon, under the sky and with reference to the river or the mountain or the forest. In this sense architecture is the primordial dwelling imperative manifested as distinct from nature.[10]

A2. *Functional imperative*. Architecture is purposeful in that it acts as shelter from the extremes of nature, establishes boundaries between distinct patterns of life, encloses specialized functions, and bestows the quality of habitat on what would otherwise have been a mere container of objects. Some architecture may have purely symbolic intent with no requirement of enclosure but in that case the functional imperative is that of a symbol, a marker, an icon, or a monument essential to maintain the shared memories and meanings of a society.

A3. *Constructive imperative*. Essential to architecture is the conscious, willful, strategic construction of spaces. Most often it is the carefully thought out bringing together of elements to make structures either support enclosures or as enclosures themselves. Sometimes architecture is an aggregation of smaller cells of space brought together through structural discipline. Other times it can be a strategic carving out, or a systematic subdivision of a larger form so that the desired spaces can be achieved. In all cases architecture challenges the transformative and connective genius of the builder in facing material resistance, tool limitations, and forces of nature, especially gravity. In this sense architecture is the result of the constructive imperative against gravity

S. Gulzar Haider

and its surrogates.[11]

A4. *Aesthetic imperative.* Beauty is the restoration of things to their rightful place with the aim of achieving a transcendent sense of pleasure, harmony, well-being, positive excitation, evocation to deeper or higher realizations about God, man, nature and time.[12] This act of restoration to a rightful place implies the belief that be it the word or windows, courtyard for sun or chimney for smoke, reverberating echo or deadening silence, green or yellow or red, all have their place in the scheme of things and the genuine aesthetic imperative is the search for that place. It is in this sense that beauty is neither a fashion nor a style but pursuit of the rightful.

The Manifold Aspects of Islamic Architecture

Now if we cross the fourfold aspects of Islam with the fourfold aspects of architecture we generate the manifold principles on which we can project our images, expectations, definitions, and critique of Islamic architecture. Using these we can develop a more focused and productive discourse on this otherwise confused and contested field. As an example, if we relate to Islam as a historical phenomenon of power and patronage (I2) and are inclined to seek the aesthetic imperative and symbolic expression in architecture (A4) we can focus on buildings like the throne rooms at the Alhambra and Fatehpur Sikri, or the citadels of Aleppo, Cairo, and Agra that encase precious royal residences. Instead of creating cumbersome and even misleading hyphenated titles like power-aesthetic to identify the crossing of two specific streams (I2) and (A4), it is more accurate and linguistically economical to identify it as the (I2 x A4) crossing on the manifold of Islamic architecture. Following this pattern, there are sixteen crossings on our manifold.

It is important to clarify that the proposed manifold is neither a matrix with a clear arrangement of sixteen types nor is it a framework for identifying causalities between ideas and their architectural manifestation.[13] Manifold does imply a hyperdimensional construct where centers of spatial cells are the crossings of different perspectives on Islam (I1-4) and different architectural imperatives (A1-4). As in any hyperdimensional imagination beyond the three-dimensional space one can experience magical events like looking around corners, escaping prison cells, peeling oranges without breaking the skin, or walking on the ceiling but arriving in the cellar, this manifold would allow us to see other crossings without abandoning the one we have chosen to place ourselves.[14] For example, while discussing the throne room of Fatehpur Sikri (I2 x A4), the symbolic seat of Akbar, the reigning "monarch of all domains," it would be possible to glance at the tomb of Salim Chishti [I4 x A1], the timeless marker of the deceased but living saint, and bring it into the same discourse without confusing the intentions of one with the other. From the saintly tombs and shrines (I4 x A1) that are centers of pilgrimage one can peek into the crossing (I2 x A1) around which most of the mausolea of the kings would be located. One can thus discuss tombs in a comparative manner and see differences rooted in their intentions rather than subjecting them to the strict Islamic legal perspective (A3) and discard them in total as forbidden (*haram*) or an innovation (*bida'at*) in Islam.

This manifold of Islamic architecture is illustrated below by listing each crossing and examples of architectural situations most representative of the crossing:

Perspective on Islam	Architectural Imperative	Crossing Symbol	Building
Cosmology	Dwelling	I1 x A1	Holy Ka'ba; global orientations of mosques; places of pilgrimage, sacred sites.
Cosmology	Functional	I1 x A2	Courtyard of mosque; dome; location of cemetery in Ottoman complex; Observatories.
Cosmology	Constructive	I1 x A3	Muqarnas; colonnades of Cordoba mosque, vaulting of lanterns and *mihrabs* like Tlemcen.
Cosmology	Aesthetic	I1 x A4	Calligraphy, arabesque, infinite or mandala - like geometries, Convergent muqarnas domes.

S. Gulzar Haider

Perspective on Islam	Architectural Imperative	Crossing Symbol	Building
Power	Dwelling	I2 x A1	Minaret; *minbar*; Sultan Hasan's Tomb, Qutub Minar, tomb towers of Central Asia.
Power	Functional	I2 x A2	Muslim city: palace, palace gates, maydan, mosque and bazaar.
Power	Constructive	I2 x A3	Comparison among the citadel of Alhambra and city of al-Baicin, Fatehpur Sikri layout.
Power	Aesthetic	I2 x A4	Throne Room, Sikri; Hall of Ambassadors, Alhambra; Baghdad Kiosk, Topkapi.
Law	Dwelling	I3 x A1	Inward quality of a Muslim house; threshold as address, courtyard as heart.
Law	Functional	I3 x A2	Historical *futawa* for property rights, privacy encroachment, sharing of common walls, roofs.
Law	Constructive	I3 x A3	Typology of mosques, elements of mosque: entrance, ablution, *mihrab, mimbar*.
Law	Aesthetic	I3 x A4	Unadorned white mosques, *mushrabiyya*: privacy screens, geometric, arabesque work.
Spirituality	Dwelling	I4 x A1	Ziyaraat, Takiyyahs, places of pilgrimage, memorials, markers.
Spirituality	Functional	I4 x A2	Gateway, threshold to the mosque, *mihrab, mimbar*, reflective pool of water for ablution.
Spirituality	Constructive	I4 x A3	Splitting of wood plank to make Rehle as the seat of the Book, Muslim city with courtyards.
Spirituality	Aesthetic	I4 x A4	*Mihrab* of Cordova mosque, *muqarrnas* dome over the tomb of Nuruddin Zangi, Sultan Hasan courtyard.

Expressed as a diagram flattened out on the surface of a paper (Figure 1), the proposed manifold has a central zone generated by I2, I3 crossing with A2 and A3. Dealing with political (I2) and legal (I3) perspectives on Islam and the functional (A2) and constructive (A3) imperatives of architecture, this zone can quite legitimately host all the discourse on Islamic architecture looked upon as the expression of Islam as a religion, a code of life, a societal protocol, and as an instrument of God's rule on earth through the state and its ruler (*ulal-amr*). Here the rulings of the religious judges and particular interpretations of the Prophet's traditions can have as much effect on the architectural and urban form as the building tradition, the architect's will, or the patron's desire.

The central zone of four crossings is surrounded by a ring of twelve crossings: I1 x (A1, A2, A3) to A4 x (I1, I2, I3) to I4 x (A4, A3, A2), and A1 x (I4, I3, I2). As can be seen in Figure 1, these twelve crossings are generated by the cosmological (I1) and spiritual (I4) perspectives on Islam crossed with the dwelling (A1) and aesthetic (A4) imperatives of architecture. Within this ring zone Islamic architecture can be discussed as an art form projecting the worldviews, deeper beliefs, collective aspirations, poetic imaginations, symbolic systems, and stylistic diversity of Muslim cultures taken as a complex weaving of traditions and ethnic lineages over a vast geography and a time span of about 1,400 years. Islam neither is, nor should be, understood as a monolith especially in I1 and I4. It should therefore surprise no one that there has been no agreement on a single architectural expression or style that could be claimed as Islamic. If in the past names such as Saracenic, Mohammedan, and later Islamic have been used to apply equally to the Dome of the Rock and the Taj Mahal, the Great Mosque of Cordova and Sheikh Lutfullah's mosque, and even the Alhambra and the Shalimar gardens of Lahore, it is because this vast

S. Gulzar Haider

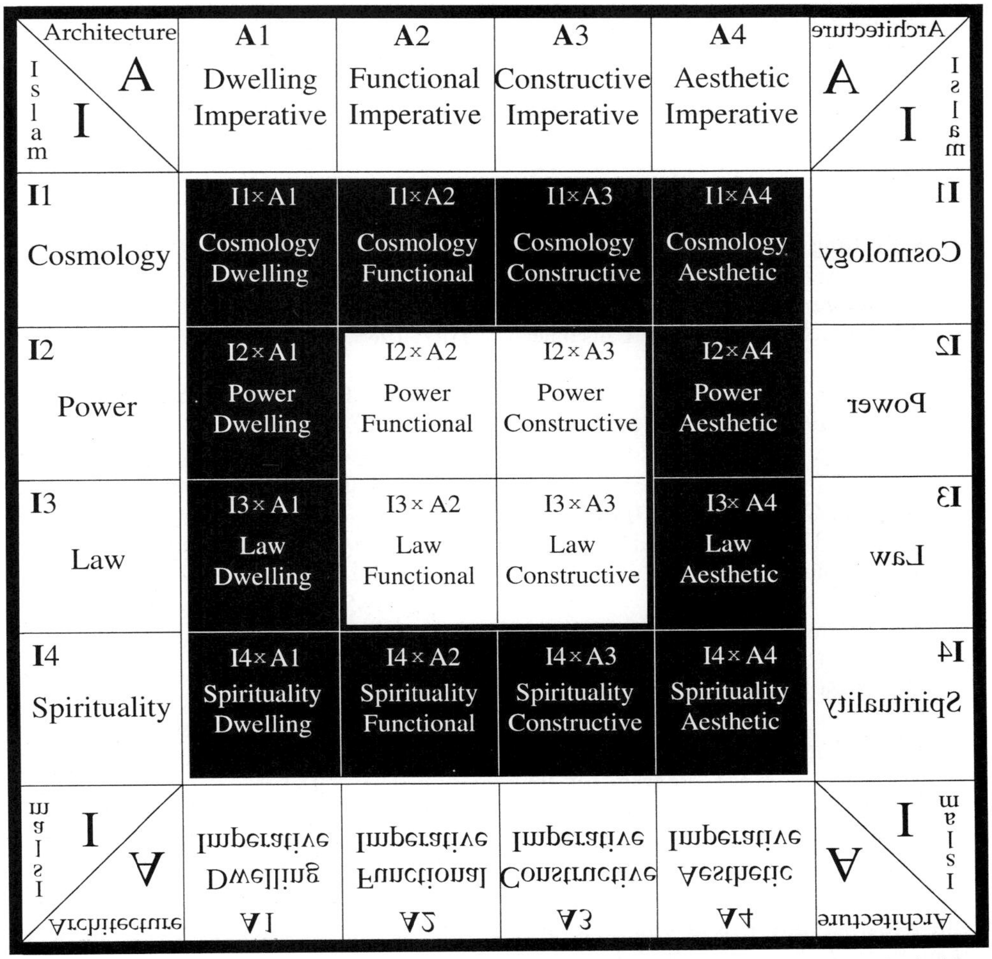

Architecture Islam **A** / **I**	**A1** Dwelling Imperative	**A2** Functional Imperative	**A3** Constructive Imperative	**A4** Aesthetic Imperative	Architecture **A** / **I** Islam
I1 Cosmology	I1×A1 Cosmology Dwelling	I1×A2 Cosmology Functional	I1×A3 Cosmology Constructive	I1×A4 Cosmology Aesthetic	**I1** Cosmology
I2 Power	I2×A1 Power Dwelling	I2×A2 Power Functional	I2×A3 Power Constructive	I2×A4 Power Aesthetic	**I2** Power
I3 Law	I3×A1 Law Dwelling	I3×A2 Law Functional	I3×A3 Law Constructive	I3×A4 Law Aesthetic	**I3** Law
I4 Spirituality	I4×A1 Spirituality Dwelling	I4×A2 Spirituality Functional	I4×A3 Spirituality Constructive	I4×A4 Spirituality Aesthetic	**I4** Spirituality
Islam **I** / **A** Architecture	Imperative Dwelling **A1**	Imperative Functional **A2**	Imperative Constructive **A3**	Imperative Aesthetic **A4**	Architecture **I** / **A** Islam

© ghaider

Figure 1. Crossings of Islam and Architecture

and complex venture has often been reduced to formal or elemental identities—dome to dome, light to light, water to water and so on. Our attempt is aimed at raising the level of discourse on Islamic architecture from oversimplicity to a befitting complexity.

Conclusion

If philosophy is the love of wisdom then the most important philosophical comment that we can offer in quest of "understanding Islamic architecture" is

to seek the wisdom underlying Islam and its texts;

to develop a fine level of discriminatory acuity in distinguishing the history of power from the history of scientific ideas and poetic imaginations of the Muslim people;

to awaken to the vast and natural distance between the unifying cosmology of Islam and the diversifying impulse rooted in the culturally accommodating nature of Islam.

This suggested shift may free the discussions on Islamic architecture from the entrenched positions of agnostic historians and believing polemicist alike.

Bibliography

Akbar, J. *Crisis in the Built Environment*, Leiden: 1988

Akbar, J. "Accretion of Decisions: A Design Strategy" in Sevcenko, M.B. ed. (The Aga Khan Program for Islamic Architecture) *Theories and Principles of Design in Architecture of Islamic Societies*, Cambridge: 1988. pp. 107-114.

Ardalan, N. and L. Bakhtiar. *Sense of Unity*, Chicago:

S. Gulzar Haider

1973.

al-Attas, S. M. N. *Prolegomena to the Metaphysics of Islam*, Kuala Lumpur: 1995.

Burckhardt, T. *Art of Islam: Language and Meaning*, London: 1976.

Gelani, I. "Muslim Housing as Built Environment for Promoting Muslim Societal Behavior" in Ozkan, S. ed. *Faith and the Built Environment: Architecture and Behavior in Islamic Cultures*. Comportments, Lausanne: 1996. pp. 59-66.

Grabar, O. *The Formation of Islamic Art*. New Haven: 1987.

al-Hathloul, S. *Tradition, Continuity and Change in the Physical Environment*. Unpublished Ph.D. Dissertation, M.I.T. Cambridge, Mass: 1981.

Haider, G. "Habitat and Values in Islam: A Conceptual Formulation of an Islamic City" in Sradar, Z. ed. *The Touch of Midas*, Manchester: 1984. pp. 170-208.

Haider, G. "Islam, Cosmology and Architecture" in Sevcenko, M.B. ed. (The Aga Khan Program for Islamic Architecture) *Theories and Principles of Design in Architecture of Islamic Societies*, Cambridge: 1988. pp. 73-85.

Haider, G. "Faith is the Architect: Reflections on the Mosque" in Ozkan, S. ed. *Faith and the Built Environment: Architecture and Behavior in Islamic Cultures*. Comportments, Lausanne: 1996. pp. 67-72.

Hakim, B. S. *Arab-Islamic Cities: Building and Planning Principles*, London: 1986.

Heidegger, M. *Poetry, Language, Thought*, New York: 1971.

Hodgson, M. *The Venture of Islam*, vol. 1, 2, Chicago: 1958.

Husaini, S. W. A. *Islamic Environmental Systems Engineering*, London: 1980.
Kaku, Michio. *Hyperspace*, New York: 1994.

Kuban, D. " Commentary" on the paper of S.H. Nasr in Holod, R. ed. (The Aga Khan Award for Architecture Seminar: Gouvieux, France), *Toward an Architecture in the Spirit of Islam*. 2nd ed. 1980.

Kuban, D. "Perspectives on Islamic History and Art" in Ozkan, S. ed. *Faith and the Built Environment: Architecture and Behavior in Islamic Cultures*. Comportments, Lausanne: 1996. pp. 31-38.

Locher, J. L. ed. *M. C. Escher, His Life and Complete Graphic Works,* Abrams, New York: 1982.

Nasr, S. H. *Islamic Art and Spirituality*, Albany: 1987.

Norberg-Schulz, C. *The Concept of Dwelling*, New York: 1985.

Rosenthal, F. *The Muqaddimah of Ibn Khaldun*. London: 1958.

Rucker, R. *The Fourth Dimension*, Boston: 1984.

Treasures of Islam, Museum of Art and History, Geneva, published by Wellfleet Press, Secaucus, New Jersey: 1985.

Notes
1. *Hariah* is the word commonly used to denote the divinely prescribed "Way of Islam" based on Koranic injunctions and elaborated in the Sunna: the example of the Prophet Muhammad in the legal, sociopolitical, and economic spheres.

2. By "forensic" I mean an attitude towards history that treats the subject matter as lifeless before the searching scalpel of the investigator. Though laudable for its detached scientific objectivity, it often yields history as a discontinuous set of facts substantiated by hard evidence.

3. Here are writers who, in contrast with the "forensic" historian, make grand claims about Islam's civilizational achievements without producing convincing evidence or argument. Their belief in the truth of Islam drives them to claim that all that has become associated with its adherents has to be good.

4. Proceedings of numerous seminars organized by the Aga Khan Award for Architecture are full of discussions that identify the protagonists of this position. Of special interest are the ideas of Dogan Kuban expressed in his commentary on the paper of S. H. Nasr in *Toward an Architecture in the Spirit of Islam*, ed. Renata Holod, 2nd ed. (Philadelphia: Aga Khan Award for Architecture, 1980), and "Perspectives on Islamic History and Art," *Faith and the Built Environment*, ed. Suha Özkan (Geneva: Aga Khan Award for Architec-

S. Gulzar Haider

ture, 1996), pp. 31-38.

5. "Manifold" implies an abstract generalization of a unity that has many diverse constituents interrelated but not in a simple, apparent way. It is a topological concept as opposed to a geometric one.

6. For a more detailed discussion on this subject, see Gulzar Haider, "Islam, Cosmology and Architecture," in *Theories and Principles of Design in the Architecture of Islamic Societies*, ed. Margaret B. Sevcenko (Cambridge, Mass.: Aga Khan Program for Islamic Architecture, 1988), pp. 73-85.

7. Two excellent examples of this perspective can be seen in respectively Oleg Grabar, *The Formation of Islamic Art*, rev. ed. (New Haven: Yale University Press, 1987); and Marshall Hodgson, *The Venture of Islam*, 3 vols. (Chicago: University of Chicago Press, 1958), vols. 1-2. Ibn Khaldun's (14th c.) view of Muslim history is a much earlier example of political power as the filter through which Islam's evolution is explained; see Franz Rosenthal, *The Muqaddimah of Ibn Khaldun* (London, 1958).

8. There have been numerous writings on the Islamicity of architecture and the environment that take a strong legalist position. Many theses, written in Arabic, in Middle Eastern—especially Saudi Arabian—universities almost as a matter of policy deny the esoteric traditions in Muslim scholarship and art and are committed to the jurisprudential and exoteric perspective. Some of the most important writings in English that represent this perspective are S. W. A. Husaini, *Islamic Environmental Systems Engineering* (London, 1980); Saleh al-Hathloul, "Tradition, Continuity and Change in the Physical Environment," Ph.D. diss., M.I.T., Cambridge, Mass., 1981; B. S. Hakim, *Arab-Islamic Cities: Building and Planning Principles* (London, 1986); Jamel Akbar, "Accretion of Decisions; A Design Strategy," in *Theories and Principles of Design* (cited above, n. 6); and idem, *Crisis in the Built Environment* (Leiden: E. J. Brill, 1988); I. Gelani, "Muslim Housing as Built Environment for Promoting Muslim Societal Behavior," in *Faith and the Built Environment* (cited above, n. 4).

9. His is the perspective of Sufi philosophers like Ibn Sina, al-Ghazzali in a later period, Ibn Arabi all the way to Mulla Sadra and Muhammad Iqbal. Among contemporary writers the best representatives of this perspective are S. H. Nasr, and S. M. N. al-Attas. In the architectural domain, see Nader Ardalan and Leileh Bakhtiar, *The Sense of Unity* (Chicago, 1973); Titus Burckhardt, *Art of Islam: Language and Meaning* (London, 1976), S. H. Nasr, *Islamic Art and Spirituality* (Albany, N.Y., 1987), and Gulzar Haider, "Habitat and Values in Islam: A Conceptual Formulation of an Islamic City," in *The Touch of Midas*, ed. Z. Sradar (Manchester, 1984); idem; "Islam, Cosmology and Architecture, cited above, n. 6; and "Faith Is the Architect: Reflections on the Mosque," in *Faith and the Built Environment*, cited above, n. 4.

10. The sense of the word "dwelling" has been borrowed from M. Heidegger, *Poetry, Language, and Thought* (New York, 1971); C. Norberg-Schulz, *The Concept of Dwelling* (New York, 1985), has elaborated the concept in a very didactic manner.

11. The concept is quite accurately conveyed by the Greek word *techne*, the pursuit of principles and methods towards the end of artful making, in contrast to *episteme*, the pursuit of knowledge and principles whose end is pure and detached understanding.

12. The philosophical writings of Syed Muhammad Naquib al-Attas, *Prolegomena to the Metaphysics of Islam* (Kuala Lumpur, 1978), very convincingly present this idea.

13. To help the imagination of a manifold in the context of this paper one may look at complex interwoven spaces in Persian miniatures illustrating episodes such as the story of Haftvad and the worm (fol. 521v of Tahmasp's *Shahnameh* (1540), reproduced in *Treasures of Islam* (Geneva: Museum of Art and History, 1985), p. 90; or the seduction of Joseph by Bihzad, in Sa'di's *Bustan* (1488), Royal Egyptian Library, Cairo.

14. To get a better grasp of strange occurrences in hyperspace, see R. Rucker, *The Fourth Dimension* (Boston, 1984), and Michio Kaku, *Hyperspace* ((New York, 1994). It might also be helpful to look at M. C. Escher's drawings like "Relativity," "Convex and Concave," and "Print Gallery" (1981) in J. L. Locher, ed., *M. C. Escher: His Life and Complete Graphic Works* (New York: Harry Abrams, 1981).

• • • • • • • • • • • • •

S. Gulzar Haider

Comments
Nader Ardalan

Structure: a "topological manifold" based on an "Islamic perspective" and an "architectural imperative" appears to be a sound structure. However, the overall diagram is possibly more complex then it needs to be. The following simplifications are suggested:

Islamic Perspective. What justifies separating "Cosmology" from "Spirituality"? The understanding of the God/Nature/man relationships could be viewed as a continuous process of self-revelation of the Divine. Therefore, within the concept of the Unity of Existence (*wahat-i-wujud*), these two categories could be considered as one and the same. Thus in this category, the four aspects might be reduced to three.

Architectural Imperatives. The author's definition of the functional imperative is beautifully all-encompassing and captures the essential purpose of architecture. As such, might it not also include the "dwelling imperative" and be entitled "Purpose," thus also reducing this fourfold category to three?

Possible simplification of the manifold. Based on the above observations, the visual form of the manifold could be simplified from a 16-square to 9-square mandala.

Disposition of three-part imperatives and perspectives in the matrix might follow an accepted pattern that vertically, the more spiritual considerations float to the top, while more material considerations are placed at the bottom. Also the left hand connotes more esoteric (i.e., aesthetic) considerations and the right hand more exoteric (i.e., constructional) ones. Please see Figure 2.

Response
The proposed manifold aims at making sense out of a wide variety of views, and often-conflicting trajectories of arguments about the "Islamicity" of any architecture. The apparent complexity is more expressive of the current state of the discourse and less of my personal position.

While Ibn Arabi's *wahdat al-wujud* (unity of existence) is one of Islam's cosmological concepts par excellence, doubts have been cast about its potential cooption of God as one with His Creations. This concern led some Muslim philosophers like Iqbal to propose *wahdat al-shahud* (unity of manifestations) in either case my use of cosmology is based on a rather uncomplicated view of the Koranic schema, and it would be expecting too much from my text to link it to *wahdat al-wujud*. My use of the word spirituality deals with an attitude towards piety and practice of Islam that has more to do with psychological states of being and imagination and less with strict dogma and law.

I deeply appreciate Nader Ardalan's suggestions about the simplification of the manifold. That he, as an architect-scholar, can extract a simpler version of this manifold by collapsing cosmology and spirituality and achieve a 3 x 3 "mandalic" diagram can be taken as a sign of the versatility of the fourfold. Maybe others can collapse other dimensions to get their own simpler and unique versions.

	Aesthetic	Purpose (Dwelling)	Constructive
Spiritual (Cosmology)	Spirituality Aesthetic	Spirituality Purpose	Spirituality Constructive
Power	Power Aesthetic	Power Purpose	Power Constructive
Law	Law Aesthetic	Law Purpose	Law Constructive

Figure 2. Model suggested by Nader Ardalan

S. Gulzar Haider

The Grand Tradition of Islamic Architecture

Abdul Rehman

The word "tradition" refers to a set of beliefs or practices common to and in current usage among a specific group. Beliefs encompass a worldview, cosmological concepts, values and ethics; practices or behavior include rituals and all forms of art, architecture, and literature. Tradition is an essential part of the living culture of people. Traditions usually pass from one generation to the next. Perhaps because of its longevity, tradition acquires a common identity with its respective social group and is deeply embedded in the culture. The fundamental principal or prerequisite for Islamic architecture is the Islamic faith upon which its traditions are built. Islamic traditions are based upon divine principals laid down in the Koran and *hadith*.

Heritage refers to the architecture produced by earlier generations irrespective of time or faith. In Muslim countries that were under colonial rule, colonial monuments also form part of the repository of heritage. But if the design concept of a monument is in total contrast to the design traditions of the land in which it was built, the monument does not form part of the tradition.

Within the same faith, people evolve different solutions determined by geology, geography, and traditional methods of construction. For example, people living in interior maritime climates have evolved wind catchers and those living in cold climates have invented roof openings that create a comfortable interior environment.

Form and meaning in Islamic architecture is Islamic if the act of creation is in the spirit of divine faith regardless of where it is built. A building can be conceived for non-Islamic cultures adopting the local forms to meet the requirements of a particular space and time. The most fundamental belief of the Islamic faith is the declaration of faith, "There is no God but Allah, Mohammed is His last messenger." This *qalma* comprises the *tawhid* and *risalat*. The *tawhid* tells us that God is one and He alone is to be worshiped; in the *risalat* the Muslim believes in the truth of His last messenger. According to Islam, man is born pure; he has been given the capacity to know the nature of the physical world, and he is the vicegerent of God on earth. This statement points to man's unlimited scope, but also defines his role in the physical world. He has to manage the earthly resources, control them for his benefit, but with wisdom and with the sense of responsibility befitting the vicegerent of God.[1] He ought not to waste natural resources or intentionally destroy any living thing, whether plant or animal. As God is creative, wise, just, and merciful, so his vicegerent ought to manage things with religious zeal.

The fundamental message of Islam to the faithful is the maintenance of unity and discipline in their lives as in their works. This concept of unity in design and composition holds the highest position in the theory of design.

Architectural forms are composed of straight and curve lines. Straight lines are static, while curved lines symbolize motion. Some art critics maintain that straight and curved lines should be composed in such a way that they compliment each other, and one is never allowed to dominate the other. Ruskin states that all forms of acknowledged beauty are composed exclusively of curved and straight lines.[2] It is the fusion of two directly opposed formal elements. In a wider sense curved lines depict life, whereas straight lines represent decay and death and also show the direction of movement. The complex of *madrasas* in Samarqand and the Taj

Mahal in Agra are composed of curved and straight lines. The composition of these monuments is such that the whole arrangement gives a unified feeling without overcoming the other. In the finest examples of architecture great use is made of the contrast between rectangles and curves, and one is never allowed to dominate the other.

In the grand tradition of Islamic architecture a scheme of beauty is presented in which the component parts are so marvelously subordinated to the whole that no single item is allowed to draw the spectator away from his contemplation of the whole building. The buildings are conceived as a whole or a single unit. The various components and volumes are balanced in both vertical and horizontal planes. Therefore the architecture not only participates in the rhythms and forces of nature, but also in her binding harmony and unity. The color scheme is selected in such a way that it complements and enhances the volumetric quality of buildings. The minor details are equally important in the whole design scheme, but this becomes apparent when the user comes closer to a building. The principle of *tawhid* prohibits idolatry. Therefore the use of sculpture and human figures is disallowed. Ornamentation is characterized by a deliberate turning away from human passions and from idolatry.[3] The content of art in the form of arabesques, floral motifs, and geometrical designs burst through the forms. The form is enhanced and accentuated through the works of art, and art without form is of course unthinkable.

There are several objectives behind the artwork that can touch the two poles at the extreme ends. On one hand, art is used as an expression of exuberance or dance of life in modern art. On the other hand, in the grand tradition it is used as a symbol of discipline and restraint, as a refuge from action and an inducement to meditation. It is a noble blending of stability and austere beauty. The purity in design concept and purposely-designed decorations and vocabulary of decorative elements make these monuments landmarks in the history of architecture. In fact, the instinct of the artists and the faithful toil of the artisans have devised and achieved a blending of perfectly correlated abstract forms that induce a sensation of mystery, awe, and infinity.

After *tawhid* and *risalat* the belief that the Koran is a sacred book is another essential prerequisite of the Islamic faith. The Koran not only provides the code of conduct for believers, but also guides them to understand the nature and realities of nature. The mathematical nature of Islamic art and architecture is derived only from the Koran and not from external historical influences.

The mathematical structure of the Koran provides an amazing rapport between Islamic intellectual and spiritual concerns and mathematics. The mathematical nature of Islamic art is in a sense the externalization of the mathematics hidden in the very structure of the Koran and the numerical symbolism of its letters and words.[4]

The Muslim also strongly believes in both the physical and the metaphysical world, i.e., both what is apparent and what is hidden. Muslims believe in both a material and a supernatural world. Therefore, the Muslim uses a great deal of astronomy, geometry, and metaphysical concepts in architecture. Muslims developed these sciences and used them in all spheres of human endeavor. The Koran says: "Such as remember Allah, standing, sitting and reclining, and consider the creation of the heavens and the earth, (and says): Our Lord! Thou createst not this in vain" (3:191).

From the philosophical point of view architectural monuments were designed on the basis of pure geometry.[5] These structures carry body and soul. The body were designed using sacred geometry, and the soul were created with the help of light, ventilation, sound effects, landscape, color, texture, and symbolism used in both the interior and exterior. These monuments, whether a historic town house, a mosque, tomb, or garden, were the result of spiritual activity.

The Muslim's firm belief in paradise is based on the teaching of the Koran,[6] which says, "And those who believe and do good works such are rightful owners of the Garden. They will abide therein" (2:82). The detailed description of the garden of paradise is given in Sura "the Beneficent" (55: 46-78). Strongly influenced by the concept of paradise, Muslim architects created an earthly paradise.

Landscape features became an integral part of site planning and architecture. The buildings are set in the landscape deliberately so that one can find himself in an idealized paradisiacal environment. The buildings are designed in a way that make them become part of the landscape.[7] These buildings not only humanize the landscape but stand there in all their simplicity of form and witness the Divine. The introduction of elements of nature is an essential part of Islamic architecture.

Light has received adequate attention in the grand tradition of architecture. Throughout the centuries Sufis sang and wrote of the significance of light as a spiritual substance.[8] The Koran teaches us that God is the light of the Heavens and the Earth, and a prophetic saying adds a cosmological dimension to this verse: "The first being created by God was light." Islamic architecture makes full use of light and shade, and the heat and coolness of wind and its aerodynamics, of water and its cooling effect, of the earth and its insulating features as well as properties of the elements. Traditional architecture remains always in harmony with the environment.

Saleh Kamboh describes the spiritual significance of Mughal monuments at some length in his *Bahar-e-Sukhan*[9] where he states that these monuments made a distinct and powerful impression upon the observer because a personality behind the masses of brick and stone had transformed their inertness into living beauty which, though rooted in the dark earth, blends with the sunshine and the breeze, the far traveled lights of moon and midnight, the trees, waters and human life. The use of rigorously defined volumes based upon geometry, precise mathematical proportions, clearly defined lines relating to exact mathematical laws were the means whereby the space of Islamic architecture, as well as its surfaces, were integrated. The principal of unity was made more manifest.

In architecture and urban design man and his relations with family and community are given high priority and this is also reflected in the hierarchy of spaces that exist in great designs. Symbolically, the room depicts the "Cube of Man," and is related to the house, as the man is related to the family unit. Just as family life, with its sense of privacy is withdrawn from public view, so the courtyard house closes itself from the outside world, preserving the privacy and sanctity of its inner surface. The courtyard is further related to communal urban spaces, which then relate to the forecourt of the mosque. This spatial hierarchy is inspired by community life as described in the Koran and the Sunna.[10]

In addition to understanding Koranic revelation and the prophetic traditions (sunna), the traditional master builders had a profound sense of the nature of the materials with which they dealt. They created masterpieces because they had a mastery of the building sciences, the physical properties of materials, and the principals of design and were thereby able to integrate them into a whole, reflecting the ethos of Islamic art. These architects designed and executed the project. The on-site design and its execution were the key to success, and this helped a great deal in achieving high quality in architecture.

Notes

1. I. G. Edmonds, *Islam: A First Book* (New York-London: Franklin Watts, 1977) page. 15-16.

2. John Ruskin, *Seven Lamps of Architecture* (1849; rpt. Mineola, N.Y.: Dover Publishers, 1995) page 8-20.

3. Titus Burckhardt, *The Art of Islam, Language and Meaning* (London: The World of Islam, 1976).

4. Seyyed Hossein Nasr, *Islamic Art and Spirituality* (New York: Oxford University Press, 1990), p. 50.

5. On sacred geometry, especially in its relation to Islamic architecture, see Kenneth Critchlow, *Islamic Patterns* (London: Thames and Hudson, 1976).

6. M. M. Pickthall, *The Meaning of the Glorious Koran* (Mecca: Al-Muslim World League, 1977).

7. Abdul Rehman, "Garden Types in Mughal Lahore according to Early-Seventeenth-Century Written and Visual Sources," *Theory and Design of Gardens in the Time of the Great Muslim Empires*, ed. Attilio Petriccioli (Leiden: E. J. Brill, 1977).

8. Seyyed Hossein Nasr, *Islamic Art and Spirituality*, p. 56.

9. Mohammed Saleh Kamboh, *Bahar-i Sukhan* (1659) ms. Punjab Public Library Lahore.

10. Abdul Rehman, *Historic Towns of Punjab: Ancient and Medieval Period* (Lahore: Ferozsons 1997).

• • • • • • • • • • • • •

Abdul Rehman

Comments
S. Gulzar Haider

Professor Rehman's attempt to distinguish between tradition and heritage is valuable in that it might be used to settle exclusive claims over monuments by nations or transnational religions. Using his argument, for example, one could safely declare the Taj Mahal to be simultaneously a treasure of Indian heritage and an expression of Islamic tradition.

In discussing the form and meaning of Islamic architecture, however, while the author amply demonstrates his personal belief in Islam, he leaves much to be desired in exhibiting precision in his scholarship. In translating the universally known Islamic creed (*kalima-e-tayyiba*): *La ilaha ill Allah....* he adds of his own the adjective "last" in front of Mohammed's messengership.

In addition, his claim that belief in *tawhid* and *risalat* somehow precedes the belief in the Koran, his assertion that the Koran is "mathematical" in nature and the exclusive source of the "mathematical nature of Islamic art and architecture," his inaccurate translation of the Prophet's statement about the first creation, and his assumptions about the Koranic and Sunnic knowledge of the Muslim architects and other similar misuses of both the Koran and history all point to a style of scholarship where zeal inundates accuracy.

References to Ruskin's claims about curved and straight lines, their parallels to life and death and their correlation with the holistic, balanced view of Muslim life are farfetched. Finally one does wonder at the conspicuous absence of Ardalan and Bakhtiar's important book, *The Sense of Unity* from the list of books referred to.

Response

Professor Gulzar Haider has raised some important questions and my responses are as follows:

First of all, Muslims believe that Mohammed (peace be upon Him) is the last Prophet and the word "last" is used in the light of Koran 33:40, which says, "Mohammed is not the father of any man among you, but he is the messenger of Allah and the seal of the Prophets."

As far as the sequence of *tawhid*, *risalat*, and the Book i.e., the Koran, is concerned, it was made in the light of Koran 4:136, which says, "O ye who believe in Allah and His messenger and the scripture which He hath revealed into His messenger, and the Scripture which he revealed aforetime." The Koran refers to the obedience of Allah and the Prophet simultaneously in several places. It is also said in Koran 4:80, "Whoso obeyeth the messenger, obeyeth Allah, and whoso turneth away: We have not sent thee as a warder over them." To me in the light of the above, the position of Prophet Mohammed is clearly stated.

I have quoted the Prophetic saying from Seyyed Hossein Nasr's translation given in *Islamic Art and Spirituality* (Albany: SUNY Press, 1987), p. 50. For a discussion of the Koran and its mathematical structure, see the same work (p. 47) and his *Introduction to Islamic Cosmological Doctrines*, pp. 47 ff.

The architects of the medieval period had a thorough knowledge of the Koran and Sunna. The books written by these architects provide a glimpse of their love for Allah and the Prophet Mohammed. For example Mehmed Aga begins his book with a "Praise of Divine Creation" and ends it with a "prayer upon the pure souls of the Prophets" (Howard Crane, trans., *Risale Mimariyye: An Early Seventeenth-Century Ottoman Treatise on Architecture* (Leiden: E. J. Brill, 1987), pp. 20-21, 108. Ustad Lutfullah Muhandis's son Ustad Ahmad Mimar Lahori, the architect of the Taj Mahal, also expressed the same feelings in his book of poems, described by Abdullah Chughtai in *Ahmad Mimar Lahori Aur Us ka Khandan* (in Urdu) (Lahore, 1965).

In 1983 Kamil Khan Mumtaz published an interview with Mistri Haji Ghulam Hussein, a traditional architect from the Potowar region of Pakistan. Kamil Khan writes, "Haji Ghulam Hussain is a devout Muslim and follower of a certain Sufi saint of Potowar." Haji expresses his feelings in the following words: "When there is fear of God in one's heart one is prepared to be compassionate with everyone. All this will be left behind here. Even the Prophet for whom the two worlds have been created had to depart from this world" (Kamil Khan Mumtaz, "Haji Mistri Ghulam Hussain," *Mimar* 10 (1983): 12.

My recent research shows that medieval architects had knowledge of the Koran and Hadith. For details, see Abdul Rehman, *The Mughal Garden: History and Architecture*, forthcoming.

Abdul Rehman

Discovering Concepts from Faith

Khalil K. Pirani

This essay proposes one possible definition of Islamic architecture. It must be established at the outset that I am neither a scholar in Islamic theology nor an academician. What follows is based upon individual learning and understanding about the faith and architecture.

Islam is a way of life. The task of understanding architecture in the spirit of Islam becomes easier when one accepts the fact that teachings of the faith Islam are not only meant for spiritual upliftment but they offer guidance for the mundane life of a Muslim. In my opinion it is a misconception that there is no such thing as Islamic architecture and that religion cannot influence architectural concepts.

Islamic architecture is a simple subject insofar as it refers to building according to the principles of Islam. It becomes complex when one realizes that the interpretation of what the principles of Islam might be is entirely subjective, and the implications for architecture of these concepts therefore extremely complex. The more I think about it the more I am convinced that a prerequisite to understanding Islamic architecture is the proper interpretation of these principles. They can then be applied to architecture in the broadest possible terms for the betterment of all humanity. It is up to each individual to interpret the principles of Islam and to apply them.

The following concepts offer one possible understanding of Islamic architecture. Each point begins with a verse from the Koran. An interpretation and its application to architecture follow. Koranic verses have been used to simply set forth the concept and not meant for literal interpretation or to give any religious significance to these concepts.

1. Dynamism of the Faith and a Constantly Evolving Search

> This day have I perfected your religion for you, completed my favor upon you, and have chosen for you Islam as your religion. (5:4)

Muslims believe that Islam is the final religion sent by God and that it is meant for all times and all places. This implies that Islam is equipped to guide people for all times and all places. Hence it has to be a dynamic faith, adaptable to any society or period. Thus, Islamic architecture cannot be a specific style as is Roman, Byzantine, or Gothic. It is the name of a constantly evolving search for design in the spirit of Islam for the betterment of all humanity. Just as God's creation is never ending, so should be an architect's search to build for the improvement of all humanity.

2. Intellect and the Use of Knowledge for Architectural Solutions

> He Who created thee, fashioned thee in due proportion, and gave thee a just bias. (82:6) He has made subject to you the Night and the Day; the Sun and the Moon; and the Stars are in subjection by His Command: verily in this are Signs for men who are wise. (16:12)

In all aspects of life, Islam encourages the use of intellect and knowledge to the utmost. In fact, intellect is regarded as an integral part of the faith. This implies that any architectural solution has to be properly analyzed, thoroughly thought through, and carefully implemented. Architects therefore should also reason and understand how architectural solutions relate to history and culture, to the socioeconomic aspects of a society, and to the local built environment of a place. It is owing to the bestowed intellect that humans have been assigned the stewardship of this earth and of God's creations.

3. Status of Man and his Responsibility of Protecting the Environment

> It is He Who hath made you (His) agents, inheritors of the earth: He hath raised you in ranks some above others. . . . (6:165) We have indeed created man in the best of moulds. (95:4) Behold, thy Lord said to the angels: "I will create a vicegerent on earth.". . . (2:30)

Humans have been created by God in the finest of forms and have been appointed to be His vicegerent on earth. This implies that man is not only responsible for taking care of God's creations such as the earth and the natural environment but also leave behind a better environment for future generations. Architects, and clients need to understand the significance of this responsibility and consider the impact of every project on the environment. Concepts such as recycling of building materials, energy conservation, and deforestation due to development are among the many to consider. Examples are the reforestation program of the Middle East Technical University in Turkey and the Menara Mesiniaga building in Kuala Lumpur, Malaysia. (Figure 1).

4. Respect for History and Tradition

> All that we relate to thee of the stories of the apostles, with it We make firm thy heart: in them cometh to thee the Truth as well as an exhortation and a message of remembrance to those who believe (11:120). There is, in their stories, instruction for men endued with understanding. It is not a tale invented, but a confirmation of what went before it, a detailed exposition of all things, and a Guide and a Mercy to any such as believe. (12:111)

For many architects history is nothing but a catalogue of old buildings to imitate. This has produced meaningless and mediocre buildings in Muslim societies. One of the most challenging aspects of practicing architecture is to understand how to extract meaning from history and apply the lessons to contemporary architecture. Understanding history is a function of the intellect. To find meaning in history, architects should utilize their intellect to the utmost and continuously search for meaning from historical buildings. The restoration of the Baltit Fort in Pakistan is a good example of how historical buildings

can have a positive influence on the contemporary built environment (Figure 2).

5. Balance in all Aspects of Life

> We sent aforetime our Apostles with Clear Signs and sent down with them the Book and the Balance, that men may stand forth in justice. (57:25) It is God Who has sent down the Book in Truth, and the Balance. (42:17)

As mentioned above Islam is a way of life. For Muslims the material life on earth is closely linked to the spiritual life hereafter and no separation exists between the body and the spirit. Without material comfort, attaining spiritual enlightenment is very difficult. Therefore, Muslims are enjoined to maintain a balance. Houses, offices, schools, parks, places of worship, therefore have an impact not only on the physical life but on the spiritual life as well. Thus, architecture should be conducive to physical

Figure 1. Kuala Lumpur, Malaysia. The Menara Mesiniaga building attempts to respond to local climatic needs through its architecture and hence provides energy savings to its client. (Photo courtesy AKTC)

Khalil K. Pirani

32

comfort, which in turn supports practice of the faith and thus elevate the soul.

6. Diversity in Tradition and Culture

If thy Lord had so willed, He could have made mankind one people: but they will not cease to dispute. (11:118) And among His signs is the creation of the heavens and the earth, and the variations in your languages and your colors: verily in that are Signs for those who know. (30:22)

God acknowledges diversity of colors, languages, cultures, traditions, and histories. Thus Islam respects diversity and teaches respect for diverse cultures and the maintenance of their architectural identity. In Islam diversity is strength and not a weakness. Hence the concept of architectural regionalism is very important. Many architects believe that Islamic architecture has to have elements such as the dome and the arch. This is not true. It cannot be true because imitating styles dilutes diversity and regionalism.

Figure 2. Hunza, Pakistan. The restoration of this 600-year-old Baltit Fort has had a positive impact in preserving the local built environment of the village of Karimabad. The fort in this village of Karimabad plays the role of a guardian for the villagers. (Photo courtesy AKTC)

Khalil K. Pirani

Figure 3. Paris, France. The Institut du Monde Arabe makes reference to the wooden screens used in several Middle Eastern societies for sun control and privacy by introducing metallic screens on windows at larger scale. (Photo courtesy AKTC)

7. No Conflict Between Science and Faith

He has subjected the sun and the moon (to His Law)! Each one runs (its course) for a term appointed. He doth regulate all affairs, explaining the Signs in detail, that ye may believe with certainty in the meeting with your Lord. (8:2) It is He who made the sun to be a shining glory and the moon to be a light (of beauty), and measured out stages for her; that ye might know the number of years and the count (of time). Nowise did God create this but in truth and righteousness. (Thus) doth He explain His Signs in detail, for those who understand. (10:5)

Islam is an all-embracing faith, and science is not excluded from it. The Koran refers to various aspects of science in a number of instances. It goes further and asks of believers to look for signs of God in all His creations. Thus the Koran enjoins upon believers to study science. All branches of science such as medicine, astronomy, physics, chemistry, zoology, and botany are devoted to the study of nature. Architecture is not only a social science but it is also a creative use of mathematics and scientific technology. Islamic architecture does not preclude

Khalil K. Pirani

using new materials innovatively and rationally. A good example of this attempt to blend technology and traditional features is the Institut du Monde Arabe in Paris (Figure 3).

8. Considering Poor and Less Fortunate People

> And be steadfast in prayer and regular in charity. (2:110) But it is righteous ... to spend of your substance, out of love for Him, for your kin, for orphans, for the needy, for the wayfarer, for those who ask. (2:177)

As a social science, architecture is a vehicle to help the poor and enhance and preserve the dignity of the less fortunate. Craftsmen and skilled laborers who at one time produced significant arts and crafts are fast becoming obsolete owing to new technology imported to developing countries. Whenever possible, architects should give preference to labor-intensive building where there is need of employment. In addition, innovative housing projects for the poor need to be developed. Examples: The Garameen Bank project in Bangladesh (Figure 4) and the Khuda Ki Basti, an incremental housing project in Pakistan.

9. Humility, Tolerance and Truth in Search for Better Solutions

> Has not the time arrived for the Believers that their hearts in all humility should engage in the remembrance of God and the Truth. (57:16) And remember it was said to them: "Dwell in this town and eat therein as ye wish, but say the word of humility and enter the gate in a posture of humility." (7:161)

Humility needs to be exercised by architects working in rural areas and designing in relation to nature and its preservation. The search for truth in all matters is the basis of the faith of Islam. Truth should be exercised in searching for the best possible solution for the client and the environment.

These are only a few of the many concepts that can be extracted from the faith and applied to architecture. Moreover, the interpretation of the holy verses mentioned above is only one of several possibilities. There are as many interpretations as there are minds. Observance of such concepts will generate an architectural trend that will guide not only Muslim societies but Western countries also. It is

Figure 4. The Garameen Bank in Bangladesh provides loans to low-income families to build their homes and provide other basic needs to improve the living conditions. (Photo courtesy AKTC)

Khalil K. Pirani

not possible to isolate one single characteristic from another to define Islamic architecture. Some characteristics such as technology or relevance to history may take precedence over others, depending on the project and type. It is the composition, the whole ensemble that acquires the characteristic and not an isolated element.

Each individual should contemplate what it is to build in the spirit of Islam. Different minds will develop different definitions and freethinking has no limits. Creativity is neither of the East nor of the West. The time has come for the dormant traditions of Islam to rise to serve all humanity as they did centuries ago.

> God is the Light of the heavens and the earth. The parable of His Light is as if there were a Niche and within it a Lamp: the Lamp enclosed in Glass: The glass as it were a brilliant star: Lit from a blessed tree, an Olive, neither of the East nor of the West. . . . (24:35)

• • • • • • • • • • • • •

Comments
S. Gulzar Haider

Khalil Pirani's paper is valuable, first and foremost, as a call against the pursuit of tightly bounded definition(s) of "Islamic" architecture within some monolithic, static and formally unique view of Islam. Whether one agrees with the specifics of his arguments or not one cannot help reading the overall message about the diversity of Koranic interpretations, the evolving nature of Islam, and its inherent ability to remain relevant and adaptable as a source of ethics and inspiration in diverse situations and times. In this sense Pirani's approach can be considered reflective of Iqbalian dynamism. The paper is also disarmingly well intended in proposing a set of nine architectural heuristics, claiming to be rooted in Islamic faith, and stated in a tone of advice for the contemporary architects. It is obvious that the concepts offered will inject ethical dimensions to the practice of architecture.

Even though the author, in the very first paragraph of the paper, tries to absolve himself of the responsibilities of a "scholar in Islamic theology" or an "academician" the fact remains that he just cannot escape the burden of the statements he makes, the Koranic verses he selects, and the correspondence he offers among these verses and the architectural concepts.

His statements that the "interpretation of what the principles of Islam might be is entirely subjective" and later "there are as many interpretations as there are minds" show characteristic misunderstanding about the highly cautious and self-critical traditions of the exegesis of the Koran. The fact that the scholars of Islam differ is not because of subjectivity or because of some self-referential exercise of one individual mind against the other.

While the verses for concept 4 and 6 fit rather well, those for concepts 2 and 5 are questionable. Also the claim about architecture being a social science serves neither architecture nor the vast and often confusingly complex matrix of social sciences. That the architecture be called upon to "enhance and preserve the dignity of the less fortunate" is a laudable goal because of its inherent ethical dimension and would be true even if architecture was put forth as an applied art as against a social science.

Response
I very much respect and appreciate Prof. Gulzar Haider's comments. My admittance of not being a scholar was intended not as an excuse but to acknowledge my relative ignorance among the highly revered collection of authors cited in this volume in particular, and in the field of architecture, in general.

The concept of individual search and interpretation stems from the notion of free will that every human being is bestowed with. This individual search has to be executed within a certain code of ethics based upon the faith. It is a fact that any artifact is bound to be "read" and interpreted differently by different individuals. The notion of what makes a building Islamic lies not only on physical characteristics but very much so on intangible characteristics such as the spirit in which it was perceived and built. The intent of the process of construction also plays a role in classifying a building to be in the spirit. Such intangible characteristics differentiate a good architecture from another.

Khalil K. Pirani

For the above mentioned reasons architecture as an applied art may not necessarily be of much help to solve societal problems and for the improvement of living conditions of human being in poor societies versus when it is being used as a social science. This needs to be further debated in a different forum.

I agree with Prof. Haider that some verses cited above do not fully relate to concepts that can be applied specifically to architecture. A more thorough study of the Koran is certainly required. In any case, the message of Islam is fairly universal aimed for improvement of the environment for all humanity just as mentioned by John Ruskin in the following: "God has lent us the earth for our life; it is a great entail. It belongs as much as to those who are to come after us, and whose names are already written in the book of creation, as to us; and we have no right, by anything that we do or neglect, to involve them in unnecessary penalties, or deprive them of benefits which it was in our power to bequeath."[1]

Notes

1. John Ruskin, *The Seven Lamps of Architecture*. Farrar Straus and Giroux, New York. 1979.

Khalil K. Pirani

Section II

MEANING FROM HISTORY

Authors in this section have used historical buildings and planning concepts to draw meaning from and to suggest how to apply lessons learned to contemporary practice. Where an answer is not available they have raised questions for readers to think about. Ronald Lewcock focuses on some basic features of Islamic cities and creates distinctions between the historical cities of Muslim societies with their Western counterparts. Ludovico Micara examines the "intermediaries" of a mosque and provides readers with examples of how to read and interpret historical buildings in their respective cultures. His essay also alludes to how Muslim and non-Muslim cultures perceive architecture. Jale Nejdet Erzen analyzes the spatial organization in Muslim societies, in general, and Ottoman architecture in particular. She further draws distinctions with European religious architecture and how it differs from its Muslim counterpart. Adhi Moersid, Achmad Fanani, Tulus Setyo Budhi and Mahvash Alemi focus on the concept of flexibility of Islam according to time and place. The Indonesian scholars examine how the faith of Islam was adopted in their new society without altering or imposing any specific style of architecture. Mahvash Alemi investigates whether traditional Persian landscape design was affected or altered with the introduction of Islam into Persia.

Cities in the Islamic World

Ronald Lewcock

...[The] streets are wholly indescribable, their narrowness, antiquity, sharp lights, and arcades of gloom, carved lattices, mat awnings, mixture of hubbub and fatalist quietude ...the modes of buying and selling....

Harriet Martineau, *Eastern Life, Past and Present.* 1848

If the early Muslims were inheritors of the Greco-Roman tradition in the countries of their first conquests outside the Arabian Peninsula—Palestine, Syria and Egypt—why did the formal urban order that belonged to that tradition disappear, taking with it its civic calm and dignity? Or, to put it another way: in those places where traces of the Greco Roman city can still be discerned, like Damascus and Aleppo, why did the regular plan become so completely broken down into an apparently disorderly plan after the Arab conquests?

The answer almost certainly is that the disintegration of the regularity of these Greco-Roman cities was due to the Muslim attitude to the organization of life in urban communities. The foundation or appropriation of any city by conquering Muslims was followed by the need to establish a system for distribution of the land within it. This appears to have been was done simply by the ruler allocating a fairly large zone alongside a main road to each of the chiefs (*sheikhs*) of the tribes or clans under his jurisdiction. This subdivision became the basis for the quarter system. Naturally, each of these newly allocated tribal or clan areas (called in various regions a *dar*, a *har*, or a *mahalla*) soon acquired an entry street, and then side streets that led to the habi-

tations. With the passage of time the land was more and more subdivided, as families split their inheritance: the urban area became more and more densely occupied and the number of dead-end lanes proliferated, to produce in the end a system of distribution streets which typically resembled a tree with branches (Figure 1).

This quarter system was the genesis of the unique urban characteristics that can still be seen in Islamic countries from Morocco to Indonesia. Unless they have been modernized, old cities in Muslim countries basically differ from Western cities in three essentials: Firstly, the urban area is divided into the quarters described above—each segregated from the other and accessed from the through streets by complicated branch-like networks that end in dead-end lanes; secondly, the streets are narrow—there are no sidewalks; animal and vehicular traffic is mixed with pedestrian, and, thirdly, there are seldom any sizeable open spaces attached to the street system—Islam had little tradition of the public participation in government that led to the creation of the Greek agora, the Roman forum and the medieval market square.

Each of these aspects of the characteristic city in Islam has significant implications. The narrowness of the streets with their mixed traffic creates a vibrant street life, full of noise and bustle, with movement slow enough to facilitate social interaction and improve shopping. (It is interesting to note the resemblance of the above characteristics to those of modern shopping malls in the West). In the traditional city in the Islamic world, because of the narrowness of the streets, vehicular and animal traffic being mixed with pedestrian crowds is forced to slow down. It sometimes constitutes a nuisance to

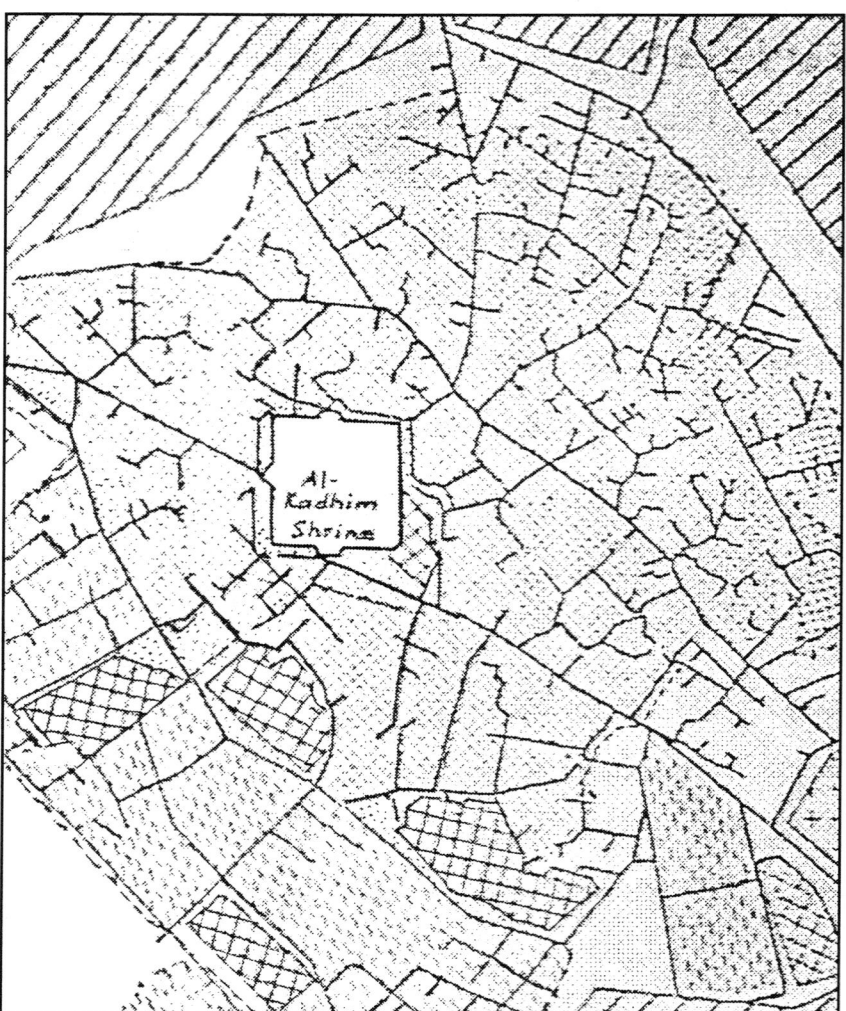

Figure 1. Sketch plan of Kadhimiyah, part of old Baghdad. Clearly visible is the pattern of main through streets, secondary branch streets, and tertiary dead-end lanes.

the pedestrians, but seldom an insupportable one. The thoroughfares are lined with shops, frequently so small that they seem little larger than cupboards. The goods sold by them are produced within the shops or in a larger workshop nearby. The vast majority of the shops in the city are grouped in a central market or *suq*, itself a quarter with its own governor, or *sheikh*. The streets of the market are organized by craft or type of goods, colorful textiles, fine carpets, polished daggers, decorated water pipes and so on. Sometimes the market, and less often parts of the through streets, are shaded with awnings or roofs to provide shade, constructed from brick or stone vaulting or made of wood, canvas or brightly colored cloth (Figure 2).

In small towns the markets and the caravanserais might be located at one or two of the town gateways. But in larger cities the main market was centrally situated near the Friday mosque. Before mod-

ern times, trading caravans with goods had to penetrate through the town to the market, which was surrounded by the caravanserais needed to accommodate the camels, donkeys, horses, goods and merchants until they departed. Inns like medieval European ones were also sometimes built. Near the markets there were small crushing mills in which animal power was used to grind commodities such as salt and sesame oil.

Each residential quarter focused on its own main street, which led to it from one of the through streets. As these quarters were traditionally closed off from each other at night, they had their own public water fountains or cisterns, shops and craft-workshops, as well as local mosques, shrines of holy men, public baths, schools for teaching the Koran to children, and possibly clinics and even hospitals. These would be arranged along the quarter's main street; from it branched side streets leading to the

Ronald Lewcock

narrow, dead-end residential lanes. The main streets would be thronged with a jostling, multi-colored crowd of men, women, children and animals, the residential lanes quiet and empty. Houses traditionally appeared anonymous and blank-walled at the street level, the only openings being the single entrance doorways, which were often polished, painted, and placed in elaborate frames. Above, screened windows like the women's veils protected the privacy of the home, while allowing the inhabitants light, air, and the possibility of outside views.

The absence of open public spaces in the traditional cities in the Islamic world was remarkable to a visitor from the West. (Samarqand and Isfahan were unique exceptions). The sometimes-mooted idea that the courtyard of the Friday mosque was a distant descendant of the Roman forum has to be abandoned when one realizes that the mosque was reserved space, with all the restrictions that that entailed. Often only Muslim men (who had performed the required ablutions) were admitted; in any case public meetings for political debate were never countenanced there (or indeed elsewhere in Muslim communities). It is important to remember that many Muslim cities had substantial communities of Christians and Jews, with sometimes only two thirds or even half the population Muslim.

The absence of wide spaces in the street system meant that Islamic architects were confronted with a particular problem in dignifying public buildings externally. They succeeded in achieving a monumental quality by using a number of architectural devices. Firstly, by the enormous scale of the door portals or *iwans* (in Cairo some of them are over fifty feet high). Secondly, by minarets placed on the street facade, so that they dominated the distant view as they broke the skyline. Thirdly, their facades were built in distinctive materials, and often striped or checkered to draw attention to their religious function (Figure 4). Finally, when it was possible, part of the facade of the public building was projected into the street so that it could be seen from a distance.

The practice of projecting a facade into the street raises the issue of whether the dense fabric of cities of the Islamic world was controlled by build-

Figure 2. The color and varied costumes in the crowded traditional market of San'a', Yemen.

Ronald Lewcock

Figure 3. Aerial photograph of the old city of San'a', Yemen, in 1972. The mosque and the market behind it, in the upper center, are surrounded by the quarters, many separated by market gardens (*bustans*).

ing regulations or laws. In fact, there were very few controls. Those that existed were "customary laws", established by local custom over long periods. These tended to vary from one country or city to another. Cities on the sites of Cairo, Damascus, Istanbul, Aleppo, Samarqand and Lahore were important long before they became Muslim. It is possible to generalize, however, and say that, because customary law was influenced by Islamic law (which was enshrined in the Koran and the *hadith*, the sayings of the prophet), cities in Muslim countries tended to share the same kinds of essential controls.

The extension of buildings into the street was considered from the points of view of the principles of tolerance and right of passage. If any citizen felt that a new construction interfered with the movement of animals and goods by unreasonably narrowing the thoroughfare, he could appeal to a *qadi* or magistrate, who would settle the issue by holding a public court, usually at the site.

Another restriction of this kind was interference with another's privacy. If anyone felt that the privacy in his building was threatened by the construc-

tion of a new building he would resort to the same appeal to law. In order to minimize this problem it was a custom to assume that any new building would have openings in its facades of the size and shape of those that had been there before. If this was not observed, a public inquiry might become necessary, with a decision from a *qadi*. Should an appeal against his decision be sought, it could be made to the governor.

Water rights were another continuous bone of contention—but this was actually true as much in the countryside as the city. Their control was a major factor in the organization of farm production and of human settlements alike.

The choice of site for a city in the semi-arid conditions of most Islamic countries—from India and Central Asia to Marrakesh—was determined principally by the availability of water. A river crossing was an obvious place. Otherwise an area traversed by streams or with natural springs would be ideal. Finally, a site might be selected because of the presence of an underground water table from which water could be tapped by digging wells, with

Ronald Lewcock

Figure 4. View of a narrow through street in Cairo in the last century, showing how public buildings were designed and treated to draw attention to their significance.

Ronald Lewcock

the water raised into cisterns using human and animal power. Whether the source was from natural springs or from such storage cisterns, it was usual, wherever possible, to lead the water through the city down the course of the thoroughfares, just below the paving of the streets, enclosed in *kanats* or *ghayls* made of masonry. In this way, fresh water supplies were ensured throughout the city. The water was either made available to the citizens in public cisterns (*sabils*) dispersed at regular intervals throughout the city, or it was actually distributed through secondary *kanats* to serve wells in private courtyards or house vestibules. Once it had become soiled or soapy, the water was either filtered into the ground using open drains or seepage tanks, or, alternatively, a further system of *kanats* was introduced solely to carry away sewerage and dirty water.

Domestic sewerage was separated within the home into wet, effluent and dry waste. The wet sewerage was handled in the way just described. The dry waste, which included human excrement, was collected in closed rooms on the ground floor, and periodically transferred outside of its city in boxes or bags—as night soil used to be in the West—or carried to furnaces within the city, where it was burnt as fuel to heat the public baths.

Cities in the Islamic world were usually surrounded by walled fortifications. Outside of the gates were the special markets reserved for noxious commodities, manure, firewood, sometimes meat and fish. Cemeteries were almost always outside the walls—as was the communal prayer ground, the *musalla*, in which was celebrated the two great dawn prayers of the Muslim calendar, one at the end of Ramadan, the other to mark the beginning of the new year; within the *musalla* a low white wall served as the *qibla* to mark the direction of prayer.

Within the city dwelt the farmers who cultivated the surrounding countryside. Some of their farms were even within the city walls. These were generally market gardens, *bustans*, taking up the spaces that were originally left open to separate the quarters, and to reduce faction fighting between residents belonging to different tribes or clans (Figure 3). In these market gardens farmers generally grew vegetables, and the two important delicacies of Muslim cuisine, radishes and spring onions. They were fertilized with the ash from the furnaces of the public bath (burnt human waste), located at the edge of each garden. Near the bath, and often also on the edge of the *bustan*, was the quarter mosque, which the public bath provided with income, according to the Islamic law of charitable foundation (*waqf*).

The policing of the city was the responsibility of the *sheikhs* of the quarters. Crime was seldom serious (Islamic penalties were severe), but particular caution was exercised in the market quarter, where the *sheikh* maintained a night watch with rooftop guard posts.

Planned cities were much more regular and rational in their layout than cities that grew by accretion over time—as might be expected. Since they generally lacked the organic system of the quarter structure, with all its complexities, it is not surprising that few planned cities survived for long in their original form. They were either abandoned or quickly modified to accommodate the pressures and complexities of daily life through the principle of subdivision and encroachment discussed above. Nevertheless, the persistence with which they were designed is evidence that Muslim rulers and city fathers valued visual order. Two bold attempts have survived until modern times. The late fourteen century Registan of Samarqand, the capital of Timur, is still a grand public square (originally a market), although the fine buildings now surrounding it arose later. The huge rectangular Maydan of Isfahan, built by Shah Abbas at the end of the sixteenth century, survives intact, lined by a double storied arcade and with great axially placed gateways to the market and the royal mosque at its ends.

Modernization has usually meant driving wide, straight thoroughfares through the traditional quarters and markets, with disastrous effects on the functioning of these essential parts of the old cities. Sections of quarters and markets that have been divided by modern roadways have quickly died, or their original functions have been replaced by strip developments of western type.

The conservation and rehabilitation of old cities in the Islamic world has not proved as difficult as might be expected, provided that there is government willingness to effect it. The traditional way of life is very resilient, and is preferred by many of the inhabitants, including even a significant number of the young and educated. In cities such as Cairo and San'a', the narrow streets have proved navigable by modern mini-vehicles for use both for service and emergencies, provided that speeds are controlled by special road surfaces and bollard systems so that the pedestrian-vehicle mix is not affected. And upgrading kitchens and bathrooms has generally given traditional housing a new lease of life at little cost without difficulty. The steady increase in the num-

Ronald Lewcock

ber of modern motor vehicles has necessitated the provision of special parking areas, usually on a peripheral ring system; the public have proved surprisingly amenable to walking two or three hundred meters (yards) to their homes, provide that certain hours of the day are set aside—usually in the evening—when cars may be driven to their houses to deliver goods.

In conclusion, the title of this essay, 'Cities in the Islamic World', was carefully chosen because this type of city is basically more ancient than Islam. Indeed, there is considerable evidence in archaeology to suggest that it closely resembles in its main characteristics the early cities of Mesopotamia, Egypt and South Asia that also developed free plans due to the system of parceling out urban lands of the leaders of tribes or regional groups. From another point of view there is need for caution, since descendants of the ancient city type exist in other cultures than Islam, notably in Hindu India.

Bibliography

Akbar, Jamel. *Crisis in the Built Environment: The Case of the Muslim City,* Concept Media, Mimar Books, 1988.

Hakim, Besim Selim. *Arabic Islamic Cities: Building and Planning Principles,* Kegan Paul International, London, 1988.

Lapidus, I. (ed.) *Middle Eastern Cities,* University of California Press, Berkeley, 1979.

Lewcock, Ronald. "Working with the Past", in *Theories and Principles of Design in the Architecture of Islamic Societies,* AKP, 1988.

Serageldin, Ismail & El-Sadek, Samir. *The Arab City: Its Character and Islamic Cultural Heritage*, Proceedings of the Symposium, Medina, Kingdom of Saudi Arabia, 1981.

Serjeant, R.B. (ed.) *The Islamic City,* UNESCO, Paris, 1980.

Serjeant, R.B. & Lewcock, R.B. *San'a' and Arabian Islamic City,* World of Islamic Festival Trust, London, 1983.

● ● ● ● ● ● ● ● ● ● ● ●

Comments
Oleg Grabar

I find it difficult now (as opposed to decades ago) to consider cities in the Islamic world as a single broad concept. The article is right in everything it says (or almost, as mosques were used for political debates and discussions!), but what comes out is a colorless and lifeless city, when movement and activity actually characterize nearly all urban centers. In fact, I feel there was no Islamic city ever except perhaps Khiva around 1800, but there were hundreds of cities with Muslims, all more different from each other than similar, all rich with a complex inner life rather than embodiments of a few abstract principles.

Response

In this very brief article I have tried to avoid sweeping generalizations while helping readers to understand why traditional towns and cities in the Islamic world appear to differ so much from the old cities of the Western World. My view is that the religio-political, social and cultural similarities between most towns and cities in the Islamic world generally imparted to them, before the twentieth century, a strong functional similarity.

Ronald Lewcock

Lofty Chambers: The Interior Space in the Architecture of Islamic Countries

Ludovico Micara

"The believers . . . will be lodged in Paradise, in lofty chambers, underneath which rivers flow."
Koran 29:58

In a recent study, *The Mediation of Ornament,*[1] the well-known historian of Islamic art Oleg Grabar sets forth an exciting "theory of intermediaries in art," intending ornament as "agents that are not logically necessary to the perception of a visual message, but without which the process of understanding would be more difficult." Among these intermediary agents that are apt to "facilitate or even compel access to the work of art, strengthening the pleasure derived from looking at something," he distinguishes "writing, geometry, architecture, nature" that "evoke . . . in viewers well-defined emotions and stances: control and forcefulness of assertion with writing, order with geometry, boundaries and protection with architecture, life forces with nature, and throughout sensory pleasure. . . ."

The chapter dedicated to "The Intermediary of Architecture" focuses on the analysis of two extraordinary images with architectural subjects from a Koran manuscript. The manuscript codex was found in the Great Mosque of San'a' in Yemen while the building was undergoing repairs and, according to scholars, belongs to the eight century. These are therefore early images, among the first in the Islamic world to have an architectural subject. The two drawings (Figures 1 and 2) are not easily interpreted as mosques. These images, in which elements of plan and elevation are juxtaposed, describe two types of hypostyle space: the first is characterized by a full height axial nave, oriented towards the *mihrab*, that cuts a series of arcades on two levels; the second is defined by a central court onto which the nave opens and by the great arch of the *mihrab*, where the symmetrical axis ends. In the lower part of the two drawings and therefore in the front part of the buildings are the doors. There are two doors on either side of a central one in the mosque with an axial nave, and only two side doors in the mosque with the *sahn*.

A series of curious details point to certain features of the building and the space of the mosque: the minbar located to the right of the space in front of the *mihrab*; the spiral stairs on the back of the building that suggest two symmetrical minarets; the staircase that elevates the first building on a podium, decorated with amphorae and spaces for ablutions; the casual cut through a thick cornice, or enclosure, of the repetitive system of the naves, that can be extended further; the design of a paradisiacal garden in the back of the mosque, composed of tall trees and flowing water at their base.

These images, beyond their ichnographic contents, are intermediary and indeed refer to something else that does not belong to the context in which they appear, that is the decoration of a text of the Koran; however they contribute additional meanings through the power of evoking architectural drawings. But in a more general way these architectures and the way they are represented suggest a particular idea of space, of a way of conceiving the environment built for man, according to a certain culture and civilization.

Let us interpret these images in a different way. The first approach is that of reading these representations as elevations, that is, as views of the exterior aspects of the two buildings. A podium with staircases anchors the building to the ground; entrance

Figure 1. Reconstruction of a frontispiece from Koran. (Drawn from Oleg Grabar, *The Mediation of Ornament,* Princeton, 1992).

doors and a series of overhanging arcades face the exterior. In the center of the elevation are loggias that are wider and higher than the arcades. At the top an *altana* concludes the vertical axis of symmetry and the hanging gardens gracefully define the relation of the buildings with the sky. One of these buildings is flanked on the roof by two light towers that contain spiral stairs.

What we have tried to describe is a plausible explanation that makes sense looking at the images. We have simply interpreted, one above the other,

the structures disposed, probably, one behind the other. But it is the very technique of representation and the adopted communicative system, largely used in miniatures, that allows this interpretation.

These different ways of reading, both justified by the concrete image to which they refer, originate from two different cultural standpoints that lead to diverging interpretations. We may observe that the first interpretation, more complex and elaborate, only partly explains the exterior form of the building, while it describes in a more extensive way its

Ludovico Micara

Figure 2. Reconstruction of a frontispiece or finispiece from Koran. (Drawn from Oleg Grabar. *The Mediation of Ornament*, Princeton, 1992).

plan and interior space. On the other hand, the second one relies mainly on the elevation as a synthetic representation of the principal aspects of the building.

These interpretations not only explain two different ways of representation, but also tell us about the underlying idea of architecture as it is expressed in two different cultures generically referred to as Islamic and Western. If we were to represent one of the most important buildings of the Islamic world, the Great Mosque of Cordoba, in a synthetic image, we would certainly choose a view of the hypostyle interior space, and of the fascinating and complex juxtaposition of its parallel naves. Certainly we would not choose an image of its elevation, which in this type of architecture, aside from the entrance portals, is a secondary aspect and at times does not exist at all. In contrast, in a representative Western

Ludovico Micara

Figure 3. Yazd. Courtyard of the Masjid-i Jum'a covered with canvas during a funeral ceremony. (Photo: L. Micara).

building, such as the Farnese Palace in Rome, the elevation and its architectural order and relative proportions is far more significant and better communicates the features of the palace.

The fundamental concept of architecture in the Islamic world is enclosure. This, in the mosque as in the house, delimits the space and separates the place of architecture from all that is without: the urban fabric, or the landscape and the natural world. The enclosure is entered through well-defined and expressive portals. These are almost the only architectural elements that characterize the external elevations. Their location in the mosque is not generally on the symmetrical axis, but is related to the urban routes and directions to which the building is connected. Only in relatively recent times did the monumental purposes of the Ottoman and Safavid empires lead to axial entrances, in addition to side ones.

Once within the enclosure, it is possible to appreciate the symbolic-communicative system of the mosque. It is based, in the hypostyle type, on the repetition or juxtaposition of spatial modules or naves, oriented in the longitudinal or transversal direction to the *qibla* wall. The analysis of the growth of the Great Mosque of Cordova or the Masjid-i-Jum'a in Isfahan shows their flexibility and the possibility of responding to an increasing demand for prayer space. The great interior public space is exalted by the juxtaposition of additional naves with different architectural features.

However, the architectural logic that underlies the composition of the mosque is not limited to the creation of a great sacred interior space, "the lofty chamber," but also includes open space, "the garden," the paradisiacal reward of the believer that, in the mosque, is synthesized in the courtyard and its water basin. Thus we can read the courtyard of the mosque as the appropriation of the external space and its modification into an "interior" one—an open space covered by the sky (Figure 3). The emphasis on the interior space of the mosque explains why some of the symbolic communicative procedures of

Ludovico Micara

the Islamic world appear so frequently here: the use of Koranic inscriptions, the so-called arabesques, and the omnipresent abstract decorations and geometries articulating, through the *muqarnas*, specific architectural spaces.

While the inscriptions symbolically associate the sacred word of the Koran to the structure of the building, contributing to the understanding of their metaphoric meaning, the geometric decoration, and in particular the *muqarnas,* resolves the points of transition between different architectural parts. The squinches or pendentives mediate between the square plan of the supports and the circular plan of the cupola. The complex vaults of the *iwan* in Persian architecture mediate between the exterior and interior, announcing the sacred values to the urban scene. In this way the interior space is presented as a harmonious architectural, decorative, and geometric unit, becoming intelligible to the believer through the divine word. The same inseparable and extraordinary unity is possible to perceive in some of the masterpieces of Safavid Isfahan, such as the Royal Mosque or the Sheikh Lutfullah Mosque.

Does it make sense to recall these values today? Is it possible to find in so-called modern architecture such an involving interest for an interior space, susceptible to becoming the source of inspiration for new projects?

When in 1911 Charles Edouard Jeanneret, called Le Corbusier, visited Istanbul during his *Voy-*

Figure 4. Chandigarh. View of the interior space of the Palace of Assembly. (Drawn from: *Le Corbusier, Architect of the Century*, Arts Council of Great Britain, 1987).

Ludovico Micara

age d'Orient, he was moved beyond his expectations by the space of the mosques. He visited the great Ottoman mosques with cupolas built by Sinan and inspired by the Byzantine model of Hagia Sophia. Le Corbusier immediately perceived the importance and quality of the interior space:

> A silent place looking towards Mecca is needed. Vast for the spirit to be at ease, high for the prayers to arise there. A great diffused light, so that there would be no shadows at all, and all over, a perfect simplicity; an immensity which should be enclosed in the forms. The space should be vaster than a piazza, not to contain crowds, but so that those who come there to pray would feel joy and respect in being in this great house. Nothing should be out of sight: on entering the immense square one sees, covered with golden ever-new straw mats, no furniture nor chairs, only some low pulpits holding the Koran, in front of which one sits. At a glance all four angles are taken in, their presence is clearly perceived, and the great cube, pierced with small windows, is thus 'constructed'. On top of this the four gigantic structures connecting the squinches rise; and then the twinkling of the bright crown of small windows of the dome is seen. Above, a vast space the form of which is not easily perceivable; the fascination of the hemisphere consists in its resisting any sort of measure. Numerous strings hang down vertically from above, almost reaching the ground, and keep the poles on which small oil lamps are hung; crystalline strings, disposed along con-centric circles, which in the evening spread a roof of light above the head of the believers. In the dark of the immense space the endless strings are lost, rising closely to the top of the dome, in the middle of the belt of the now-dark windows. The *mihrab*, in front of the entrance, is nothing but a door to the Ka'ba; has no protruding elements or volume. All this exists in the majesty of white plaster. The forms are clear; the faultless construction shows all its severity....[2]

This experience, probably the most involving in the *Voyage d' Orient*, changed completely Le Corbusier's way of looking at architecture; "It was as if the veil of my tabernacle was torn apart," he asserts, leaving "the conquered and beloved city." Looking at the interior space of the Palace of Assembly at Chandigarh (Figure 4), we can understand how deeply this experience has affected him and how the space of the mosque, through the reinterpretation of Le Corbusier, becomes one of the primary components of the "modern."

Notes

1. Oleg Grabar, *The Mediation of Ornament.* Princeton University Press, Princeton, NJ. 1992.

2. Giuliano Gresleri, *Le Corbusier, viaggio in Oriente.* Marsilio Editori—Fondation Le Corbusier, Venice-Paris, 1984.

• • • • • • • • • • • • •

Comments
Attilio Petruccioli

a) Le Corbusier's discovery of the mosques in Istanbul is read through the eyes of an architect. This consideration is not intended as a negative judgment on his reading, but it does need to be mentioned. In fact Le Corbusier read the mosque as a project requiring an evaluation, rather than objectively as a building arising from a specific situation to satisfy certain functional and aesthetic needs.

His attitude is deeply antihistorical. He decontextualizes spatial images in which he is interested; he cuts off the connections with the culture and the society that had produced them in order to manipulate these images in his own projects. One can therefore come to the conclusion that the relevance of the interior space as the characterizing form of the architecture of the mosque does not necessarily originate from the reading of Le Corbusier in *Voyage d' Orient.*

b) The idea of space developed over a very long period of time. By the advent of Islam in Yemen, however, the concept of space, architecture, and landscape were already substantially formed. It would be

Ludovico Micara

important to know whether the images analyzed here and the ideas underlying them were the creation of Islam, or a revised manifestation in content and form of an archetype that already existed in the pre-Islamic cultures.

Response

a) It is true that Le Corbusier read the architecture of the mosque in a subjective way, attending to his personal interests and creative instincts rather than the objective features of the space. His reading is a sort of discovery of a dimension of architecture unknown to him until then. His descriptions of the mosques are closer to that of a project that is on one's mind than to that of an existing building.

This attitude is revealed in a curious misunderstanding in his description of the Eski Jami in Adrianople (Edirne), in the second *Carnet* of the *Voyages d'Orient* (Charles-Edouard Jeanneret Le Corbusier, *Voyage d' Orient, Carnets*, ed. G. Gresleri [Milan-Paris: Electa-Fondation Le Corbusier, 1987]). In this mosque, which is a typological variant of the Ulu Jami at Bursa, the repetitive system of the plan is composed of square spatial modules, covered with cupolas. It contains an exception in the central row in axis with the entrance and the *mihrab*. These spatial modules are in fact higher than the others, because of a different solution in the passage between the square and the circular cupola. Such a system, though repetitive, is transformed in the sketched section by Le Corbusier into a central space, a space that, being higher than the others, becomes hierarchically more relevant. What is revealed is a "desire of cupola" that is what Le Corbusier basically expects from Ottoman architecture (see Ludovico Micara, "Le due Rome di Le Corbusier" in *Groma* 2, Dipartimento di Architettura e Analisi della Citta dell' Universita degli Studi "La Sapienza" [Rome, 1993]).

When deeply creative minds are attracted by certain architectural features revealed by particular buildings, then it is true that these features of the buildings are contained in their genetic code. The fact that there is need for the sensitivity and creativity of an architect to grasp and appreciate these features does not mean that they belong only to the person who reads the buildings and not to the object that is read. On the contrary, the highly formal quality of these spaces is understood in their full richness only by a particularly sensitive and attentive public.

b) The dating of these images is not certain. They are thought to belong to the first or second Islamic century, but Professor Grabar prefers a later date. In any case, the level of elaboration of these images seems to be quite sophisticated and already within the Islamic culture, considering that we are able to read the "representation" or better, in the words of Grabar, the "evocation" of the building of the mosque.

Certainly this type of representation manipulates, with great facility, the decorative need, the "terpnopoietic" effect (providing pleasure, according to a neologism of Grabar's) of the image, with the intent of evoking the text, the sacred Koran. This manipulation is successful down to the slightest detail, if we notice how the margin of the drawing, which is also the enclosure of the mosque, encloses the hypostyle system of the parallel naves. In fact the arcades, constituting the principal decorative theme of the image, are interrupted haphazardly against the margin according to current decorative modules, often used, for example, in the design of carpets. Yet this haphazard interruption also evokes with great finesse one of the principal spatial features of the mosque: the continuity of the hypostyle architectural system that cannot be contained integrally inside the image.

It is probable, then, that certain features of the space and architecture suggested by particular methods of abstract representation were already in use before the advent of Islam; but this new culture systematizes, applies, and potentiates these features in order to meet new expressive needs and above all spreads out uniformly those features in areas and cultures that are broader than the ones that generated them.

Ludovico Micara

The Aesthetics of Space in Ottoman Architecture

Jale Nejdet Erzen

Spatial articulation corresponds to or defines a society's orientation in the world and its relation to the environment. Ordering, manipulating, and building the environment corresponds to patterns of seeing and understanding and are objectifications of projected cultural meanings. As making and revealing, space is a poetic construction. Regardless of geographical place, spatial articulations render identity to architecture without depending on regional effects. Therefore, it is the contention here that an understanding of the formal mechanisms of spatial articulation in sixteenth-century Ottoman architecture and site organizations, as well as other forms of articulation in Islamic architecture, can guide today's architects of the Islamic world in creating forms and living contexts that are congenial to their culture and that can be modern without losing qualities belonging to their culture.

When an art form becomes highly articulate, it contains its culture's understanding of its orientation in the world. This is true of sixteenth-century Ottoman architecture and miniatures. Both can be studied as expressions of Ottoman poetics of space. Except for the directionality towards the *qibla*, the organization is not as easily legible in architectural experience as it is in the pictorial world. Some aspects of Ottoman miniatures can even be seen as illustrations of spatial organization in Ottoman architecture. Close familiarity will reveal distinctive aesthetic qualities of space, experienced as unique to this cultural atmosphere. These qualities concerning both interior and exterior space can be categorized according to (1) movement and circulation, (2) use and accessibility, (3) sequence and succession, (4) symbolism and meaning.

Movement and circulation. One can safely generalize that often in the Islamic world circulation is not direct. This means that between the point of departure and the point of arrival the path chosen is not the most immediate, the fastest, or the straightest. This has very frequently been noted for Ottoman neighborhoods and for approaches to large mosques. Anyone who has walked to the mosque of Suleyman in Istanbul (1557) has experienced how difficult it is to find the right path leading to it. The paths, which have not changed since their original conception, are patterned as circulating around the building rather than leading directly to it. Even when there is a ceremonial entry, or a monumental portal, as in the mosques of Selimiye (Edirne 1574) and Suleymaniye, there are no major roads that lead into these directly. In the Selimiye mosque the main entry to the court is from a side street on a slope. The present organization of entries and streets around the mosque is still the original one, and it is easy to observe the circumambulatory system. In the Selimiye another entry is from the south, through the cemetery, and faces the blind *qibla* wall; one has to go around the building to enter it. One would often haphazardly find oneself entering the precincts from a side entrance that happens to join a street. There would be several such entries, each fashioned according to the topographical and local exigencies of the site.

The Suleymaniye complex also has many entrances in addition to the main north portal; they are up stairs or through kiosks and at different levels. But even a smaller mosque, such as the Kadirga Sokollu (Istanbul, 1571) situated on a steep hill, will offer similar experiences. Assuming that dignitaries,

Jale Nejdet Erzen

57

as well as many visitors, came to the mosque from the direction of the Topkapi Palace, the path is certainly indirect and winding. One has to go down the street to the lowest level and then up the steps to the courtyard. If we look at other examples of religious complexes built in the time of Mimar Sinan, we will find similar situations. The experience will always be one of circling around the building and its precincts through the circular pattern of streets, rather than walking directly to the main entrance. This can be seen as a circumambulatory movement.

The spiral and concentric fashion in which space is experienced as one circulates around and within religious complexes is also true of spaces within other kinds of buildings and interiors in general. The sensation of always being in the center and being surrounded by space, which is typical of sixteenth-century Ottoman architecture, is created by a very specific arrangement of architectural elements. If we study interior plans of mosques, baths, courts, and *madrasas* we see that spaces are organized around a core, whether a courtyard with rooms en-circling it, a hospice with rooms around an open court, or a mosque which has its essential space under a central dome surrounded by secondary spaces. These encircling spaces with their structural supports often also act as the structural buttressing of the core baldachin. Thus the circular pattern that becomes a circumambulation is also a structurally and functionally practical scheme. The pattern of concentric rings of spaces is also an aesthetic form: galleries surrounding a closed unit and opening it to the exterior, arcades providing semi-open, sheltered or shaded spaces around a sunny open court. The pattern can as well be seen in the organization of roofs, as the smaller domes encircle the central main dome.

Although patterns of movement that are indirect and often in the form of a spiraling path can be found in most medieval organizations, in Ottoman architecture they became a systematic design scheme in both structure and site layout. In traditional societies where religion dominated life and intellectual patterns, the symbolism of the circle was

Figure 1. Sinan, Zal Mahmut Pasa Mosque, Istanbul (1585). Lower courtyard, showing a concentric, continuous series of spaces. (Photo: Author)

Jale Nejdet Erzen

of primary importance. In European architecture axiality became increasingly important with the development of perspective, but in Ottoman art and architecture, with the state's support of orthodoxy, the tendency was to systematize circular patterns. This is obvious in the case of the special emphasis placed on the central dome and the enveloping of spaces in concentric series, or the joining of *madrasa* and mosque around a common court, which are systems of circumambulation that are not as obvious in earlier examples.

Since such rules were handed down orally and in practice from master to apprentice, we do not have texts explaining the principles that created them. The reasons must have been basically symbolic. Circumambulation of a sacred site or religious building was certainly proper and the kind of movement that would be desired because it would provide access to the spiritual realm by repeating the movement of the heavens and the movement around the Ka'ba.

Ottoman miniatures can help us understand how this organization was the outcome of a basic and common cultural attitude. In many miniatures the scene is organized with figures situated in a spiraling arrangement around a center.[1] In contrast to the perspectival ordering of space in European visual fields, in the miniatures the observer's point of view is within the pictorial field. Comparative studies of medieval European pictorial works even before the use of perspective will show that figures were generally placed according to a vantage point outside the frame of the picture. In the Islamic visual field space does not fall into a sequential order up to the horizon, as it does in the Western visual world. Rather, it surrounds the observer, as it would in a mosque or courtyard.

Besides any symbolic or religious meaning that such a pattern or design principle may have, it will still today create the conditions for certain experiences that are important in the perception and appreciation of, and relation to, the environment and to the development of a meaningful relationship between the building and its surroundings. Circumambulatory circulation is itself a kind of continuous link where the movement outside the building is continued inside, winding in a spiral until it reaches its goal at the core of the building under the dome, after winding in spiral fashion.

Each culture, era, or functional need will create its own patterns. What these can teach today's architect is how and in what ways relations between building and site, between the human aspect and the physical setting, can be created.

Use and Accessibility. The experience and character of spaces vary according to use and to accessibility. Intermediary spaces which complete an irregular contour and which are not necessarily entered or used can function as buffer zones (against noise or perhaps exposure). One can also assume that such spaces are especially well-guarded or off-limits, or even taboo. The inaccessible courts which frame *madrasa* rooms or exterior galleries on mosques and are not given any specific function other than being fill-in spaces between arch buttressing in large mosques are an example. The two *madrasa* buildings on the west of the Suleymaniye as well as the stepped *madrasas* on the east have such inaccessible walled-in spaces adjacent to their rooms.

The three-dimensional layering of spaces that take advantage of the topography with sloping terrains also creates different qualities in spatial experience by the degrees of accessibility created at different levels. In the Atik Valide Mosque in Uskudar, which is a late Sinan design, one can look down from the court of the mosque and see the lower court of the *madrasa* directly from above.

As we circumambulate the periphery of a complex to find the entry, or as we encircle the mosque, we pass by many different exterior spaces that are defined, transparently walled-in, but not readily accessible: the cemetery seen across a screened wall, the court of a *madrasa*, the exterior court of the mosque or of a mausoleum. We are made to experience the environment as ordered into different territorial zones. Often these are formed as circular rings. Within the arrangement of concentric rings there are several centers differing in hierarchic importance: the mosque, the mausoleum, the main *madrasa* room and the courts, the mosque's court being central.

All these different spaces create various ways of protecting, encircling, defining, enveloping the core, whether it is the sacred space of the mosque, the interior of a mausoleum, or simply an open court. The analysis and understanding of these articulations and the gradation of accessibility reveal that their architect approached each place and site with a kind of respectful apprehension, and tried to bring forth the invisible life force of the site. Space was evidently a kind of entity with its protected inner identity; it could not simply be manipulated and indiscreetly entered. The word *harem* that denotes privacy is

Jale Nejdet Erzen

Figure 2. Sinan, Suleymaniye Mosque, Istanbul (1557). Inaccessible *madrasa* spaces adjacent to a street wall. (Photo: Author)

also the word for inner space. This implies that space also has its own privacy that cannot simply be invaded.

Sequence and succession. The spatial orientation of the beholder is not conditioned by a perspectival system. Yet it differs from other visual constructs that also lack perspective, such as medieval European painting and illuminations, or from the architecture and planning of medieval Europe. In fact, the systematic progression of European visual systems towards a perspectival organization was very much prepared by the stage-like setting that was dominant both in architecture and in pictorial representations. In the Islamic world, the visual field is laid out as a map, or as a stage that is standing vertically, and the beholder is in the center of it. The beholder is the actor being watched rather than the audience looking at a frontally staged event. This position also implies self-consciousness about being watched by the ever-seeing eye of God. Many scenes depicted in miniatures illustrate this: sometimes the main event is taking place around the center of the picture surrounded by landscape or architectural elements from behind which people or natural features like clouds,

rocks, or trees seem to be watching.[2] This kind of central orientation is vital to the organization of architectural spaces that are concentrically arranged with soft, transparent boundaries in between them. The arches and columns of the central structural system, which is a baldachin in principle and which supports the dome, create such transparencies: the outer limits of a building with its usually large fenestration at lower levels creates another such transparent boundary; then come the courts and the exterior spaces or courts which surround the mosque and which have walls with large openings. This succession continues until we reach the limits of the religious complex.

This aesthetic organization is also a practical necessity created by the arched buttressing structure. The encircling principle of form that creates flexibility in expansion and contraction and transparencies and soft boundaries refer to a conception of the universe as a limitless spiral and to its core symbolized by the dome.

Does this kind of progressive, differentiating process through space, especially in and around a religious site, not convey a sense of pilgrimage from the ordinary to the supra ordinary? As one finally

Jale Nejdet Erzen

Figure 3. Sinan, Zal Mahmut Pasa Mosque, Istanbul (1585). Inner space surrounded by arcaded and gallery spaces. (Photo: Author)

Jale Nejdet Erzen

61

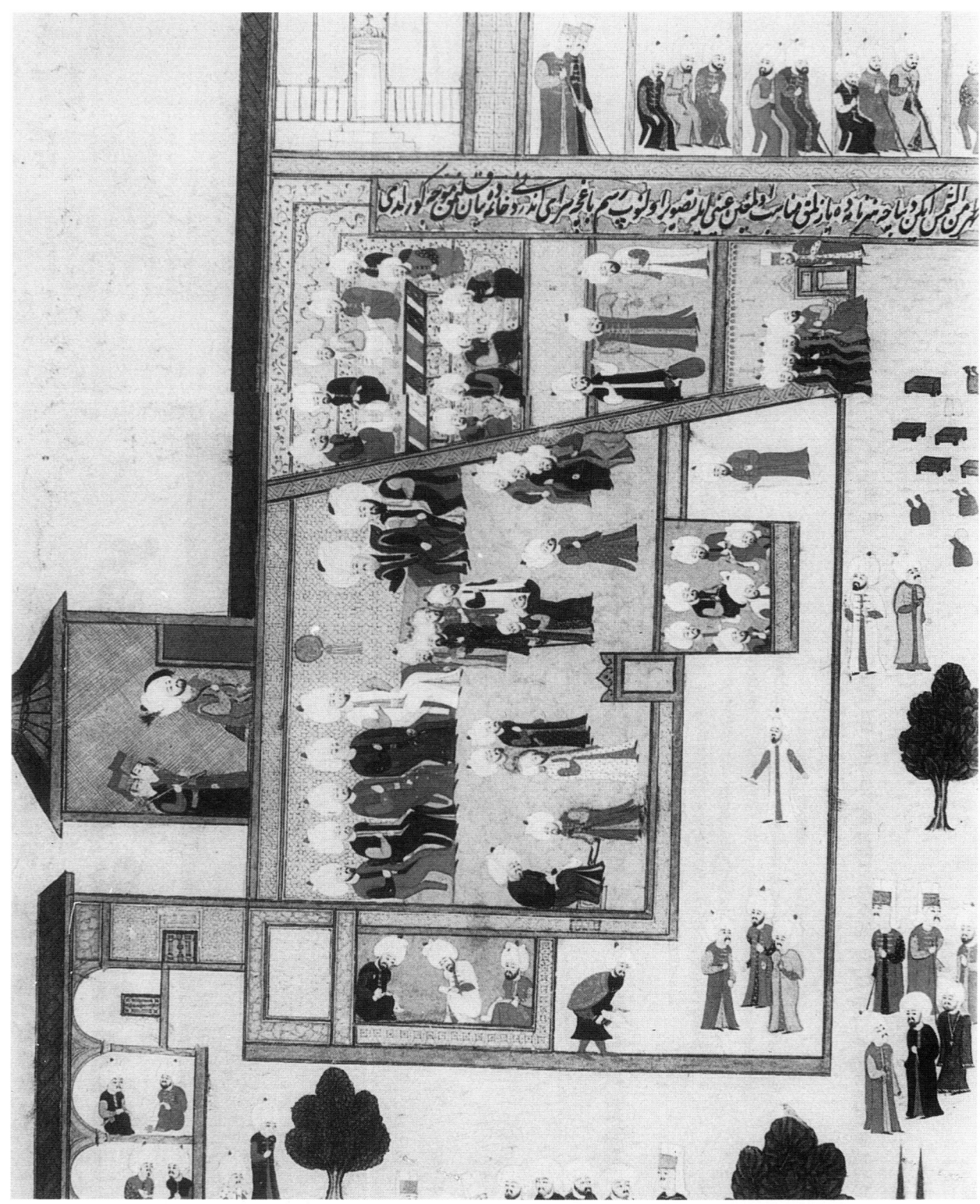

Figure 4. Partial image of a miniature from the *Hunername* - Hazine 1523. Date 1584. (Courtesy of Topkapi Museum, Istanbul). (Photo: Author)

enters the innermost core, one has gone through a process of purification, of slowing down and making the passage from the quotidian to the religious realm.

On the other hand, generally speaking, most neighborhoods in Islamic cities do have in their street patterns not a homogeneous distribution of equally accessible streets or alleys, but rather a progression from the public to the most private on a dead end.

Symbolism and Meaning. The importance of architecture in the visual and experiential world is matched by poetry in the realm of discourse. As a civilization that gave importance to the lived experience rather than to intellectual reasoning and conception, literature developed especially in poetry and in metaphoric discourse. Therefore, the evaluation of architecture is found in metaphoric descriptions in Islamic poetry and literature rather than in any theoretical writing. Sinan's records of his work testify to the poetic assessment of space in his approach. Man is happy if he can find a semblance of paradise on earth.[3]

As a sacred space, the interior of a mosque is made to remind one of paradise, of a garden of fragrant flowers and crystal ponds. A light ambience, sparkling, scintillating, reflecting surfaces, tones of blue on vertical planes to give a sense of peace and harmony, rugs of vibrant colors on the floor to resemble meadows full of flowers, all in all an atmosphere of joy and peace was sought and emulated with the decoration and use of materials.

Elements using water were always abundant: fountains or tanks, usually decorated with marble reliefs of floral patterns, cooled the air in the heat of summer or offered a drink to the passers- by. In the mosque of Selimiye at Edirne, a fountain is placed directly under the dome's center. It reminds one of the little ponds placed directly under the clerestory opening (oculus) in Seljuqid *madrasas*. Water reflecting the sky or a pond receiving the blessing in the form of rain were common symbols used to give meaning to space.[4]

The sensuous qualities created by light, color, reflection, transparency, by the varieties of tactile experiences in the quality of surfaces like tile, stone, wood, or the carpet on which the forehead was lowered to the earth in prostration for prayer, all transformed the physicality of architecture into a sensory, aesthetic experience and into an immaterial world.

Space is differentiated primarily according to its degree of purity. This kind of zoning of the environment dialectically into sacred and profane, pure and impure, peaceful and chaotic, the abode of Islam and peace and the abode of war and strife also differentiate it as alien or intimate, as congenial or unknowable. This is reflected in distinct zones in architecture and urban planning that grade the environment according to its closeness to or distance from the sacred, or God. The door, the passage, the threshold all had a special power and meaning as the defining element between the private and the common, the inward and outward, the core and the periphery.

The door plays an important symbolic role determined by its form, scale, size, and the inscription on it. It creates a rite of passage and establishes conditions and rules governing the space inside for the person who enters to abide by. In earlier monastic buildings, prayer rooms with very low small doors forced a kind of prostration in entering the room.

One of the main lessons to be drawn from these examples should be about the spiritual satisfaction and aesthetic pleasure that spatial variety can offer. These spaces are still used today, often for similar functions, and, as in the case of the Rustempa'a caravanserai built by Sinan in Edirne, which is now used as a hotel, they are often more successful and suited to their purpose than their modern equivalents. Yet, one important fact that is often overlooked when inspired by such historic examples is that in their time, they were all innovative and even experimental. Sinan's continuous search for new forms and structural solutions was the key to his ability to create an architecture that was unique each time, even within traditional norms.

Architecture that symbolized the ideal order of the world as perceived and understood by Islam created a guide for behavior and for man's relations to the environment by categorizing spaces according to a value system. The essential character and atmosphere of the Islamic world were created by meanings given to the environment through the organization of space. The capacity of transforming the material world into a spiritual one through infinite variety in this kind of sensory articulation has not been equaled in any other culture. With such a heritage, the modern architect of the Islamic world has all the necessary guidance needed to create once again an environmental quality where man becomes elevated by inhabiting the world. Not imitation, but analysis of how forms relate to functions and to values, is the only way in which architecture in the Islamic world

Jale Nejdet Erzen

today can recapture some of its old significance.

Notes

1. For spiral organization in miniatures, see A. Papadopoulo, *L'Islam et l'art musulman* (Paris: Editions d'Art Lucien Mazenod, 1976).

2. Such animated landscapes abound in the epic about Suleyman; Esin Atil, *Suleymanname: The Illustrated History of Suleyman the Magnificent* (New York: Harry N. Abrams, 1986).

3. Texts on Sinan's works, *Tezkiret-ul Bunyan*, *Tezkiret-ul Ebniye*, and *Tuhfet-ul Mimarin*, collected by Zeki Sonmez, *Mimar Sinan ile Ilgili Tarihi Yazmalar Belgeler* (Istanbul: Mimar Sinan Universitesi Yayynlari, 1988); and Howard Crane, *Risale-i Mimariyye: An Early-Seventeenth-Century Ottoman Treatise on Architecture* (Leiden: E. J. Brill, 1987), are full of descriptions of mosque interiors resembling paradise.

4. *Rahmet*, the word for rain in Turkish, also means blessing.

• • • • • • • • • • • • •

Comments
Sibel Bozdogan

This is an original approach to Ottoman architecture from the perspective of an artist and aesthetic theorist; it offers valuable insights for the practicing architect, without collapsing into "operative theory". It is a kind of "history of mentalities": an attempt to understand the experiential and sensual qualities of space as part of a larger cosmology that manifests itself equally in the plan of the mosque complex and the pictorial arrangement of the miniature painting.

How transhistorical and how transcultural are these aesthetic and spatial sensibilities? Are they unique to Ottoman culture (as the subtitle of the article suggests)? To all Islamic societies past and present (as suggested by the hope that "they can guide today's architects of the Islamic world")? To all pre-modern (pre-Renaissance, pre-perspective) societies (as suggested, for example, by the reference to the significance of "the symbolism of the circle" for all "traditional societies")? Or are they simply timeless, poetic principles of design anytime, anywhere (as the main title suggests)?

If "an art form manifests a culture's understanding of its orientation in the world" *only when* it becomes "highly articulate," how do we escape the implied essentialism? If the "essence" of Ottoman culture is embodied only in the sixteenth century, what are we to make of other periods? Are they "less authentic"? "less true"? and, of "less value" to today's architects?

Response
The aesthetic and spatial forms mentioned in my essay may have been preferred by certain cultures, but to the extent that they relate to the biological, organic, or natural inclinations of living beings towards order (such as the golden section) they can be transcultural or transhistorical. The spiral and the concentric are such basic orders that natural forces seem to prefer them, although this should not be taken to mean that nature is always orderly. Some forms may be cultural rather than natural preferences, such as the separation of opposites by Islamic cultures in contrast to the integration of opposites by Hindu culture.

Within the representational and qualitative system certain forms may be more articulate or more intense stimuli. Each culture may have special reasons for preferring certain forms, yet, on an individual level, all such articulation may be universally effective.

On the other hand, one may well ask whether people used to digital, quantitative, and conceptually contextualized cultural media may be less sensitive to these orders of the representational and qualitative system. The forms mentioned might simply be more readily appreciated by members of Islamic societies who may be more traditional than others are today.

The idea of "timeless" values is always questionable. As for guiding architects today, one can say that forms to which people can easily ascribe symbolic meanings create "thick" spaces constituted by focal elements and qualities, whereas arbitrary or merely practical choices or orders may end up in "thin" spaces that are alienating (see Borgman, 1984).

Jale Nejdet Erzen

Changes in the Islamic Religion and Their Effects on the Built Environment: Two Cases from Indonesia

Adhi Moersid, Achmad Fanani, and Tulus Setyo Budhi

When Islam spread to various parts of the world, it did so solely as an ideology, with little, aside from language, of its Arabic origins. Wherever it took hold, it utilized various local forms for its identity.[1] How did this process of combining Islam and local culture work? What effect did the shift from pre-Islamic religions to Islam and from Islamic to a more orthodox version have on the built environment? The following study will try to answer these questions, using two cases from Indonesia: the first describes the transformation from a pre-Islamic to an Islamic society, and the second the re-Islamization of an already Islamic society.

Pondok Pesantren: The First Muslim Community in Java

Muslim merchants from India established the first Muslim community in Java along its north coast (Gresik, Tuban, Jepara, Demak, Cirebon, Banten), led by the *walis* (the *ulamas* of that time), who were identified by Drewes as Sufi followers of an extreme mystical sect.[2] The Islamic religion managed to penetrate into Java's hinterland sometime after 1400, where it found fertile ground for the promulgation of education that included Islamic values. The *walis* assumed a strategic position in the *ashrams* as *ajars* (an *ashram's* head teacher). The conversion of the *mandala* education into an independent and self-supporting Islamic educational institution gave birth to a settlement in which the religious teacher, later called the *kyai* (the admired and revered), and his disciples, called *santri*, constructed a complex of buildings consisting of dormitories, workshops and shops for craftsmen, and places of worship.[3] This initial process of Islamic educational establishments in the hinterland shaped the subsequent development of the Islamic community in the country.

For religious purposes, this first generation of *pesantren* (lit. place of the *santris*) made the necessary adaptations of the educational system, religious worship, and the instruments and requirements to be assimilated with the local tradition and pre-Islamic primitive usage. The *walis* then engaged in intensive cultural engineering by bringing the various literary and cultural products into the educational environment.

According to Winsted, as quoted by Taib Osman, the primary task of the walis was to replace the Hindu epics with stories about Islamic heroes.[4] A comparable process went on in architecture. Almost all forms of space as well as the placing of building elements in the *pesantren*s were left unchanged; they referred to the older forms related to pre-Islamic beliefs, though with renewed messages containing the spirit of *tawhid*. The cosmic figures in the primitive classification system and the composition of the Hindu-Javanese cosmology formed part of the architectural expression that also contained newly introduced values. For example, the preference for the numbers 4 and 5 was retained, but reinterpreted as a symbol of God's oneness; His four aspects--material, characteristics, name, and works -- were combined within a single one. This is reflected in a number of designs, for instance, the concept of *mancapat* remains but is expressed anew as four *khalifa sejati* (*al-khalifa al-rasyidun*), the four principal disciples of the Holy Prophet, with the Prophet himself at the center. Similarly the four *imams* who founded the orthodox Muslim *madhhab* (Hanafi, Shafi, Hanbali, Maliki) are the four pillars, with the

Holy Prophet as the central unifier. The principal approach to the religious belief in God is reflected in the application of the four pillars of religious practices, i.e., the *shari'at, tariqat, hakekat,* and *ma'rifat.*

This phenomenon was repeated in a variety of situations; everything was given a different name, but otherwise remained essentially the same in that it refers to the One and Only, the absolutely highest reality, God. The part played by the four cardinal directions of the compass (north, south, east, west) in locating the *kyai*'s house, the mosques, and the dwellings of the *santri*s, reminds us of the Lokapala concept concerning the position of the gods on the eight corners,[5] but evidently refers to the important part played by the number 4 in the primitive classification of Mancapat and Mancalima.[6] While the ancient belief refers to the four positive elements—the *guru* in the north, the *wali* in the west, *pandita* (the law expert) in the south, and the *ratu* (king) in the east—controlling the negative evil (*syetan*) at the center, the *pesantren* utilizes the pattern by placing the four main elements as follows (Figure 1):

—the *kyai*'s house, symbol of science and education, at the position of the guru,

—the mosque as the place of worship at the *wali's* position,

—the houses of the revered elders, symbol of law and order, at the *pandita*'s position; usually reserved for the *kyai* to spend his last days, or for his parents,

—the *santri*s' dwellings at the position of the *ratu*. According to the *pesantren* tradition, the *santri* as a pursuer of knowledge is the most respected agent, like a king whom everybody should serve well.

This phenomenon of reusing ancient symbols is also evident in the architecture of the *pesantren* mosques, the horizontal and vertical pattern of placing the elements: the rooftop (crown), the storied roof, the main pillars, the verandah, the pond, up to the gate (Figure 2). The horizontal room division with the difference in floor height refers to the principles of the megalithic *punden*, a stepped-roof construction.[7] The three-story building with two or three hanging roofs reminds us of the old principles of Triloka and Tribhawana in Hindu-Buddhist mysticism.[8] But a message was inserted between these

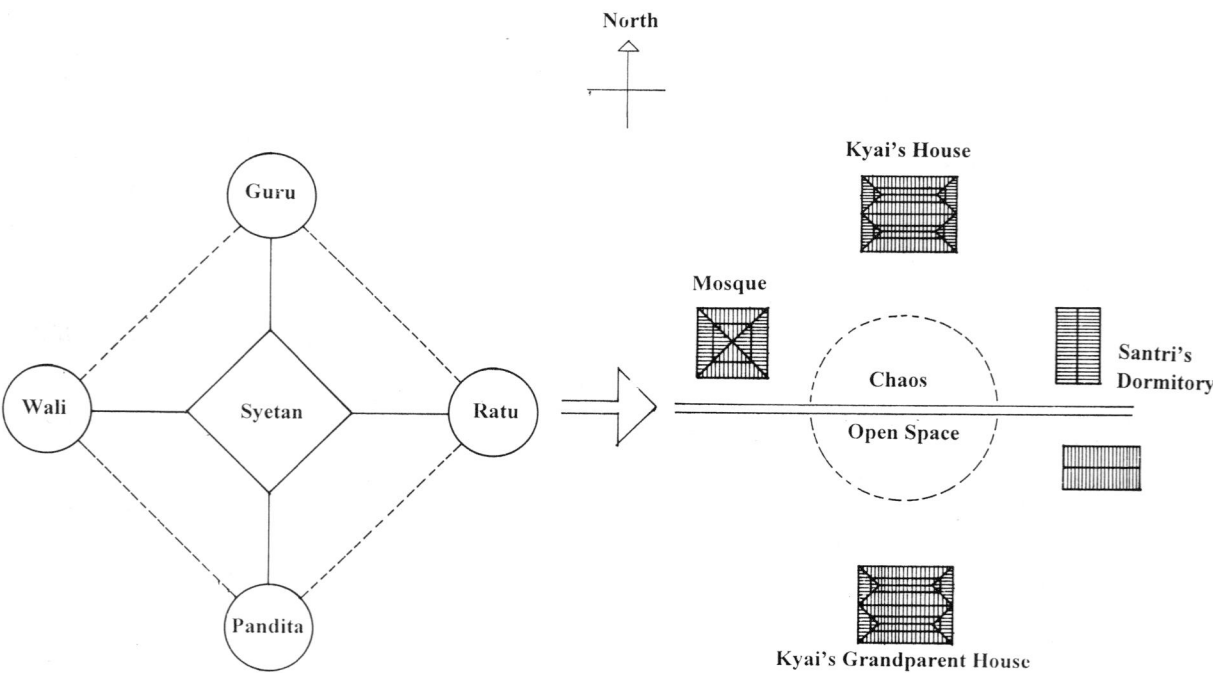

Figure 1. The concept of *mancapat* and its transformation into the Pondok Pesantren layout.

Adhi Moersid, Achmad Fanani, and Tulus Setyo Budhi

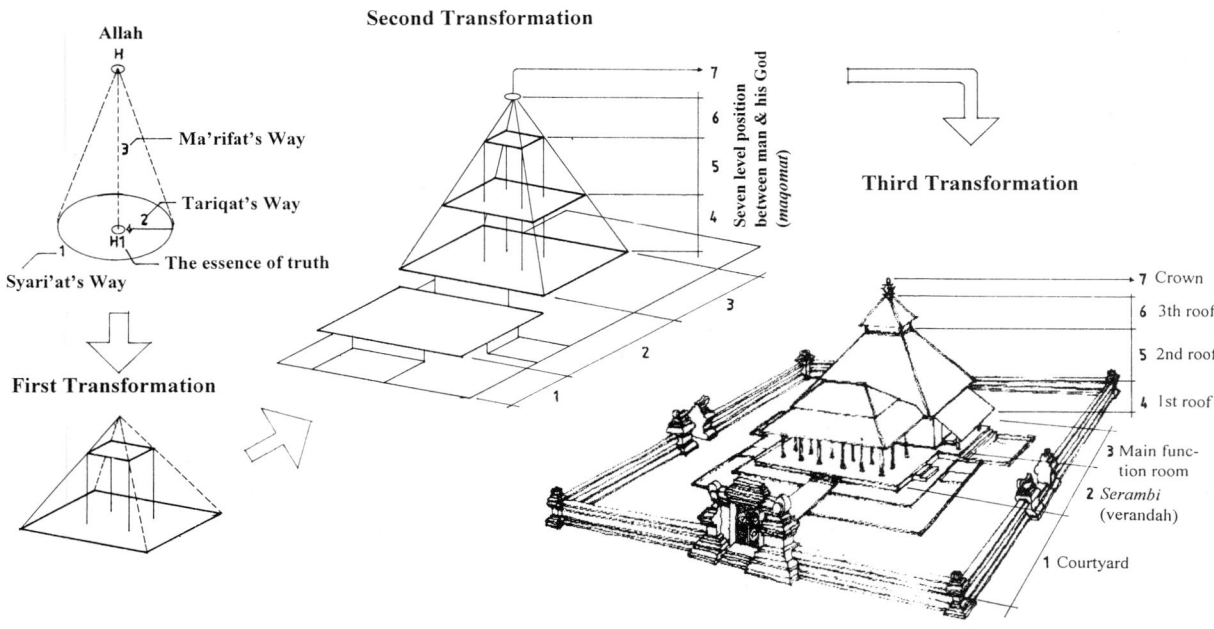

Figure 2. The Sufi idea of the approach to God and its transformation into architectural form.

elements concerning the (abstraction of) the *tawhid* belief transformed into the degree of piety, translated through the *maqomat* concept, i.e., the relationship between man and his God after having undertaken various exercises and spiritual interventions, physical as well as mental. The training proceeds from three to seven positions, with four preliminary treatments. This is in accordance with the *maqomat tujuh* concept leading to the highest stage where no spiritual distance (*hulul*) exists in the communication between man and his Creator.[9]

By brilliantly utilizing the ancient symbols, giving them a new, characteristically Islamic meaning, applying changes where necessary, and leaving out elements or parts that were in opposition to Islam, the Sufi philosophers or *walis* achieved the smooth flow of communication with the believer society, though in its turn, a too enthusiastic engineering of this mystic Sufi approach opened up the opportunity for pantheistic styles, which deviated from the monotheistic Islamic *tawhid* doctrine. Hurgronye observed that the upper-class community tended to drift towards pantheism, and among the common

people and laymen various superstitious beliefs emerged.[10] Nevertheless, the first generation of the Islamic community was reported to have managed to raise Muslim religious awareness, working from a mystical religious base.[11]

Kota Gede: The Re-Islamization of a Javanese City

Kota Gede is a small town, southeast of Yogyakarta that still maintains the characteristics of a Javanese traditional town. According to the Dutch historian, H. J. de Graff, Kota Gede was built in the mid sixteenth century by Ki Gede Pemanahan, a high-ranking officer of the kingdom of Pajang, the first Islamic kingdom in central Java.[12] Pemanahan died in 1584 and was buried in the mosque's graveyard behind the city wall. His son Sutawijaya, who succeeded him on the throne and was known by the titles *ngabehi loring pasar*, *panembahan senapati*, and *sayidin panatagama* (prince from north of the market, commander-in-chief, royal religious administrator), destroyed Pajang, built his own kingdom, Mataram, and made Kota Gede the headquarters of

Adhi Moersid, Achmad Fanani, and Tulus Setyo Budhi

Figure 3. The north entrance gate of the mosque and the graveyard complex of the Mataram kingdom in Kota Gede that shows the Hindu-Java style. (Photo: Tulus Setyo Budhi).

Adhi Moersid, Achmad Fanani, and Tulus Setyo Budhi

his *kraton* (royal administration) in 1587.[13]

The city-planning pattern of this first Islamic Mataram kingdom resembles that of the Hindu kingdom of Majapahit in thirteenth-century East Java, which turned out to have features similar to ancient Indian city planning, i.e., an open space at the center, the *kraton* facilities at the south, the holy building (mosque) at the west, and the market place at the north.[14]

Although Kota Gede was abandoned as the kingdom's capital by the subsequent Mataram powers, it did not decline into an ordinary village: it still functioned as a crossroads of religious as well as secular traffic and maintained its position as a center of worship, being the burial place of the ancient Mataram kings, and as a center of commerce and Javanese handicraft.[15] When it ceased to be a town of royal bureaucracy, Kota Gede became a center of trade and commerce.[16]

In 1925 the Kota Gede branch of the Mohammediya, an organization devoted to Islamic renaissance and purification, was established. It had its headquarters in Yogyakarta. To the Muslims of Kota Gede, it was the beginning of a golden era, particularly because of the great success achieved by the Mohammediya in preaching throughout the country that was later recognized as the Kampung Islam, the Muslim Village.[17]

But this was not achieved without conflict. The effort of the Mohammediya to exercise their authority over the Great Mosque of Mataram, which belonged to the royal *kraton* of Kota Gede, and their perseverance in purging Islamic learning of its local superstitious beliefs and practices (*takhyul, bid'a,* and *khurafat*) was resisted by the *kraton*. The conflict culminated in the mid 1930s, as recorded by Nakamura: "When the Mohammediya tried to renew the traditional practices of the Friday prayers and preaching, which ended up in the construction of a new mosque, Masjid Perak (Silver Mosque), so called after the fully supportive local silver craftsmen."[18] In his doctoral thesis for Cornell University, Nakamura wrote:

> The Masjid Perak is a symbol of freedom and separation of the avant-garde Muslim leaders from the royal religious administration and the traditional Islam. In the newly built mosque they have attained their freedom and right of self-administration: outside and different from the traditional spiritual order.[19]

Quoting a Mohammediya member, "The Masjid Perak, referred to as 'Firaq' or independent mosque,

Figure 4. A winding narrow pathway in the traditional Javanese Kota Gede settlement. (Photo: Tulus Setyo Budhi)

symbolizes the freedom of the followers of the Muslim faith from the dirtiness and chill of the past."[20]

The conflict gradually subsided; the Mohammediya even gained the support of the majority of the Kota Gede community, not only owing to the benefits they obtained from the order's religious, social, and educational activities, but also from the sympathetic approaches they used utilizing Javanese idioms. Thanks to the services of two *kraton* monks approached by the Mohammediya, the administration of the Great Mosque was handed over to this organization,[21] where it remains to this day. The Mohammediya are still the dominant religious and social organization in Kota Gede.[22]

Kota Gede has long attracted many visitors, particularly because of its historical importance as a Javanese traditional city. The Mataram civic center is still recognizable with its royal graveyard and Great Mosque in a single complex surrounded by a wall around 2.5 meters high with a Hindu-Javanese gate at each entrance (Figure 3). As is common among the important burial places of the Muslim

Adhi Moersid, Achmad Fanani, and Tulus Setyo Budhi

kingdoms in Java, this settlement shows symptoms of syncretism: it combines the Hindu *candhi* concept of the original Javanese ancestor-worship with Islamic ritual modes and facilities.[23] On certain days, usually Fridays, the air is filled with praying voices and the aroma of flowers and incense spreading out from offerings at the graveyards.[24]

Other interesting features of the heritage in Kota Gede, in addition to the location of the graveyard and mosque in one complex, are the traditional Javanese villages and houses. The houses are spread over all corners of the city, but hidden among amazingly winding narrow pathways (Figure 4). A Javanese house in Kota Gede generally consists of the *pendapa* (ceremonial space) and the *dalem* (main living facilities) with additional buildings on the left, right, and rear, and the entry from the yard (see Figure 5). Every morning and afternoon one can encounter women sweeping or chatting in the yards and pathways, while the men look after their cattle and the children play around. Kota Gede has become a town that encourages the socialization of

children and the reproduction of Islamic Javanese values.[25]

All the traditional Javanese houses in Kota Gede face south in honor of Nyai Roro Kidul (Queen of the South Seas), and also because the common people believe it improper to face the same direction as the *kraton*, which faces north.[26]

The community in ancient Kota Gede was divided into groups according to profession, social status, and degree of religious piety. There were quarters known as *santri* quarters (occupied by pious Muslims), such as Kudusan, Boharen, Purbayan and Ledok. The so-called *abangan* quarters, where the non-Muslims or the "superficial" Muslims lived, are Jagalan, Prenggan, and Keboan.[27] But these groups no longer exist today. There is no significant difference between an *abangan* and a *santri* house, except for the *senthong*, the most sacred room in a Javanese house. For the *abangan*, the *senthong* is a room for burning incense and for meditation; for the *santri* it serves as the place for prayer.[28]

Another phenomenon in Kota Gede's physical

Figure 5. An example of a traditional Javanese house in Kota Gede with *pendapa* at the front and *delam* in the rear. (Photo: Tulus Setyo Budhi).

Adhi Moersid, Achmad Fanani, and Tulus Setyo Budhi

70

environment is that every kampung has its burial place and mosque. The inventory recorded sixteen graveyards and thirty-five *musallas* (small mosques) in the main quarter of the town, and thirty-eight mosques in all.[29] According to A. Charris Zubair, who has made a series of studies on Kota Gede, the large number of graveyards and places of worship is evidence of the community's high appreciation of the spiritual life. "In daily life man is constantly reminded of the existence of death and life hereafter. Have the real-estate businessmen ever thought of providing a graveyard for the occupants of their thousands of hectares of modern constructions? The answer seems to be no. Even worship places are built in the last stages only."[30]

Nevertheless, in spite of the ever-growing number of beautiful Muslim places of worship, some prominent locals observed that "there is a decline in the social intimacy and the religious spirit among the people."[31]

Relations between Islam and the local culture at the time Islam entered Java seemed quite harmonious. The *walis* seized the opportunity to interpret the local culture in Islamic terms for the purposes of their mission. In the case of the re-Islamization of Kota Gede, the reformers initially had some conflict with traditional Muslims groups, but it slowly faded and finally even the management of the royal mosque, a symbol of traditional authority, was handed over to the reformers. The case of Kota Gede also shows how a local tradition can exist alongside a reforming tradition.

The other fact worth noting is that the religious transformation from pre-Islamic to Islamic (case 1) and from a faithful to a more orthodox Islam (case 2) seemed not to change the built environment of the society in any significant way. The *walis* used the local architectural language to build the early Islamic community, and Panembahan Senapati used the same language when he built his Islamic Kingdom Palace. The new generation of *santri* reformers who occupied the Javanese traditional house also did not change its physical form; they only changed the function of the *senthong* from a place of offering to a place of prayer.

Islam was tolerant toward the local culture, and provided a broad range of choices for its followers to adapt, reinterpret, and transform. Islam was ready to utilize various local architectural treasures for its physical identity. From this we can understand why so many traditional buildings in the various ethnic societies in Indonesia who followed Islam soon became mosques and why new mosques were built according to the plan of the local traditional house. Finally, we can understand how Islamic culture, especially Islamic architecture, became so rich from Spain and the Maghrib to Arabia and Southeast Asia.

Notes

1. Adhi Moersid, "Konsep Disain Masjid Said Naum," design report.

2. G. W. J. Drewes, "Indonesia: Mistisisme dan Aktivisme Islam," (Indonesia: Misticism and Activism of Islam) in G. E. Von Grunebaum (Ed). *Islam Kesatuam dan Keragaman (Islam, Unity and Diversity)*, Yayasan Perkhidmatan, Jakarta, 1983), p. 355.

3. Koentjaraningrat, *Kebudayaan Jawa* (Jakarta: Balai Pustaka, 1984), pp. 60-61.

4. M. T. Osman, "Pengislaman Orang-orang Melayu: Suatu Transformasi Budaya," *Islam di Asia Tenggara* (Jakarta, 1989), p. 94.

5. Isma'oen, Banis, "Konsep Triloka dalam Bangunan Tradisional Jawa" (Sualu Tinjauan Singkat) (Concept of Triloka in Javanese Traditional Building, A Short Desting), paper delivered to the Regional Planning Board Seminar, Yogyakarta Municipality. March 1990.

6. F. D. E. van Ossenbruggen, *Asal-usul Konsep Jawa tentang Mancapat dalam hubungan dengan Sistem Klasifikasi Primitif* (Jakarta: Bhratara, 1975), p. 12.

7. Soediman, Local Genius dalam Kehidupan Beragama (Local Genius in Religious Life) in Ayatrohaedi (Ed.) Local Genius (Pustaka Jaya, Jakarta 1986).

8. Isma'oen, Banis, "Konsep Triloka dalam Bangunan Tradisional Jawa" (Sualu Tinjauan Singkat) (Concept of Triloka in Javanese Traditional Building, A Short Desting), paper delivered to the Regional Planning Board Seminar, Yogyakarta Municipality. March 1990.

9. Achmad Fanani, "Pondok Pesantren Pabelan: Pendekatan Simbol pada Perancangan," (Pabelan Islamic School: Symbolic Approach in Design), Bachelor graduate end project, Department of Architecture, Gadjah Mada University, 1990, p. 23. Unpublished.

10. S. Hurgronye, *Islam di Hindia Belanda* (Jakarta: Bhratara, 1989), p. 13.

Adhi Moersid, Achmad Fanani, and Tulus Setyo Budhi

11. Kuntowijoyo, *Dinamika Sejarah Umat Islam Indonesia* (Yogyakarta: Shalahuddin Press, 1985).

12. H. J. de Graaf, *Awal Kebangkitan Mataram: Masa Pemerintahan Senapati* (Jakarta, 1985).

13. M. Nakamura, *Bulan Sabit Muncul dari Balik Pohon Beringin: Studi tentang Pergerakan Mohammediya di Kota Gede-Yogyakarta* (Yogyakarta: GMU Press, 1983), p. 18

14. De Graaf, *Awal Kebangkitan Mataram*; A. C. Zubair, "Nilai Budaya Masyarakat Jawa di Kota Gede Yogyakarta sebagai Landasan Etika Linghungan Hidup," M. A. thesis, University of Indonesia, 1988, p. 181.

15. H. J. van Mook, *Kuta Gede* (Jakarta: Bhratara, 1972), p. 10.

16. Achmad Charris Zubair, personal communication, 1997.

17. M. Nakamura, *Bulan Sabit Muncul dari Balik Pohon Beringin: Studi tentang Pergerakan Mohammediya di Kota Gede-Yogyakarta* (The Crescent Arises over the Banyan Tree: A Study of the Mohammediya Movement in a Central Javanese Town), Yogyakarta, GMU Press. 1983, p. 118.

18. Ibid., p. 116-20.

19. Ibid., p. 121

20. Ibid., p. 121-122.

21. Ibid., p. 122.

22. Tulus Setyo Budhi, "Kota Gede Field Studies," 1997.

23. A. Bagoes P. Wiryomartono, Seni Bangunan dan Seni Binakota di Indonesia, Jakarta, P.T. 1995.

24. Tulus Setyo Budhi, "Kota Gede Field Studies," 1997.

25. Ibid.

26. Tulus Setyo Budhi, "Kota Gede: Berapa Lama Engkau Akan Bertahan?" Gelanggang, No. 3, 1982. Maret. p. 1-12.

27. A.C. Zubair, Nilai Budaya Masyarakat Jawa di Kota Gede Yogyakarta sebagai Landasan Etika Lingkungan Hidup. M.A. Thesis, University of Indonesia, 1988. (Unpublished) and Tulus Setyo Budhi, "Kota Gede Field Studies," 1997

28. Department of Architecture, Gadjah Mada University, "Studi Perumahan Tradisionl di Yogyzkarta dan Sekitarnya," research report; R. A. Wondo and S. B. Sigit, *Kotagede between Two Gates*, research report, Department of Architecture, Gadjah Mada University, 1986; T. S. Budhi, "Kota Field Studies". 1997.

29. Tulus Setyo Budhi, "Kota Gede Field Studies," 1997.

30. A. C. Zubair, personal communication, 1997.

31. Tulus Setyo Budhi, "Kota Gede Field Studies," 1997.

• • • • • • • • • • • •

Comments
Nadia M. Alhasani

Within the unifying faith of Islam, diversities exist resulting from the conditions of a particular regional habitat and particular cultural practices. These conditions open up possibilities for a display of distinct regional expressions. What becomes fundamental for these communities is the associations drawn from the construction of specific symbols that relate to particular lands, people, and beliefs—in this case, the Muslim communities in Indonesia. To what extent are these natives responsible for the preservation of the built culture of the place? How are the elements that are universally Muslim distinguished from those that are traditionally Javanese? If the distinction is obvious, may one assume that the transformation process is a failure? Or, conversely, if the transformation is complete then what makes this Islamic architecture Javanese?

Several pre-Islamic buildings such as Hagia Sophia have been reused with only minor modifications. The authors fail to make a distinction between existing buildings being adapted and new buildings

Adhi Moersid, Achmad Fanani, and Tulus Setyo Budhi

being built. What is this process of transforming a native dialect into an evolving architectural language? How is it different from establishing a new vocabulary? Reorienting a space to align it with the *qibla* is fundamentally different from replacing a painted symbol with verses from the Koran. In spite of the two stages of Islamization and re-Islamization, isn't the power of local cultural practices undermined? Where and how do Muslim faith and Javanese practices come together in this architecture?

Response

We presented two cases we considered as representative of the process of Islamic religious transformation from pre-Islamic to Islamic conditions (Pondok Pesantren) and from Islamic conditions to a more orthodox Islamic attitude (Kota Gede). The first involved the development of a new environment for the first Islamic community in Java. We based our description on our 1989 field research in ten old *pesantren*s in East Java, which could illustrate conditions at that initial stage (the first *pesantren* in Java dates to the fifteenth century, but no reliable reference to it is available). All the *pesantrens* have a similar layout, i.e., the yard at the center, the mosque on the west, the *kyai*'s house on the north, the *santries'* dormitory on the east, and the dwelling of the *kyai*'s parents on the south. When we analyzed this pattern, we came to the conclusion that it was a clever interpretation of the *mancapat*, i.e., the space classification and division in pre-Islamic Java based on the four points of the compass, each of which in Java had a particular meaning. For instance, the north is the seat of Wishnu, symbol of the sun, its color is yellow, and its meaning is the source of life (Frick, 1997: 85). The development of the new environment of the *pesantren* used in this case the old space design concept but with contemporary contents, i.e., referring to Islamic values. A similar principle was also followed by the *walis* when they built the very first mosques in Java. They borrow the old idioms but changed their contents into the Islamic soul and spirit.

In the second case, the reformist Mohammediya undertook the re-Islamization of Kota Gede, a purification of Islamic teachings in Javanese society. A large part of that society were already Muslims, but living in a traditional Javanese environment. We tried to picture their attitude towards that old Javanese built environment. They did not make any significant changes in the dwellings or settlement, aside from changing the function of the sacred room used for offerings and meditation into a space for the required five daily prayers. We did not describe the construction of the new houses in Kota Gede which differed considerably from the old, since we assumed that these differences could be attributable to any number of factors, including modernization, changes in life style, technological progress, and new building materials.

The native people were responsive to the efforts of preservation and conservation of the old cultural environment, as shown in the Kota Gede case.

If the "universal elements" in Islamic architecture refer to things like the focus on inner space, the absence of specific architectural forms for specific functions, the presence of domes and minarets, the Muslim built environments in Java (*pesantren*, mosques of the *wali*s, and the traditional houses in Kota Gede) are clearly very different, since they are typically Javanese. But we assume they have Islamic soul and nuances, since they were built with Muslim concepts in mind and maintained for use by Muslims.

Local cultural practices based on old religious rituals did weaken in Kota Gede as a consequence of the purification action by the Mohammediya, but the inhabitants continued to respect their old architectural heritage, as is evident from the absence of significant change in their old built environment.

The harmonious joining of the Islamic belief with Javanese ritual practices is represented by the mosque and the royal graveyard being in one complex, which combines the Hindu concept, the original Javanese ancestor worship, with Islamic rituals and facilities. We would like to emphasize that our position is that of practitioners who have observed the Islamic religious transformation in the built environment that is to us a most valuable lesson as a contributory input for the environmental design process and the search of a new design language. We do not pretend to present this as an academic theory; we would rather share this Indonesian view which we presume could serve our common purpose.

Additional notes:

Heinz Frick, *Pola struktural dan teknik bangunan di Indonesia*. Yogyakarta, Kanisius. 1997.

Denys Lombard, *Nusa Jawa: Silang Budaya*. 3 vols. Trans. of *Le Carrefour Javanais: Essai d'histoire globale*. Jakarta, PT. Gramedia Pustaka Utama. 1996.

Adhi Moersid, Achmad Fanani, and Tulus Setyo Budhi

Persian Gardens and Courtyards: An Approach to the Design of Contemporary Architecture

Mahvash Alemi

ver since I have been in Persia I have been looking for a garden and have not found one."[1] Vita Sackville-West was sitting in a Persian garden while she was writing these words; it was her way of introducing the difference in conception between an English garden and a Persian one. "Garden? We say; and think of lawns and herbaceous borders, which is manifestly absurd. There is no turf in this parched country; and as for herbaceous borders, they postulate a lush shapeliness unimaginable to the Persian mind." She then explains that after a ride in summer for days across plains and mountains, "when you come to trees and running water you call it a garden. It will not be flowers and their garishness that your eyes crave for, but a green cavern full of shadow, and pools where goldfish dart, and the sound of little streams. That is the meaning of a garden in Persia".

This was what a Persian garden meant to Vita Sackville-West and probably to most of us today when we first encounter one. But what was its meaning to Cyrus when according to Xenophon he personally planted the trees in his pairidaeza in a quincuncial order? Thomas Browne implies that Cyrus was acting as God, the ordainer of order in nature, in imposing the quincuncial order as well as by the personal act of fecundating the earth.[2] The reception of the produce of earth at *nawruz*, the first day of spring, sculpted on the stairs of the palace at Persepolis, as well as the banquets offered by Cyrus to the tribes, revealed, as André Motte suggests, the king's supreme royalty and omnipotence, since the dispensing of food is a divine prerogative.[3]

Was the pairidaeza the re-creation of the earth according to the Zoroastrian *mundus imaginalis*?[4] Corbin implies that the cultivation of a garden as-

sumes a liturgic meaning as a mental recomposition of paradise and a consortium of celestial beings. All the elements of the Zoroastrian visionary landscape appear in the garden-paradise: the different terraces symbolize the Cosmic Mountain; and on the highest level, the throne in the *iwan* of the royal pavilion represents the glittering residence of gods. In front of this, the water basin is the Cosmic Ocean, source of all the waters that run in small channels like rivers. Around it trees and flowers of all kinds complete the *imago mundi*.

With the advent of Islam these meanings change. The paradise of the Koran[5] is different from the Zoroastrian one. How does the new cosmography affect the forms of the Persian garden in the Islamic period? The archaeological traces of the palace of Cyrus at Pasargadae induced Stronach to find affinities between the layout and elements of the pairidaeza and the Islamic gardens called *chahar bagh*.[6] The remains at Pasargadae define a rectilinear layout of water channels in stone, interspersed with basins and pavilions that opened on four sides through porticoes. The garden was presumably planted with fruit trees on a quincuncial pattern and was fragrant with perfumes, as Xenophon says of the pairidaeza at Sardis.[7] On the other hand, the question whether *chahar bagh* was a type of garden planted with fruit trees and divided into quarters by intersecting water channels representing the four rivers in the Koran is controversial.[8] Nevertheless we can detect certain common physical features in the two gardens, that can essentially be reconducted to an enclosed orchard with pavilions opening towards watercourses and basins.

One of the features of the design process in Persian architecture is that it combines different components.[9] The comparatively large amount of evidence we have for garden pavilions of the Safavid period enables us to sustain that in that period a *talar* was often used in front of the garden pavilions.[10] This component would extend the space of the *iwan*, the *shah nishin* or seat of the king, towards the garden, providing additional space for guests. George Perrot[11] finds analogies between the description by Polybius of the Achaemenid hypostyle halls and the Safavid *talar* of the Chihil Sutun. Where the model for such a distinctive component as the Safavid *talar* lies has still to be investigated. What is remarkable is that the Safavids, who made Shi'ism the state religion, would build their *talar(s)* with an eye on the Takht-i Jamshid (Persepolis), as the use of the mythical lion sculptures around the basin in the *talar* of the Chihil Sutun suggests. The hypostyle halls at Persepolis were made of lapidary columns; the Safavid *talar* is supported by slender wooden columns that confer to it a totally different air. The archetype of *talar* was therefore reinterpreted to fit the architectural taste and needs of the Safavid kings.

These elements seem again to disappear after the Safavids. We can detect a more diffused use of an *iwan* supported on two columns in the pavilions of the Zand and Qajar kings. The decorations of the Zand pavilions in Shiraz also draw upon the near Persepolis reliefs. Certain Western Baroque features can be distinguished in the Qajar pavilions of the nineteenth century. These changes in the composition of pavilions in different periods reveal that it is true that the garden pavilions continued to be built along the same concepts as those found by Stronach in Pasargadae, but that the archetype was reinterpreted continuously, reflecting the cultural context in which it was embedded. Did these continuities and changes reflect a similar continuity and change in cultural context?

Was the reproduction of the Shahnama of Firdawsi, in the Safavid court just a matter of political power as is suggested by Robert Hillenbrand?[12] Or were the traces of the ancient cult so profound that there was need for reviving the latent meaning of the cosmic battle between good and evil through the poems recounting the battles between heroes or kings against the tyrants? Were there, as Gray suggests, Zoroastrian elements in Mohammedan theology?[13] Would the Islamic kings celebrate *nawruz* and give public audiences, and accept the offerings of the fruits of the earth as Cyrus because of the myth of the Persian Empire? Or was there also a continuity in meaning, as Corbin suggests a continuous medita-

tion on the figure of the Angel of Earth in the Islamic Iranian theosophy, from Suhravardi in the twelfth century to Sadr ud-Din Shirazi in the seventeenth. These affinities between meanings could be the reason for a continuous thread between the pre-Islamic *pairidaeza* and the successive royal gardens, or continuity in forms of rituals could be devoid of ancient connotations? These questions await further research. The evidence we have today suggests that the archetype was continuously reinterpreted to respond to the new cultural context in which it was embedded. It is therefore the new cultural context for which a garden is designed that dictates the rules of its composition.

Let us go back to the *talar* and examine two cases in two cultural situations completely different from the Safavid one, where it has been reinterpreted in the design of a garden pavilion.

The first case is a project by Fischer von Erlach. In 1712 he presented to the Emperor Charles VI the manuscript for Entwurff Einer Historischer Architecture.[14] In its third book, devoted to Turkish, modern Persian, Siamese, Chinese and Japanese architecture he reproduces a view showing the Maydan-i Shah and the pavilion Ali Qapu. The *talar* of Ali Qapu is placed above a four-iwan building, the main gate of the royal gardens in Isfahan. It overlooks the great Maydan. Seated under its lofty intarsiated wooden ceiling among its forest of slender octagonal columns, the shah and his guests could be seen in a magnificent setting watching the spectacles taking place in the *maydan*. It could be a game of polo (*chawgan*), an archery contest (*qabaq andazi*), an animal combat, or a military parade. It was, however, also the perfect lookout from which to view, beyond the city, the mountains to the south of the river and return to dwell upon the tiled domes of the mosques around the *maydan*, and in the bazaar.

Although he had only seen this pavilion through the eyes of other travelers, Fischer von Erlach nevertheless used it in his design for a garden pleasure house for Schloss Klesheim, which he labeled "Project eines Gartten-Gebau neu persianischer bauartt",[15] where the facade of Ali Qapu is quoted integrally and flanked by two convex buildings. It was to function as a gate loggia from where carriages coming to the palace could be seen and also as a place from which to watch spectacles in the garden. The effect of combining this architecture with a Baroque architectural language was bizarre. The vocabulary needed to be changed. He solved the problem in other projects of garden pavilions by continu-

Mahvash Alemi

ing to propose a central part with arcades and belvederes on the upper terrace, but with a more coherent and synthetical Baroque vocabulary. If the passage of the Persianate drawing for the pleasure house were not there, it would be difficult to read Fischer's projects of the successive garden pavilions as a reinterpretation of the Ali Qapu type.

The second case is a garden we designed in Rome;[16] far from the Isfahan of the Safavid kings. Within its enclosure, a place was needed from which different views could be organized; it had to be lofty so that the great cliff covered with Roman pines could be exalted, as in a picture by Claude Lorraine; it needed to have shade, for the garden in this spot had no trees. It was an area paved with stones of different textures where the canopo of Hadrian[17] lay along one of the many traces that one's eyes could follow, while meditating on the memories of Via Flaminia. On this paved surface, as in the calligrames of Apollinaire, a visual lirism was sought through the juxtaposition of artificial and natural forms, of surreal, exotic and archaeological memo-ries. The image of the *talar* of Chihil Sutun[18] was evoked and it appeared to conform to the idea. There were certain affinities. Its slender wooden columns formed a lofty space and the wooden trellis roof provided the necessary shade (Figure 1). It was airy. It was no longer used as a king's audience hall, but it provided a pleasant place for the Romans who happened by to sit in its shade.

The proportions are there, but the spatial relationships have changed. The *talar* is no longer looking towards the main axis as in the Safavid garden, but it is organizing views that are Roman in their essence. The *talar*, abstracted to its essential form, deprived of its context and meanings, is part of a series of memories articulated in multiple correlations. Open on four sides, it offers a wide view that moves from the stone paved surface to the portico of the auditorium; it sweeps over to the open theatre populated by De Chirico-inspired characters and dwells inevitably on the cliff in Borghetto Flaminio, which is indeed a sublime sight.

The above examples show an approach in which

Figure 1. Pavilion in the garden of Borghetto Flaminio, Rome (Drawing by Author)

Mahvash Alemi

a single component of the Persian garden is quoted and reinterpreted as an archetype in the design of a pavilion, but in a totally different cultural context and given rules and meanings of its own. Let us now examine a typological approach.

In all Persian building types the courtyard is the core, the place to refer to. The mosque, *madrasa*, caravanserai, and house are all enclosed spaces built around a *hayyat* that cuts out just the right amount of sky necessary for the life within. Here unity and architectural order are achieved. The composition grows from the interior of the courtyard outwards. In the house, the *iwan* mediates the passage between the sky and the room; the denomination of certain rooms as *panj-dari*, or *seh-dari*, defined in terms of the number of doors opening into the courtyard, expresses clearly that the courtyard is the place to refer to.

The traditional Persian house, when it was lived in by more than one family, was organized around interconnecting courtyards. The model has changed since the 1930s giving way to a type of multiple-family house with a different morphological relationship to the city. The street has gained in importance, resulting in urban fabrics with a completely different morphological aspect. If the house is to be designed for a plot to the north side of a street, its courtyard is in the southern portion of the plot and a building beyond. If the plot is on the south side of the street, the scheme is reversed: the building is on the street side with the courtyard beyond. But these courtyards do not play the same role as they did in the traditional courtyard houses. This morphological organization is reinforced by a series of town-planning rules that would make it more and more difficult for a house to be designed around a courtyard. In two projects in Iran for multifamily housing, I have tried to return to the model of the courtyard house and make the courtyard the core of the whole composition while still observing the town-planning restrictions.

For a residential complex for ten families at Velenjak, north of Tehran, we arranged the units around two courtyards on different levels, further elaborated with smaller courtyards operating as vestibules for the apartments.[19] Here it was possible to use a variation on the theme of courtyard house for multifamily housing because the model was not treated as a rigid element. Certain characteristics of the model were maintained giving the building a pleasant air of traditional house, although the apartments were organized according to a scheme that differed from the historical model.

In a similar project at Punak,[20] west of Tehran four larger units are stretched around a first courtyard leaving a second one to the south of the plot. They could have been designed with a more compact organization, one to the north and the other to the south of the first courtyard with the same functions, but this option was discarded. I preferred the elongated plan for the unit—where the two parts of the house, devoted to day and night, were connected with a verandah that bridges across the courtyard -

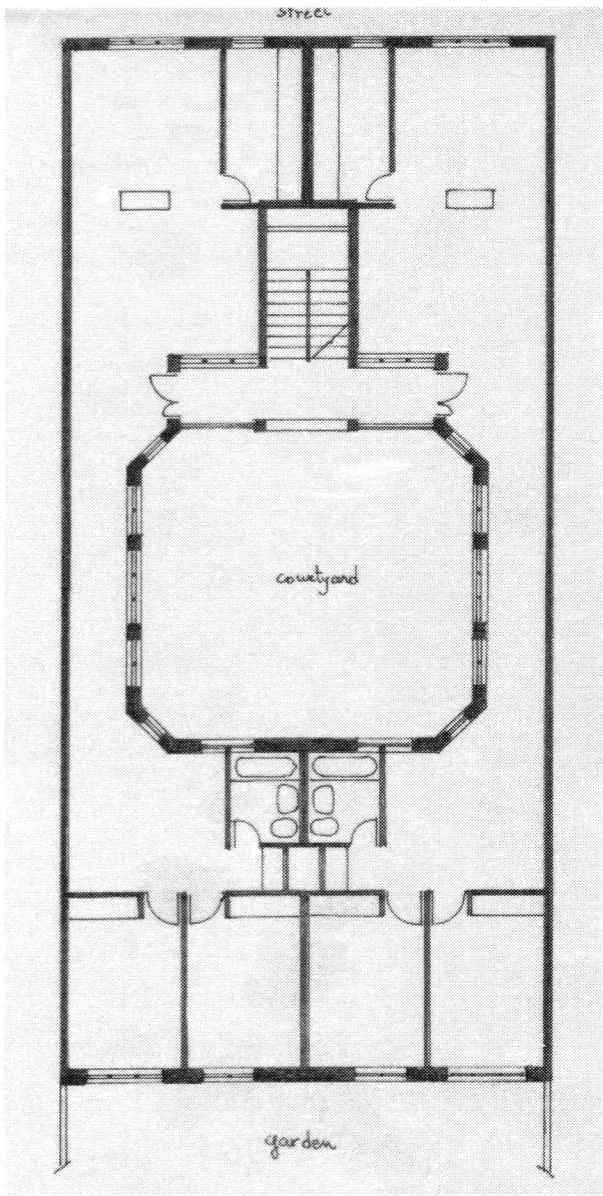

Figure 2. Plan of the housing project at Punak, Tehran (Drawing by Author)

Mahvash Alemi

because this arrangement seemed to adhere better to the idea of the court as the core of the composition. The verandah is where the pleasure and the appreciation of the qualities of the space generated by the presence of the archetype can best be perceived.

Historical models can be an important source of inspiration for contemporary projects, providing they are adapted to the different situations and are given new life by meeting contemporary requirements and cultural solicitations. In the rich and exciting environment that would be desirable for our cities, we need to perceive the echoes and breathe the air of our distant and marvelous past. Perhaps this was what T.S. Eliot had in mind when he wrote:

> Time present and time past
> Are both perhaps present in time future,
> And time future contained in time past.[21]

Notes

1. Vita Sackville-West, *Passenger to Tehran*, (London, 1926), p. 90.

2. *The Prose of Sir Thomas Browne, Religio Medici, Hydriotaphia, The Garden of Cyrus*, ed. Norman Endicott (New York, 1968).

3. André Motte , *Prairies et Jardins de la Grèce Antique. De la Religion à la Philosophie*, (Bruxelles, 1971).

4. Henri Corbin, *Corpo spirituale e Terra celeste: Dall'Iran mazdeo all'Iran sciita*, (Paris, 1979), trans. Gabriella Bemporad, (Milano, 1986); John R. Hinnelis, *Persian Mythology*, (New York. 1985); L. I. Ringbom, "Three Sasanian Bronze Salvers with Pairidaeza Motifs", in *A Survey of Persian Art*, Arthur Upham Pope ed., (Tehran, London, New York, Tokyo, 1967) vol.14.

5. Annemarie Schimmel, "The Celestial Garden", in *The Islamic Garden*, ed. E. B. Macdougall and R. Ettinghausen, (Washington, D.C.: Dumbarton Oaks Trustees for Harvard University, 1976); William L. Hanaway, Jr." The terrestrial Garden in Persian Literature" in *The Islamic Garden*, (1976); James Dickie," The Islamic garden in Spain', in *The Islamic Garden*, (1976); Maria Jesus Rubiera y Mata, " Il giardino come metafora del paradiso" in *Il giardino Islamico*, ed. A. Petruccioli (Milano, 1994).

6. David Stronach, "Caharbag" in *Encyclopedia Iranica*, ed. Ehsan Yarshater (London-New York,

1989), 4: 624; idem, "The Royal Garden at Pasargadae: Evolution and Legacy" in *Archaeologia Iranica et Orientalis Miscellanea in honorem Louis Vanden Berghe*, (Ghent, 1989) pp. 475-502; idem,"Excavations at Pasargadae, third preliminary report" in *Iran*, Journal of the British Institute of Persian Studies, 3(1965).

7. Xenophon, quoted from Fabio Roscalla, trans. Senofonte, Economico, (Milano, 1991), p. 103.

8. Many papers have been dealing with the Irshad al zira'a, an agricultural treatise in the eight chapter of which the layout of a *chaharbagh* is defined: Qasim ibn Yusuf Abu Nasr-i Haravi, *Irshad-al Zira'a*, ed. Muhammad Mushiri (Tehran, 1968); Ralph Pinder Wilson, "The Persian Garden: Bagh and Chaharbagh" in *The Islamic Garden*, (cited above, n.5); Mahvash Alemi, "Chaharbagh", *Environmental Design, Journal of the Islamic Environmental Design Research Centre*, (1986) no. 1; Jurgen Jakobi, "Agriculture between Literary Tradition and First hand Experience: The Irshad al-zira'a of Qasim b. Yusuf Abu Nasri Haravi" in: *Timurid Art and Culture Iran and Central Asia in the Fifteenth Century* , ed. Lisa Golombek and Maria Subtelny (Leiden: E. J. Brill, 1992); M. E. Subtenly, " A medieval Persian Agricultural Manual in Context: the Irshad al-Zira'a in *Late Timurid and Early Safavid Khurasan"* Studia Iranica 22, no.2(1993); M.E. Subtenly, " Mirak-i Sayyid Ghiyas & the Timurid traditions of Landscape Architecture, "*Studia Iranica* 24 (1995).

9. Lisa Golombek and Donald Wilber, *The Timurid Architecture of Iran and Turan*, 2 vols. (Princeton, 1988).

10. Mahvash Alemi, "Il giardino persiano, tipi e modelli" in *Il giardino Islamico*, ed. A. Petruccioli (Milano, 1994).

11. George Perrot and Charles Chipiez, *History of Art in Persia*, (London 1892; rept. Tehran, 1976).

12. Robert Hillenbrand, "The Iconography of the Shahnama-yi Shahi", in *Pembroke Papers* 4(1966) 53-78.

13. L.H. Gray, "Zoroastrian Elements in Mohammedan Theology", *Muséon*, new series 3 (1902); A.V. Williams Jackson, Zoroastrian Studies, (New York, 1928).

14. Vienna, Osterreichische Nationalbibliothek, Handscriftensammlung, Cod. 10791. The book was first published in 1721, Tav. IX.

15. G. Kunoth, *Die Historische Architektur Fischers*

Mahvash Alemi

von Erlach, (Dusseldorf, 1956). See plate. 153, reproduced from the drawing conserved in Universitatsbibliothek Zagreb.

16. The project for the garden of Borghetto Flaminio was designed by Myself and Ludovico Micara in the year 1995 for an international competition for designs to improve the area near the Porta del Popolo, by providing a garden with cultural and commercial activities, an archeological walk and an underground garage.

17. William Macdonald and John Pinto, *Hadrian's Villa and its legacy*, (Yale University Press, 1955).

18. Donald Wilber, *Persian Gardens and Garden Pavilions*, (1962, 2nd ed. Washington DC, 1979); Elizabeth B. Moynihan, *Paradise as a Garden in Persia and Mughal India,* (New York: George Braziller, 1979); Jonas Lehrman, *Earthly Paradise: Garden and Court-yard in Islam*, (Berkeley: University of California Press, 1980); John Brookes, *The history and Design of the Great Islamic Gardens*, (London, 1987); Mahvash Alemi, "The Royal Gardens of the Safavid Period: Types and Models", in *Gardens in the Time of the Great Muslim Empires: Theory and Design*, ed. A. Petruccioli (Leiden: E. J. Brill, 1997).

19. The Velanjak housing was designed by myself and Ludovico Micara in 1977 and is published in *Architettura nei paesi islamici, seconda mostra internazionale di architettura*, La Biennale di Venezia, (Rome: Electa, 1982).

20. The Punak housing was designed by myself in 1994.

21. From "Burnt Norton" The Four Quartets (1935).

• • • • • • • • • • • • •

Comments
Attilio Petruccioli

The observation of Sackville-West refers to an environmental situation rather than a formal scheme. The garden is " trees and running waters" in a prevalently arid environment. How important is this issue in the Persian garden tradition, considering that Western travelers describe the city seen at a distance as an oasis full of trees, as opposed to its arid natural context?

Is the same garden type found in the different parts of the Islamic world? Or does it vary according to the regional traditions? The paper's general approach seems to imply the second hypothesis. Is it therefore possible to talk of an Islamic garden?

The adoption of a talar in different post-Safavid projects seems to take into consideration a sort of quotation rather than a revival of the spirit of the Persian garden. Don't you think that other elements are more important in reproposing the atmosphere of a garden as, for example, the enclosure that defines the interior as separate from the exterior? A feature that is common between the garden and the courtyard.

Response
The paradisiacal nature recreated within the walls of the garden as opposed to the hostile nature outside the walls reflects the Persian genius loci. This spirit of the place is best understood if we refer to the representation of a garden rather than the garden itself. In the miniatures representing a garden, a decorated pavilion is placed on an elaborately paved platform with geometrically defined watercourses and basins, exalting artifice through abstraction and geometry; but the trees and flowers in the background are depicted as essential or metaphoric features in a rather naturalistic composition. The aligned trees, found in the layout of a garden, are never illustrated as such. In the pairidaeza in Taq-i Bustan, within a geometrically defined enclosure a natural scenery with trees, waters and fauna is represented. The Persian poet as well exalts the recreation of the paradisiacal nature, the variety of fruit trees, scented and colorful flowers, the perfection and height of its building and the purity and light in its water. The ideal of a varied and luxurious nature, so precious in the arid environment of the highlands, recomposes thus the image of paradise as a garden.

As for the cities appearing as oases, in the central highlands the presence of an agglomeration was synonymous of water, gardens and trees. In this respect the fact that the Persian building types are always comprehensive of a courtyard, or are located inside a garden is revealing. Pietro della Valle reads

Mahvash Alemi

the formal structure of a garden in the addition of Shah Abbas to the city of Isfahan, where the Chahar bagh promenade and the river divided the city in four parts.

The Islamic culture is quite widespread. As Grabar concludes, "the formation of Islamic art can be seen as an accumulation and novel distribution of forms from all over the conquered world, as a conscious sorting out of the meanings associated with the forms, and as a creation of a limited number of new characteristic forms." In the artistic explosion that followed the early Islamic period Iranian forms played a singularly important part. Nevertheless there was a great amount of contamination between regional traditions and cultures and the new artistic impulses. It is time to study the specific regional gardens in order to define beyond a stereotyped concept of Islamic culture the role of both parts and to define the balance between provinces in the creation and development of Islamic art. The treatise and theoretical contributions should be as precious as the study of the layouts of each garden. The Persian gardens within the archetype of an enclosed orchard display great structural and aesthetic variety, achieving individuality distinct from all other Muslim countries.

What is in a Persian garden that a designer should refer to? It is possible to refer to the essence of the space, to its symbolic meanings, to its proportions and forms, to its relationships with the context or to its memory. I believe that the design process is autonomous and that one may follow in different projects different ways. In the project of Borghetto the sense of enclosure, essential in the Persian garden, was achieved by a wall building on the sides of the plot that were along the streets. But of greater importance was the envisaged picturesque character of the garden at Borghetto, that solicited an exotic atmosphere, a memory of the Persian garden, suggested by the proportions and forms of one of its components, within a Roman picturesque spot.

Section III

CONTEMPORARY TRENDS

Essays in this section discuss the current trends in architecture, education, and the socioeconomic aspects of various Muslim countries. Suha Özkan discusses the effects of colonization on Muslim societies and raises issues such as how Modernism and Western models have dominated design concepts in Muslim societies, what were and are the reasons for the rapid adoption of Western models in Eastern societies, and what role regionalism plays in diverse Muslim cultures. He also outlines the contributions of a few prominent architects in Muslim countries. Ali Shuaibi emphasizes the need for architects to draw meaning from the local vernacular built environment and take advantage of tools such as computer systems. He also cautions architects not to imitate Western models blindly. Along similar lines, Rasem Badran encourages investigating local cultures for design guidance, supporting his arguments by providing examples of projects from current practice. Eugenio Galdieri discusses the "confusion" in oil-rich countries of the Middle East and, with the intent of guiding practicing architects, raises issues such as imitation versus innovation in Muslim societies. Kamran T. Diba provides his version of what type of buildings do not or cannot belong in Muslim societies and Arif Hasan discusses the latest socioeconomic and development trends in developing countries and how architects can help direct this rapid development in the proper direction. Kausar B. Ahmad alludes to problems faced by educational institutions in Muslim countries and outlines why education is important for the future of architectural practice and what measures can be taken to address these problems.

Modernity and Tradition: Problem or Potential

Suha Özkan

In architecture, as in most forms of artistic expression, any analysis must be conditioned on temporal boundaries; in other words, societal and economic factors can only be formulated and validated when placed within the perspective of time. When discussing contemporary architecture those temporal boundaries include both colonialism and modernism.

Colonialism has two aspects: political colonialism, which can be placed within a particular span of time, and intellectual colonialism, which remains outside temporal bounds and is not so simple a matter as political colonialism.

With two exceptions political and economic colonialism have governed the Islamic world for the last two centuries—the exceptions are Iran and Turkey, which were themselves colonial powers. Beginning in the fourteenth century, the Ottomans began their conquests that ended in the colonization of the fertile lands of Eastern Europe with the mission of expanding Islam, and occupation of the Holy Land and northern Africa, where they remained for centuries. When the Ottomans failed to adapt to industrialization in the nineteenth century, their military and economic power weakened, and their territories were effectively ceded to the European colonial powers—Italy, France, and Britain—who became the new colonizers of the Middle East. The rest of the Islamic world, from Pakistan to Indonesia, was mainly colonized by the British, the Portuguese, and the Dutch. Iran, however, remained within its own historical boundaries and its influence was more intellectual and cultural than political.

Colonialism imposed a pattern of cohabitation of local population and colonizers; they not only had to live together and share the same environment, but were committed to the yields of the same lands and seas. The only differences lay in their backgrounds and identities, and ultimately their loyalties.

Where architecture was concerned, in contrast to the political and economic controls of the colonial setting, colonial approaches were rather considerate of the cultural values and climatic requirements of the occupied lands; colonial Dutch architecture in Java and colonial British architecture in the Indian Subcontinent yield evidence of architects trying to understand the architectural heritage and vernacular settings of the new lands and using them as inspiration for a new architecture. The results were an often-intriguing synthesis of the values of the Western heritage and the overpowering environment of the East.

With the end of colonialism in the twentieth century, the next wave of influence from the West was modernism, with its new values for living in an industrial society, which not only contrasted with existing traditions, but also distanced itself as much as possible from traditional societies and values, often to the point of denying or suppressing cultural continuity altogether. The dictates of newly developed modes and expressions of Western societies that modernism imposed were not limited to architecture or design, but also affected music, literature, drama, and the plastic arts, but obviously architecture was the genre that most affected people's lives.

After World War I expressions of modernity were introduced without much difficulty into traditional Islamic societies, along with new technologies such as photography and motion pictures, which enormously strengthened the impact of new influences by directly communicating real-life images and sounds. For the most part the transition to modernity caused little disruption since it did not seem to conflict with traditional values and even seemed to offer improvements in comfort and efficiency. In some cases, however, modernism was introduced as a strategy with a strong political agenda: it was the centerpiece of governing politics for Kemal Atatürk in Turkey, Gamal Abdul Nasser in Egypt, Habib Bourgiba in Tunisia, Reza Shah Pahlavi in Iran, Muhammad Ali Jinnah in Pakistan, Jawaharlal Nehru in India, and Ahmad Sukarno in Indonesia, all of them forceful leaders who uncompromisingly placed modernity at the core of their political discourse. Their conception of modernism implied industrialization, efficiency, and the improvement of living standards; "progress" would be the reward. In a political context, most of the values that had been cohesive in these societies were overlooked and, in many cases, suppressed and denied. Communism, the most forceful of the new doctrines, and its leaders Lenin and Stalin in the USSR and Mao Zedung in the People's Republic of China, disregarded cultural plurality, especially of those peoples with strong ethnic roots and traditional values. The new political doctrines replaced them with ideological uniformity and the homogenization of values. Tradition, history, and geography had no place in the modernist discourse, which instead focused on uniformity, equality, and a universally valid mode of life.

Countries which had gone through painful struggles to gain independence from colonial powers saw modernism as the only viable avenue, and with this forceful and persuasive objective in mind, the appropriateness of modernism was not challenged, either politically or technically. Whole sectors of society took its value and validity for granted.

Architecture played a major role in this transformation. In the 1930s the overpowering spread of modernism in almost all cities, East and West, was represented in the beginning by the iconic modes of building professed by the Bauhaus and such pioneering modernists as Walter Gropius, Ludwig Mies van der Rohe, and Le Corbusier. The principles of functionality and of quality with simplicity were initially adhered to. During the reconstruction period following World War II, however, when demand for new building was very great, it was most often met with simplistic derivations of badly understood and badly interpreted "modern" architecture. New built environments were carelessly transformed by this mundane and worthless architectural idiom which purported to be modern, but which in fact violated

nearly every tenet of modernism. Alongside this simplistic uniformity, meaning in the built environment was further diminished by the gradual but massive demolition of the surviving architectural heritage and with it the symbolic content and meaning it had always provided.

The phenomenon of rural-to-urban migration that affected nearly all third-world cities, beginning in the 1950s and continuing until today, greatly accelerated the transformation of environments in the Islamic world. Novel modes of building for urban survival became widespread, and squatter settlements and unlicensed or informal building added a harsh new reality to the rapid transformation of the urban fringes, even as their historical cores were being destroyed from within.

Whose fault was it? The question remains permanently unanswered. Is it the modern movement in architecture which caused this degeneration, or is it modernity itself and its licensing of meaningless uniformity? Or did it come about as the result of hidden forces in society that pursued selfish or political short-term goals and disguised their efforts in the name of modernity? Since the late 1970s, these questions have been endlessly debated, and the debate will probably continue indefinitely, perhaps because architects and architectural thinkers like to adopt strong, partisan attitudes rather than try to understand the forces that brought the situation about.

Charles Jencks, one of the most profound and prolific of the modernist critics draws an analogy to religion: "Modernism is one of the strongest religions—indeed in the nineteenth century it was the most potent of Post-Christian faiths. With the rise of secularism, Darwinism and atheism and the attacks on Christianity of Feuerbach, Marx and Nietzsche, most intellectuals become skeptics."[1] This conviction may be the reason why many of the proponents of modernism like Gropius and Mies van der Rohe gave lip service to the right-wing politics of the time. Perhaps they recognized that building with modernist conviction required a heavy-handed political power, and yielding to that they violated the ethical aspect of modernism, which is perhaps its strongest point.

Jencks also challenged modernism as a basis for constancy and its aspirations of predictability: "...the Modernists with their mechanistic models emphasize predictability, but the cosmos is much more dynamic than either a pre-designed world or a dead machine."[2] One cannot disagree with Jencks on the aspect of predictability which modernism demands;

Suha Özkan

86

the parameters of that predictability are what is at issue, especially in the view of its long history, during which modernism has endured many challenges.

It is important to distinguish first between bad or thoughtless architecture and modernism. The modern movement has never represented or condoned bad architecture. On the contrary, its simplified but extremely demanding and sensitive criteria for quality require the highest standards from designers. Simplicity is a goal, and functionality is a required rationale, but the great strength of modernism lies in its respect for structure, materials, and site; honesty of expression is perhaps the most important criterion but also the most difficult to attain.

Regionalism and the Islamic World

It is not easy to discuss developments in the Islamic world as a whole, since each setting has its own dynamics and priorities. However, a number of categories can be formulated for consideration, and examples from each discussed. In the 1980s, once the hype and the noise of post-modernism had subsided, serious thinking about relating the built environment to cultural context began to emerge. This focus on regionalism turned into a search for architectural identity within a given cultural, historical, and climatic context.[3] Regionalism was not conceived as an approach to challenge modernism, but as a contemporary discourse that the internationalist vein of modernism did not address. Noted architects such as Charles Correa, Balkrishna Doshi, Geoffrey Bawa, and Hassan Fathy among many, declared the importance of context over art (i.e., over building). Serious critical thinking on the topic of regionalism, such as Kenneth Frampton's "critical regionalism," began to appear, culminating in a debate in which my own contribution aimed at situating regionalism within the intellectual tenets of modernism.[4] As the use of earlier styles in architecture—Neo-Classicism, Art Nouveau, Art Deco, etc.—receded, modernism became the common language of the architectural profession. It developed a valid and consistent model for architectural education, building design, and criticism, and was successful in formulating the concepts of time and progress, in integrating architecture and industry, in its emphasis on function, its search for subtle aesthetics, honesty of form, and logical reasoning. Most important, and in contrast to such short-lived fashions as Post-Modernism, modernism was erected on a strong and noble ethical foundation and a commitment that are hard to challenge, and perhaps impossible to dis-

agree with.

In a subsequent attempt to catalogue regionalism,[5] the taxonomy conceived of it within the framework of history and classified various approaches as historically derivative or transformational. Derivative approaches are those that build upon vernacular architecture and, by definition, historical precedent; all the norms, technologies, and patterns of spatial organization have their origins in historical architecture. Design efforts aim to distinguish between historical forms that are still valid and those that have now become obsolete. Derivative regionalism, or, in simpler terms, vernacularism, had the work of Hassan Fathy (1900-89) as its inspiration.

Early in his long career, Fathy designed in a modernist idiom,[6] but he later came to doubt the validity of the movement, and began to advance a notion that he expressed as "building of the site" as opposed to building on it.[7] His village planning and architectural experiments were not entirely successful sociologically, since he was in no position fully to understand the mentality of the inhabitants; as a consequence, villages such as New Gourna and Bariz remained under-occupied for many years, and their failure was used against Fathy by his opponents. However, Fathy's ideas attracted adherents internationally, and successive generations of younger architects adopted his pioneering approach that challenged the validity of modernism, especially the use of imported materials, and the disregard for cultural differences and common identity.

Fathy wholeheartedly believed that materials to build with were available on any site; he thought that it was the responsibility of the architect to figure out how to use and develop appropriate technology to transform local materials into buildings. According to Fathy, an architect is the person who brings the expertise to assist people in creating their own buildings. To prove his theories he used ancient Nubian techniques for the construction of vaults and domes in simple, readily available, and inexpensive materials. This technique did not require wood for formwork, and was therefore also viable ecologically and ethically, as well as architecturally. These ancient construction techniques were successfully applied, but provisions for infrastructure and maintenance were unfortunately poorly considered.

Fathy's commitment was political and ethical as well as architectural, though his talent and professionalism were always in the fore; he demonstrated his versatility equally well when building in materials other than earth and for clients other than the

Suha Özkan

87

poor. He hoped that if his wealthier clients would accept traditional techniques and materials in their houses so then would the poor, an idea that seems to be becoming a reality. In addition to his architecture, the prophetic vision of his influential book, Architecture for the Poor (1978),[8] continues to guide and inspire.

Fathy's oeuvre earned him an international following. The French architect André Ravereau focused on the contextual importance of Fathy's work, and his medical center[9] (1976) in Mopti, Mali, became a seminal building in Sub-Saharan Africa for the provision of modest facilities in rural settings. Fathy's approach was also taken up by a younger generation of architects who were committed to using their talents and intellects for the benefit of the underprivileged. Groups such as the Development Workshop[10] (based in France, England, and Canada), CraTERRE,[11] (France), and ADAUA[12] (Geneva and West Africa) became notable for their development efforts within the confines of Fathy's ideology. Each of these groups has a different way of working, but in most cases they secure funding from international agencies and develop projects either as demonstration efforts or in response to environmental or social crises. Though they are all dedicated to vernacular expressions of technology based on the use of existing materials and methods of construction, the architectural forms they have developed are bold and novel. Particularly, the plasticity of form which characterizes their efforts firmly places them in the current discourse of architecture. Only time will tell, however, whether these forms will be accepted or rejected by local populations and thus whether the experiments have succeeded.

The Development Workshop's "Building without Wood" project in Niger, CraTERRE's primary school in Somalia, and ADAUA's Housing for Refugees in Rosso and hospital in Kaedi, Mauritania, are all fine examples of this approach. In a similar line of development, UNESCO's experimental work in Senegal under the direction of Kamal el-Jack for the Agricultural Training Center in Nianing,[13] and Raoul Snelder in the Daara School in Malika, and the Muhanna brothers' experiments in Syria[14] reveal the development of building systems which employ locally abundant natural materials.

Figure 1. Irfouane, Niger. Development Workshop, woodless construction program. (Photo: John Norton/ AKTC)

Suha Özkan

Figure 2. Istanbul, Turkey. Sedad Hakki Eldem, Social Security Complex. (Photo: Argun Dundar/AKTC)

These experiments aim at using local materials in prototype buildings in order to introduce a more suitable response to local environmental conditions and have yielded novel architectural expressions as well.

The climatically and culturally sensitive concerns of all these people found its most mature architectural expression in the Kaedi Hospital by Fabrizio Carola.[15] Carola not only provides for cultural specificity and the technological demands of modern health care, but also fully explores the expressive, structural, and economic potential of a single structural material—load-bearing brick.

These and other approaches that have grown out of Hassan Fathy's teaching can all be considered as modern, even though their appearance may seem to place them in a different stream of thought. Ironically, they conform to modernist discourse, since they are solely the expression of the functions they accommodate. Structure is expressed as boldly and directly as possible.

In Turkey, Sedad Hakki Eldem (1908-87) worked in a tradition similar to Fathy's, but in a completely different vein. He belonged to the second generation of Turkish architects trained in the modernist discourse and had worked with such leading architects of the modern movement as August Perret and Le Corbusier. He was drawn to the work of Frank Lloyd Wright, Charles F. A. Voysey, Sir Edwin Lutyens, and Herbert Baker.

Eldem continuously studied and documented the Anatolian architectural heritage, convinced that traditional domestic architecture contained the seeds from which an appropriate and contemporary new Turkish architecture could emerge. His work, particularly his large residences and embassies, reflected but never copied Anatolian architecture, but reinterpreted it. He disagreed with Fathy's approach, which he considered reductionist building, not architecture. Eldem believed that advanced design skills were needed to create proper architecture, but shared Fathy's belief in the imperative relation of architecture to culture.

Eldem's architecture derived plans and structural and proportional systems from traditional architecture; he believed that all other components

Suha Özkan

should reflect contemporary concerns and values as fully as possible in order to accommodate the functions and amenities of modern life. Eldem's architecture showed great integrity, and he refused simply to replicate or imitate the built heritage. His work showed such a high level of sophistication that only he could achieve such accomplished architectural design; very few others could even attempt to aspire to a similar level of excellence, and the attempt was made even more difficult by Eldem's charismatic presence and professional stature. Following his death in 1987, a number of architects tried to emulate him and create a new style of building in Turkey, but sadly, most of these efforts have failed. The results are mostly inferior and, since developers have adopted them, these poor imitations now mar the landscape, particularly along the shores of the Bosporus.

Comparable to Eldem's contribution in Turkey are those of Nader Ardalan and Kamran Diba in Iran. Like Eldem, Ardalan was also committed to research. Ardalan's work was not, however, limited exclusively to the physical aspects of historical form, but encompassed the philosophy and mysticism of Sufi traditions in Iranian architecture. In A Sense of Unity, Ardalan and Laleh Bakhtiar tried to convey some idea of the hidden order that had determined Iranian architectural morphology.[16]

The work of Ardalan's architectural firm, called Mandala, reflected these explorations. In the late 1960s and early 1970s, they sought to rediscover and reestablish "order" to bring about new spatial existence. The influence of Louis I. Kahn's School of Management Studies (1972) on Ardalan's Imam Sadegh University in Tehran is evident.[17] Ardalan based his design on a traditional open space (a courtyard garden) and employed traditional Persian mandala cosmograms to determine the spatial configuration.

Ardalan and Kamran Diba worked together on the Tehran Museum of Contemporary Art (1976), where the influence of Louis Kahn can be observed even more vividly. The boldness of expression, the honesty of exposed finishes, and the domination of the plan by geometry were more international than local or Persian. In Shushtar New Town (1977), Kamran Diba committed himself to exploring the existing socio-architectural realm of Old Shushtar, and eventually produced perhaps one of the world's finest housing schemes. Diba not only studied the physical patterns of building in Old Shushtar, but also explored the social and economic characteristics, as well as issues of ecology and culture.

Mohammad Makiya (b. 1914) of Iraq is among the pioneers who showed the relevance of modernism to tradition and culture. His Rafidain Bank

Figure 3. Jaipurhat, Bangladesh. Muzharul Islam, Jaipurhat C-Type Housing. (Photo: Architect/AKTC)

Suha Özkan

90

buildings in Kufa and Karbala (1968), and the Diwan al-Awkaf Library (1967) in Baghdad[18] are undeniably modern, even though referring to traditional form. Later in his career, these references become so direct that they are of relevance to Post-Modern architectural discourse.

The boldness of the solid brick walls and the stark openings in the early works of Makiya have an affinity with the work of Louis Kahn, whose influence was considerable in parts of the Islamic world, but especially the subcontinent, where the work of Balkrishna Doshi, Achyut Kavinde, and Muzharul Islam all reveal Kahn's influence.

Muzharul Islam of Bangladesh has had a distinguished career; he is an international figure, perhaps not so well know as Fathy, but certainly more so than Eldem. He is a talented architect himself, but his efforts to secure commissions for leading architects to work in Bangladesh are even more extraordinary: Alexis Doxiades, Paul Rudolph, Stanley Tigerman, and Louis I. Kahn were all given projects as a result of his efforts.

In his own architecture, Muzharul Islam's dormitories, housing complexes, and public buildings are sublime expressions of structure, material, and function, but at the same time also statements about the harsh social and economic conditions of life in Bangladesh.[19] His work has aimed at novel but simple expressions in modest but abundant materials such as brick and tile. The simplicity of form and attention to climatic comfort are firmly based in the local culture. Islam's works have set new standards for subsequent generations of architects.

Islam's commitment to the intellectual enrichment of younger architects has been extraordinary. The working group which he founded, Chetena (which means consciousness or awareness), was one of the few intellectual fora in the Islamic world where issues could be openly debated on an interdisciplinary platform. Over time, Chetena has gained a greater international reputation than any other architectural institution in Bangladesh. Its members are concerned with people; writers, poets, and artists have also gathered around Muzharul Islam to debate and develop their ideas.

Other searches for a contemporary expression were cultivated in the subcontinent. Charles Correa in Bombay, Balkrishna Doshi in Ahmedabad, Raj Rewal in Delhi, and Kamil Khan Mumtaz and Nayyar Ali Dada in Lahore devoted attention to the values inherent in their cultures. Correa gave high priority to Sullivan's maxim that "form follows function," but rephrased it to read, "form follows climate." His idea of "open to sky spaces" contested box-like, contained architecture and sought new expressions of culture- and climate-based configurations. Correa's determinants of climate and cultural values not only nourished his novel architecture but also placed him among the top architects worldwide. The concentration of ideas in his book, The New Landscape,[20] became one of the most important influences in contemporary architecture and planning during the 1980s. Instead of professing architectural ideals, Correa pointed out the fallacies of badly interpreted modernism. He explored the dynamics of rapid urbanization and proposed new attitudes for understanding third-world realities so far addressed using Western recipes that had no basis in deep-rooted cultural values. Raj Rewal, also from India, has a more exclusively architectural approach to regional identity.[21] He uses the Mughal heritage of northern India as his primary source of inspiration; spatial configurations are built around courtyards and refer to such seminal historical sources as the seventeenth-century palaces at Fatehpur Sikri. His reinterpreted use of materials such as beige and red sandstone as untreated cladding brings a fine touch to his buildings and firmly relates them to their sites.

Nayyar Ali Dada, in his seminal building in Lahore, the Alhamra Arts Center (1973), used exposed brick to clad a reinforced concrete structure. The windowless architecture with high walls is reminiscent of the Lahore Fort and the tomb of Shah Rukn-i Alam, and Dada thus relates the new arts complex directly to Lahore's historical heritage. His later works also place strong emphasis on integrating building with landscape.

Kamil Khan Mumtaz has experimented with small-scale projects to demonstrate the potential of climate-sensitive architecture. In his series of private houses in Pakistan, he exploits the principles of tropical architecture, where buildings contribute to reducing the use of energy with natural means of cooling. He also experiments with novel contextual expressions for one of the culturally richest regions of Pakistan.

Although not designed by a subcontinental, one of the best conceived, designed, and built examples of architecture in the Islamic world is the Aga Khan University Hospital and Nursing College in Karachi designed by Thomas Payette. The campus reflects all of the intellectual, aesthetic, and architectural demands of post-1970s regionalism. While designing for a highly sophisticated and very technical brief,

Suha Özkan

91

the architect relates his work to the context without engaging in any of the superfluous trends that marked most buildings during the same period.

Climate and vernacular modes of building as sources of inspiration are perhaps most prominently displayed in Southeast Asian architecture. The Tanjong Jara[22] hotel complex in Kuala Terranganu, Indonesia was one of the pioneering efforts in this development that has since become an identifiable movement throughout the region. The firm of Atelier Enam, notably in the work of partners Adhi Moersid and Rubi Sularto, has continuously developed this attitude in Indonesia and consistently opposed the parallel trend of massive, high-rise blocks that continues to scar the country.

The most novel expression in Southeast Asia has come from Kenneth Yeang of Kuala Lumpur, who has dedicated his career to developing climate-responsive architecture and urban design.[23] After many experiments with high-rise buildings using permeable skins that permit natural ventilation and passive cooling, his Menara Mesiniaga tower[24] perfectly embodies his radical commitment to tropical architecture within a high-tech vocabulary.

The development of architecture totally conversant with the values of Islam has flourished in the Arabian Peninsula, thanks to clients who have engaged the finest talents. The region has been fertile ground for the development of some of the finest expressions of contemporary architecture, both avant-garde and conservative. Abdel Wahed el-Wakil, a pupil of Hassan Fathy, has pursued the contextual-classicist discourse propagated by Maurice Culot, Quinlan Terry, and Rob Krier, and defended by Krier's younger brother, Leon. The Kriers believe that innovation in the production of new forms in architecture is unnecessary; all the possible forms to achieve good architectural solutions have already been produced and are available for architects to build within any context. El-Wakil demonstrates this same approach in the series of mosques he has designed in Mecca and Medina.

El-Wakil believes that the architecture of the Hijaz has throughout history been characterized by the importation of the very best examples of architecture brought by its successive rulers, especially the Mamluks and Ottomans. In his contemporary works, El-Wakil thus strives to reinterpret compo-

Figure 4. Jakarta, Indonesia. Triatno Yudo Harjoko, Faculty of Engineering, University of Indonesia. (Photo: Suha Özkan/AKTC)

Suha Özkan

nents of seminal historical buildings and strongly opposes the widespread attempts to Islamicize buildings by the superficial application of slapped-on pastiche. Instead, he employs the authentic technologies and building processes that are intrinsic in the historical buildings to which he looks for inspiration. His mosques on the corniche of Jedda are noted for their sensitive design and are among the outstanding examples of classicist buildings of recent years.[25]

A widespread attitude towards design in the Arabian Peninsula during the building boom of the 1970s was the Islamicization of buildings by the use of reinforced cast-concrete arches and domes of dubious origin and validity. However, more authentic and serious efforts have also taken place, among them the architecture of Basem Shihabi, Henning Larsen, Gordon Bunshaft, and Kamal Kafrawi. First, however, the Riyadh Development Authority and its long-time director Mohammad al-Sheikh must be commended for encouraging architects to offer the best of their talents and abilities; equally important has been their commitment to architecture in harmony with climate and landscape. The landscaping of the new Diplomatic Quarter in Riyadh is perhaps one of most important landscaping projects of our century. Richard Bödeker and his colleagues undertook meticulous sieving of the desert sand and then incubated the fine dust in order to regenerate some of the now-extinct plant species which had resisted the violent climatic changes of the desert over hundreds of thousands of years. The seeds and spores obtained in this fashion were then germinated in incubators and have now been nurtured and planted again in extensive, non-irrigated areas of landscaping. The use of naturally abundant materials such as rocks and boulders to contain the desert sand and dust, along with the newly revived plant species, is a novel and revolutionary approach to dealing with the harsh climatic conditions that characterize almost the entire Arab world.

Within a similar scope and understanding, Basem Shihabi and his colleagues in the firm of Omrania created the Tuwaiq Palace (formerly called the Diplomatic Club), which merges a new approach to landscape with a radical new architectural solution. The continuous wall-like building, clad in local yellow limestone, defines a free-form courtyard which is conceived as a lush, green, oasis-like garden to contrast with the harsh and dry landscape outside. The design language and exaggeration of curvilinear forms are peculiar, but the boldness of this grand idea makes it an architectural solution that is one of the most important interventions of recent decades.

In a similar vein, but with a different understanding and spatial configuration, Gordon Bunshaft of Skidmore, Owings and Merrill encapsulated an architectural formation much like Shihabi did a natural one in his National Commercial Bank[26] in Jedda. There the oasis is represented by three courtyards in the air inside a high-rise building. Bunshaft's simple spatial configuration, which carves courtyards into a triangular-plan building, unfolds and is articulated into various functional and climatic solutions. This building was a new conception of high-rise buildings in harsh climatic conditions.

Architects who gave priority to traditional architectural forms and references have matured in many regions. Ali Shuaibi in Saudi Arabia and Rasem Badran in Jordan have worked towards the regeneration of urban fabric with traditional volumes but with contemporary technology. In Riyadh, Shuaibi's al-Kindi Plaza and Badran's Old City Center Development are particularly important, as they were realized at a time when motorways and cars already dominated urban spaces and community life. Both architects refer in their works to the Najdi architectural heritage and use the traditional forms and colors of the region.

The aspect that most unifies all these architects is that they have neither denied nor challenged modernism, but have accepted it as the lingua franca of contemporary architecture. They are united in the belief that it is the responsibility of individual architects to relate modernism to every particular locale and region. Their achievement is comparable to what Alvar Aalto achieved in Finland and Luis Barragan in Mexico. Their architecture employs modernism, but at the same time is profoundly embedded in the cultural milieus where their buildings are located. The degree of abstraction is probably the measure that relates these architects on a scale that has modernism at one end and traditionalism at the other.[27]

Since the rejection of the Parisian Neoclassicism championed by J. N. L. Durand,[28] the theory and discourse of modernism have remained unchallenged. Modernism's well-established tenets of architecture encompass education and the organization of the architectural profession, as well as both theory and criticism. The challenges[29] to modernism that arose during the 1970s first contested its relevance and then attributed to it all the ills of the con-

Suha Özkan

93

temporary built environment. The architectural equivalents of these challenges were Post-Modernism and classicism, and they have affected recent architectural media and building considerably.

Post-Modernism benefited from the failures of and boredom with Internationalism, but was nonetheless short-lived. In order to comply with its search for meaning and identity through links with the past, Post-Modernism licensed any architectural contribution including copying the past, regardless of intrinsic architectural value. When this criticism was finally raised, differentiation between worthless pastiche and respectable building was made by terming the former "Po-Mo" and the latter Post-Modern. The movement, which protested the tedium and homogenization it assigned to modernism, itself very quickly became boring, as the criteria for quality disappeared.

Among Post-Modern proponents, one of the more significant was Rifat Chadirji of Iraq. Chadirji gave priority to the existence of buildings in their primarily urban contexts. He therefore challenged a basic axiom of modernism—the expression of function. Instead, he professed that plan (function) and elevation (the expression of plan) could be considered separately, since the most important aspect was the appropriateness of any building to its context. This approach, consciously or subconsciously, was perceived as a call to Islamicize buildings. The widespread use of clip-on Islamicizing features found theoretical justification, as well as a measure of validity, under the auspices of Post-Modernism. Chadirji's profound theory was misconstrued, abused, and made the pretext for superficial contextualization. The damage is architectural, and has been very great.

On more theoretical grounds, Post-Modernism accepted the validity of opposites[30] and basic agreement with chaos theory. The premise that architecture (or design) should discover, express, or determine "order" was denied. Neither in the Muslim world nor in the world at large did Post-Modernism yield any masterpieces. Perhaps its worst effect was to give the unenlightened nouveaux riches a pretext to justify their unsophisticated tastes.

Classicism is definitely a nobler act. It is pure; it seeks authenticity; it respects materials and technology. In other words, it has modernist concepts at its base. However, it professes that forms should be derived from the past, since they have endured the proof of time; however, present-day technology,

materials, labor, and needs have changed substantially and confront classicism with new challenges. Labor, knowledge, and skills are all different today, and to continue to produce architecture as if nothing has happened since the development and reign of classicism is only an elusive dream, albeit a very pleasant and enticing one.

In the traditionalist environments of Islamic societies, classicism has found echoes in architectural rhetoric, but in most cases, it is basically Post-Modernism that has been more at the essence than classicism. Only El-Wakil has attempted genuine classicism, and only he has found support on both the international and regional levels.[31]

The dilemma of classicism is that in Western classicist discourse and practice (in the work of Quinlan Terry and Rob and Leon Krier), what is basically referred to as the late Renaissance period, when classical architecture reached full maturity. This period of development has thus been asserted as the valid point of departure for all contemporary emulation. Direct references are usually made to the works of Andrea Palladio and his Four Books. Palladio is the genius (or, alternatively, the schoolmaster[32]), who simplified the rich and complex currents of Renaissance architecture by proposing more conveniently applicable orders to the various norms. Palladio made High Renaissance classicism internationally valid and accessible. Was Palladio a modernist at heart?

Modernism spread through the world like a new colonizing force. The difference between the political colonialism of the eighteenth and nineteenth centuries and the modernism of the twentieth is that modernism exists only in the mind. It is the free choice of new values. Even though it may seem to contradict the intrinsic values of tradition, that is not true. Instead, it respects time and has a simple motto: every generation or civilization must create its own expression. That which is in the past belongs to history and is good and valid as a contemporary expression of the past; the past should not, however, dictate the future.

Notes

1. C. Jencks, *What is Post Modernism?* (1986; London: Academy Editions, 1996), p. 21.

2. C. Jenks, *The Architecture of the Jumping Universe* (London: Academy Editions, 1995), p. 7.

Suha Özkan

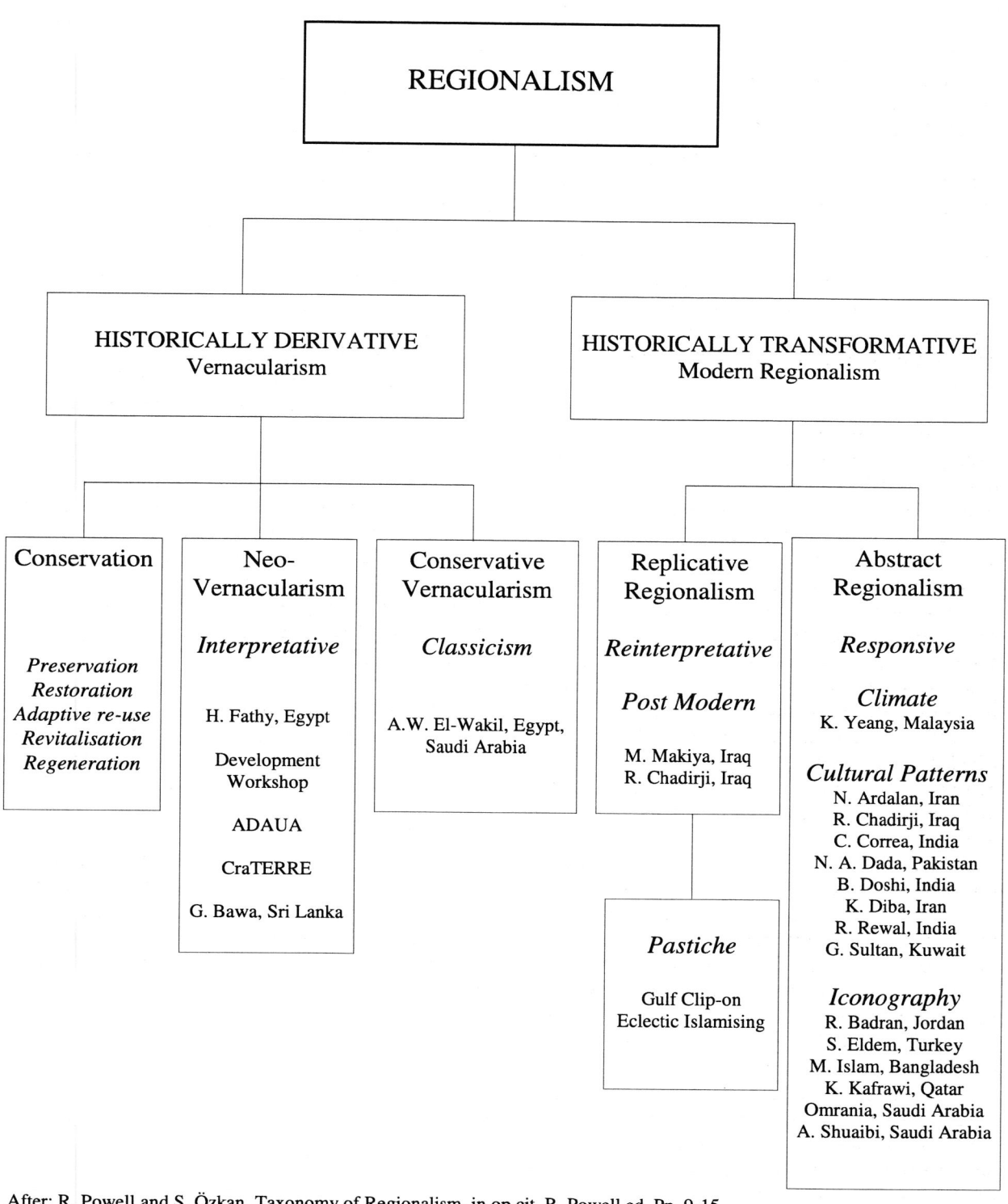

REGIONALISM

HISTORICALLY DERIVATIVE
Vernacularism

HISTORICALLY TRANSFORMATIVE
Modern Regionalism

Conservation

Preservation
Restoration
Adaptive re-use
Revitalisation
Regeneration

Neo-Vernacularism

Interpretative

H. Fathy, Egypt

Development
Workshop

ADAUA

CraTERRE

G. Bawa, Sri Lanka

Conservative Vernacularism

Classicism

A.W. El-Wakil, Egypt,
Saudi Arabia

Replicative Regionalism

Reinterpretative

Post Modern

M. Makiya, Iraq
R. Chadirji, Iraq

Pastiche

Gulf Clip-on
Eclectic Islamising

Abstract Regionalism

Responsive

Climate
K. Yeang, Malaysia

Cultural Patterns
N. Ardalan, Iran
R. Chadirji, Iraq
C. Correa, India
N. A. Dada, Pakistan
B. Doshi, India
K. Diba, Iran
R. Rewal, India
G. Sultan, Kuwait

Iconography
R. Badran, Jordan
S. Eldem, Turkey
M. Islam, Bangladesh
K. Kafrawi, Qatar
Omrania, Saudi Arabia
A. Shuaibi, Saudi Arabia

After: R. Powell and S. Özkan, Taxonomy of Regionalism, in op.cit. R. Powell ed. Pp. 9-15

Suha Özkan

3. Here the establishment of the Aga Khan Award for Architecture in 1977 as an organization searching for excellence and meaning in the contemporary built environment without ignoring the realities of Modernism must be cited.

4. Suha Özkan, "Regionalism within Modernism," in *Regionalism in Architecture*, ed. R. Powell (Singapore: Aga Khan Award for Architecture and Concept Media, 1985), p. 8-16.

5. R. Powell and S. Özkan, "Taxonomy of Regionalism," in R. Powell, ed., *Ken Yeang, Rethinking the Environmental Filter* (Singapore: Landmark Books, 1989), p. 9-15. The subject was subsequently developed in a dissertation by Powell.

6. See J. Steele, The *Hassan Fathy Collection* (Geneva: Aga Khan Trust for Culture, 1989), p. 11-12.

7. Hassan Fathy, *Lectures in Middle East Technical University* (Ankara, 1973).

8. We may regard his *Architecture for the Poor* (Chicago: University of Chicago Press, 1973) as his *magnum opus*; in it he writes up his twenty years of experiments and ideas to influence generations to come.

9. See Renata Holod and D. Rastorfer, *Architecture and Community* (New York: Aperture, 1983), p. 77-87.

10. The Development Workshop was founded in 1973 by John Norton, Alan Cain, and Farrokh Afshar. The group worked in Iran, Sub-Saharan Africa, Vietnam, and Angola.

11. CraTERRE is the center for research in earth construction at the School of Architecture in Grenoble, France. It aims to make construction in earth both feasible and more durable. Patrice Doat and Hugo Houben are among its most active members. Jean Dethier of Center Georges Pompidou, Paris, is a strong supporter of this group. They have built a number of experimental projects abroad.

12. ADAUA was an association established by Jak Vauthrin in Geneva; the name is an acronym for architecture and urbanism for Africa. It had a decentralized structure with centers in Mali, Mauritania, Senegal, and Burkina Faso.

13. See Holod and Rastorfer, *Architecture and Community*, p. 63-75.

14. See J. Steele, ed., *Architecture for a Changing World* (London: Academy Editions, 1992), p. 156-63.

15. C. Davidson and I. Serageldin, eds., *Architecture beyond Architecture* (London: Academy Editions, 1995, p. 101-11.

16. Nader Ardalan and Laileh Bakhtiar, *The Sense of Unity: Sufi Tradition in Persian Architecture* (Chicago: University of Chicago Press, 1973).

17. Louis I. Kahn was acknowledged, "for having kindly reviewed the manuscript and confirmed the conceptual approach there," ibid., p. xvii.

18. Ibid., p. 92f.

19. It is sad that no one has written a definitive book on Muzharul Islam's architecture and thinking. He is the person who dominated the architectural scene in East Pakistan/Bangladesh and left his mark in the form of hundreds of disciples. The attempt of Kazi Ashraf to display his work internationally is commendable.

20. Charles Correa, *New Landscape* (Singapore: Concept Media, 1985).

21. For details, see Brian Brace Taylor, *Raj Rewal* (London: Concept Media, 1990).

22. Tanjong Jara Beach Hotel and Rantau Aband, in S. Cantacuzino, ed., *Architecture in Continuity* (New York: Aperture, 1985), p. 138-45.

23. Ken Yeang, *Tropical Veranda City* (Singapore: Concept Media, 1990); idem, *Designing with Nature: The Ecological Basis for Architectural Design* (New York: McGraw Hill, 1995).

24. "Menara Mesiniaga, Kuala Lumpur," in Davidson and Serageldin, *Architecture beyond Architecture*, p. 94-101.

25. See "Corniche Mosque," in Steele, ed., *Hassan Fathy Collection*, p. 110-15.

26. C. H. Krinski, *Gordon Bunshaft of Skidmore Owings and Merrill* (Cambridge, Mass.: MIT Press, 1988).

27. A survey by the author covering the Arabic Peninsula, Iran, and Turkey has recently been published in D. Cruickshank, ed., *Sir Banister Fletcher's "A History of Architecture"* (London: Architectural Press, 1996),

Suha Özkan

p. 1445-47.

28. J. N. L. Durand, *Précis des Leçons d'architecture* (Paris: Ecole Polytechnic, 1802).

29. Peter Blake, *Form Follows Fiasco: Why Modern Architecture Did Not Work* (Boston: Little Brown and Co. 1977).

30. Robert Venturi, *Complexity and Contradiction in Architecture* (New York: Museum of Modern Art, 1966), is the seminal work that anticipated Post-Modernism and laid the theoretical foundation for the movement.

31. The Prince of Wales in his provocatively conservative book on architecture, *A Vision of Britain* (London: Doubleday, 1989), referred to El-Wakil and Hassan Fathy to support his view of classicism.

32. R. Bloomfield, *Seven Architects* (1939; New York: Books for the Libraries Press, 1966), p. 25: "After the giants came the schoolmaster to put everything in order."

• • • • • • • • • • • • •

This article was reviewed by Prof. Charles Jencks. Due to the fact that the review comments far exceeded the word limit set by the editors, the comments could not be published. In addition, the author opted not to respond to the comments.

Suha Özkan

The Search for Appropriate Architecture

Ali Shuaibi

Contemporary architecture tends universally to be influenced by trends in the West (Europe and North America) and to ignore the rest of the world. Initially modern architecture brought strength, good plumbing, electric lighting, and conveniences to buildings in the third world, just as industrialization brought convenient transport and infrastructure and the promise of abundance to all. But the situation quickly turned into extreme dependence on electrical cooling, heating and lighting, higher cost and running expenses, reduced local employment, and increased deficits in housing and public buildings; it also worsened the quality of life in the city and undermined the safety and convenience of its inhabitants.

The advantages of contemporary architecture and city planning stemmed, not so much from Western models of architecture and urban planning, as on advances in Western technology. Contemporary universal forms were therefore rejected by governments of newly independent states in the third world as being inappropriate for their identity. To find a substitute inevitably architects in general and those working in Muslim countries in particular looked back to a glorious past.

For architects in the Muslim world, the situation was particularly complex. Art historians had identified the styles of monumental architecture in the great centers of Muslim civilization in Spain, Egypt, Turkey and Asia, and many took them to be the right models for architecture. Later, under the influence of nationalism in the newly independent states, the local classical and vernacular styles and models of pre-colonial or pre-industrial periods were considered to be useful sources for theoreticians and designers. These were useful in some cities like Cairo or Baghdad, but they did not help in many other Arab cities like Mecca, Jedda or San'a' that had a different climate or context. In addition, the set of local characteristics that was thought of as rules for Muslim architecture were taken from buildings in the Middle East and were inappropriate in equatorial Muslim countries like Indonesia. Finally, their forms and rules were often difficult to re-create where land-subdivision practices had become dominated by Western grid systems for streets and planning regulations that required building setbacks.

It is in this context that contemporary architects have been practicing, and unlike theoreticians and art historians, in their search for appropriate architecture they have to come up with a design that will meet all the restrictions and complex relationships of their clients, comply with government and city regulations, and work within labor conditions, contractual procedures, site conditions, availability of building materials, and many other factors, including their fellow engineers and their own knowledge and experience, or the lack of it. Some of these problems will be illustrated using projects designed by Beeah, the firm partnered by Abdul Rahman Hussaini, and myself during the past twenty years.

The projects mainly concentrated on adapting contemporary Western architecture to local conditions. The Muslim World League Headquarters (Rabita) is an example (Figure 1). This meant designing buildings with small openings to reduce exposure to the sun and creating relatively flexible interiors. The early excitement with the results was quickly dulled as we discovered what happened when we used an exposed compact mass appropriate for cold countries, instead of traditional architecture, with its contiguous mass, penetrated only by small courts and the extensive use of transitional spaces in the form of shaded arcades, which was more suited

Figure 1. Most modern buildings are cold-country models, with limited facade treatments to suit local climates. (Photo credit: Beeah)

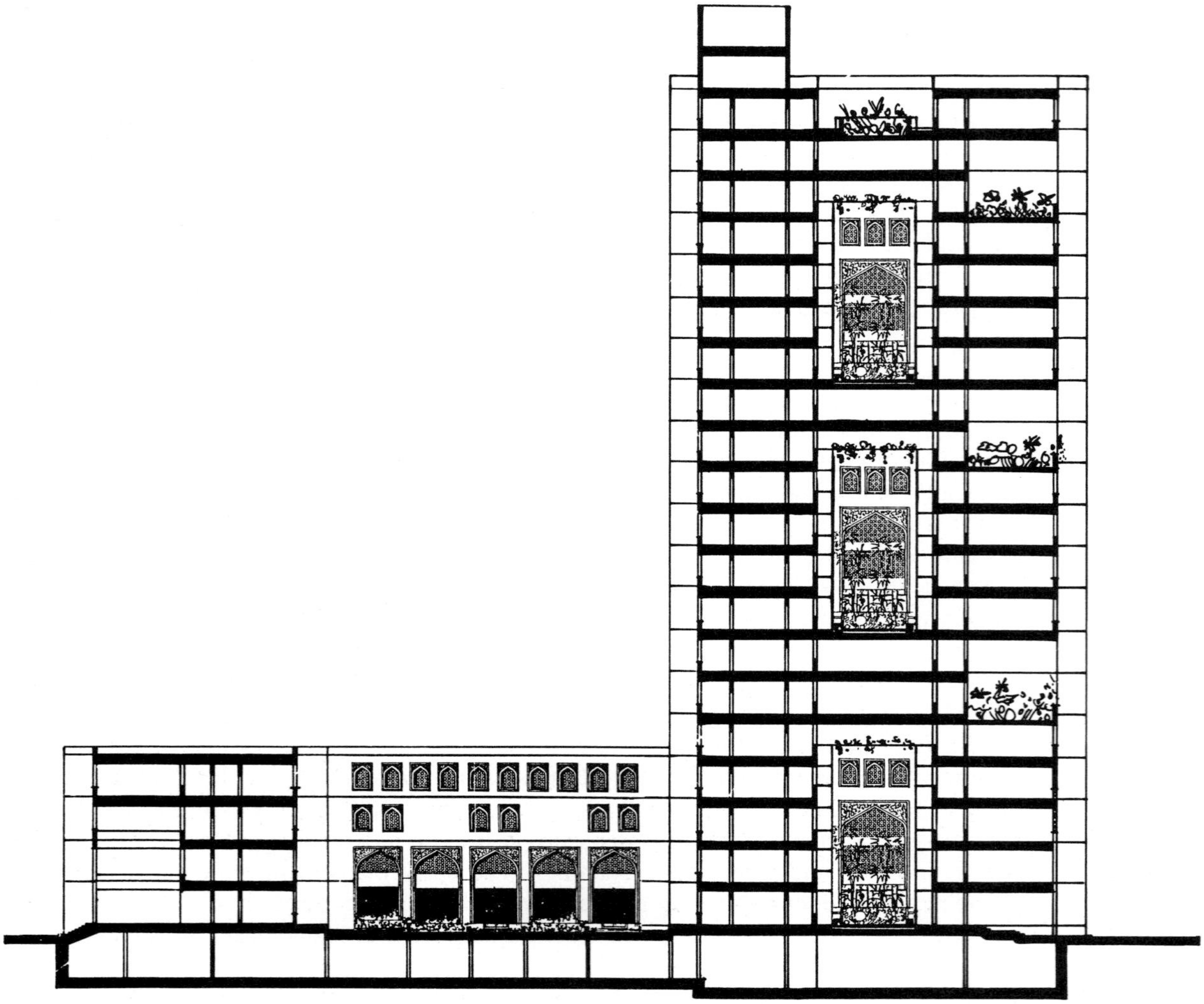

Figure 2. Modern urban structures demand new building types that had no equivalent in traditional architecture. Appropriate new forms can still be derived from traditional models. (Drawing by Beeah)

Ali Shuaibi

for our hot arid climate. The use of indigenous materials, of stone or mud, blended and aged nicely in its local environment in contrast to the harsh glaring white Greek marble we used in the Rabita project.

While on a site visit to San'a' preparatory to designing the Saudi embassy in Yemen, we observed that the comfortable weather of San'a' and the severe arid climate of the desert in Riyadh had resulted in totally different forms in the traditional architecture, even though the regions were contiguous. The traditional buildings in San'a' also needed no air-conditioning, but the rooms of the new centrally air-conditioned hotel there were intolerable whenever the power failed, which was often. These observations taught us a most important lesson about the dominating influence of climate on the built form. As a result, for the design of the embassy we adapted the traditional tower form of San'a' with its south-north orientation in addition to the use of stone in construction and local glass ornamentation.

Resorting to traditional models provides useful solutions to many design problems when the new context is similar to the traditional conditions that created them. But when confronted with new situations, such as a high-rise tower, different ideas are needed. In the competition for the SAPICO building, a twenty-story tower in Islamabad, Pakistan, the idea was to create human scale and exciting interior spaces to avoid the monotonous interiors of typical high-rise buildings (Figure 2) by breaking the tower into five buildings, each having its own atrium or court and capable of functioning with natural light-ing and ventilation. The geometry and art were derived from Mughal architecture to provide a link to its context and location.

Saleh al-Hathloul has directed attention to the dynamic nature of Muslim architecture by showing how the Shari'a permitted the built form to change from open courthouse to covered *qa'a* to full facade wood-window (*mushrabiyya*) high-rise buildings without the need for waivers to change regulations or the permitted or favored building form. In that spirit, the limited competition entry for the Municipality of al-Madina al-Munawwara (Amana) was developed (Figure 3). The design for Amana, which was similar to Rabita in function and scale, was an attempt to achieve economy through the use of the locally abundant lava porous stone as filler for the exposed finish walls and the use of local fired brick for domes and vaults and to cover major spaces. Buildings were arranged in a contiguous form penetrated by transitional open courts that provided attractive public spaces and modified the microclimate. Shallow office spaces permitted the use of daylight and natural ventilation whenever possible. It also provided shaded arcades for the public passing along the edge of the project.

A competition for the Ministry of Education (Wazara) in Riyadh provided an opportunity to carry the same principles that led to the design of Amana a step further (Figure 4). The building blended into the landscape of desert plants, fruit trees, and flowers designed in the tradition of Muslim gardens; these grounds also acted like a lung, filtering out the

Figure 3. Traditional rules of space organization and construction techniques are still valid for most modern projects. (Photo credit: Beeah)

Ali Shuaibi

Figure 4. Architects, once relieved of imitating traditional or alien forms, adopting traditional wisdom with appropriate technology, can produce new, locally appropriate architecture that responds to the economic and ecological challenges of today. (Photo credit: Beeah)

pollution generated by the traffic in and around the project. The use of recycled water and collected rainwater in this garden reduced the pressure on the limited water supply. The orientation of windows, shallow spaces, thermal solar collectors, evaporative cooling, the integration of mechanical and natural ventilation, artificial light and daylight in the building control system reduced both peak and total power requirements to a fraction of that in similar projects elsewhere.

The design intentionally avoided any apparent reference to traditional architecture. But Jamel Akbar, a member of the Aga Khan Award's master jury, commented, "it is the most local and traditional building in spirit."

The architecture of cities, their centers, and their neighborhoods is far more influential in urban life than single buildings. Sahat al-Kindi (the central

area of the Diplomatic Quarter in Riyadh) was an attempt to reconcile the conflict between the high quality of the pedestrian environment in traditional town centers and the convenience of using modern vehicular service, in addition to providing appropriate context for buildings to work together rather than compete with each other (Figure 5). The design reinterpreted the structure of traditional cities, where the mosque, the school, the governor's palace, and the *maydan* formed the center of the city, to which all the main roads that came from the city gates led.

In the old city there were no blind facades or long fences. There were only shops and entrances to specialized markets or houses. The project was therefore also designed as a contiguous mass so that the blind facades of office buildings were covered with shops and houses above them, leaving only enough space for entrances. Buildings looked into

Ali Shuaibi

their private courts or atria instead of to the outside, as with most contemporary buildings, which thereby invade the privacy of neighbors. Vehicular traffic was limited to the boundaries; it allowed vehicles to penetrate from the sides as far as was needed to provide services or to park, but they are never allowed to interfere with pedestrian movement in the walkways or plazas. Service vehicles pass under the *suqs* where all utility lines were located.

Sahat al-Kindi has become a center of attraction for the city dwellers. Families congregate, even picnic, there, while their children safely run around, roller-skate, or bicycle. The buildings are humble; the whole environment is congenial to human activity. It has attracted local and international attention.

The greatness of Muslims architecture stems from the freedom it had to shape the environment and respond to a variety of climates and building materials under different economic conditions. Through that it created many models and developed techniques that are still relevant today. But its real greatness lay in the spirit and courage it displayed in assimilating suitable ideas from other cultures. Today architects everywhere can still do the same: rejecting traditional architecture or copying it blindly is the extremes that prevent architects from responding to the challenge of population growth and dwindling resources. Today architects have analytical and modeling tools that traditional architects did not have and that can help re-create and evaluate traditional models or parts that do not exist any longer and are inaccessible for evaluation, as well as to explore and assess new ones. They also can compensate at least partially for limited experience.

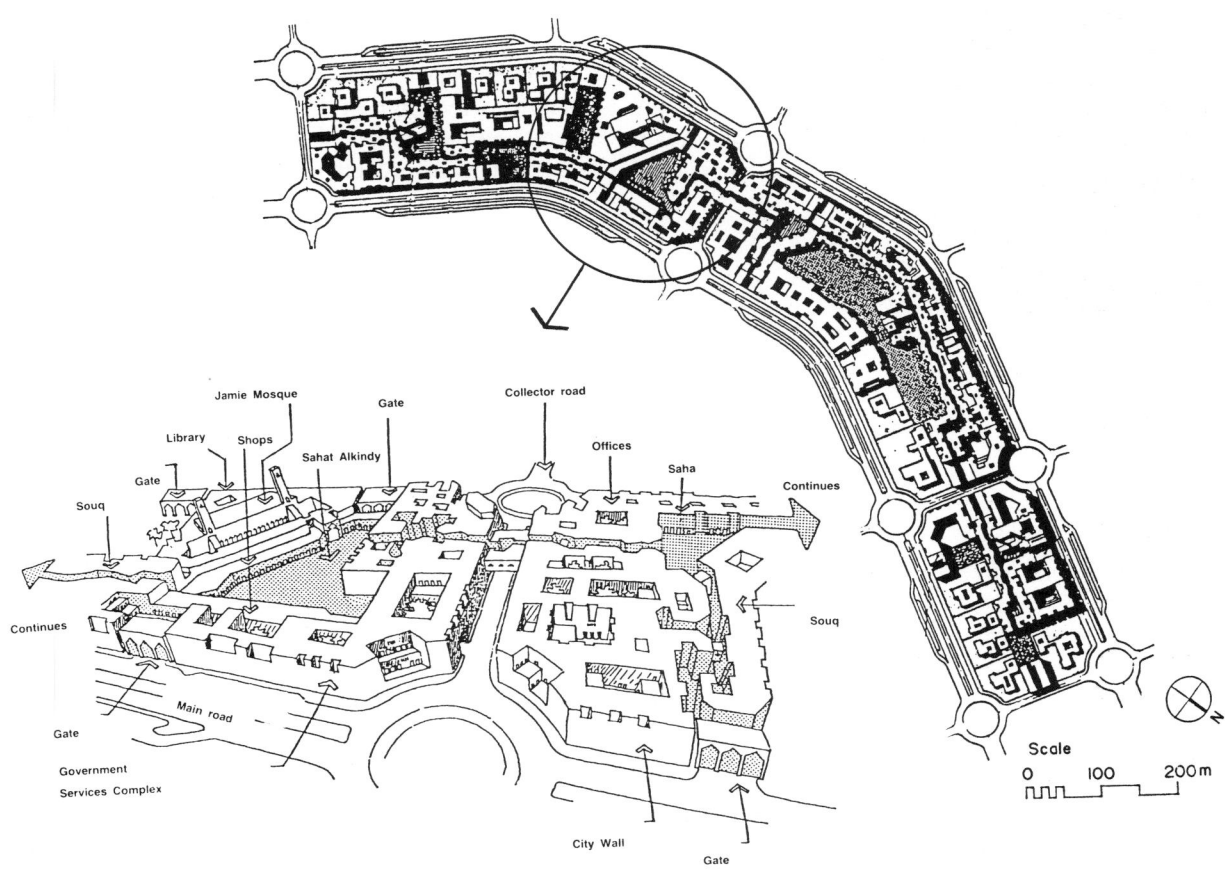

Figure 5. Most arguments that apply to design of buildings are valid for city form, its centers and neighborhoods. (Drawing by Beeah)

Ali Shuaibi

Comments
Khalil K. Pirani

I agree with Ali Shuaibi that blind imitation and acceptance of science, technology, and Western models have led to a loss in quality of communal life in some Muslim societies. At the same time, in this age of globalization, science and technology are inevitably becoming integral parts of every society. Since Islam has no conflict with science, will it be appropriate to say that contemporary Muslim societies have to find the delicate balance between maintaining the continuity with their respective history, culture, and tradition while taking advantage of recent scientific developments and utilizing them to improve, wherever possible, the quality of life?

If the answer is affirmative, how do you suggest practicing architects in Muslim societies should try to achieve this delicate balance between science, technology, and culture?

Response
Today architects are fortunate in having the advantage of developments in computers and science. In the past architects had either to rely on traditional (tested and evaluated) models or on highly subjective speculations on the expected behavior of new forms or approaches in architecture. Today computers provide the architects with superior analytical and modeling tools. These tools are becoming more and more sophisticated and easier to use. Architects can now test (animate) the visual experience and the impact of every project in its context. They can also evaluate daylight behavior, thermal interaction and energy consumption and even simulate natural ventilation in and around their buildings. In addition, they can model ideas and concepts of sophisticated and complex geometries that were almost impossible to do a few years ago when plans, sections, and elevations were the only tools they had. The conflict between the traditional and the modern (that is, maintaining traditions versus innovation) is no longer valid as architects do not have to copy superficially the traditional or import blindly the modern in any local environment. They can innovate or assimilate and rigorously test different ideas to achieve the highest level of harmony with nature and appropriateness to their culture and local conditions in an affordable manner.

Ali Shuaibi

On the Poetics of Place:
The Communicability of an Architectural Image

Rasem Badran

Looking at well-known historical cities in the Islamic world such as Marrakesh, Cairo, Jerusalem, Baghdad, Jedda, Riyadh, Dubai, and San'a', one can sense the diversity of their environments despite their commonalties derived from a shared historical background. This leads us to ask the inevitable question: How can one deal morphologically with architectural images in these environments despite this diversity in expression?

If we claim that architecture is the product of the interaction of culture, society, economy, and environment and that these aspects are vital in giving architecture the fundamental and integral characteristics and continuous existence that distinguish one place from another, then we might understand the sensitive and important role of the architect. I believe that the architect's role is not to impose his personal style, which would detract from the place's individual character, but rather to encourage an inquiry that investigates and excavates deeply into the secrets of the place and uncovers its tools and media of expression. This in turn will help architecture to occupy its appropriate place in global civilization.

The aim of this approach is to emphasize the relationship between man and place in the context of changing times; creativity becomes the tool that connects the heritage and contemporary events and builds bridges to the future. This allows us to avoid the confusion that faced architecture after the eighteenth century, when it ceased to be a craft and became an industrial product, thus ending the cooperation between creativity, perception, and implementation. We can assume that there are a number of characteristic elements in any man-made environment that generate morphological patterns resulting from the interplay between environment and behavioral,

social, cultural, and technological characteristics. For example, some structures can be viewed as the result of an ecological framework, such as climate; others as manifestations of a cultural impact that adds character to cities such as Cairo, Marrakesh, Kairawan, and Baghdad.

The socioeconomic character of some old cities, such as San'a' and Shiban in Yemen and Jedda in Saudi Arabia, reflects their individual and particular solution to civic and urban demands reaching a stage of awareness and realization ahead of its time in responding to contemporary models of land utilization. The value of this urban socioeconomic framework is judged according to its continuity and vitality in the local as well as the global sphere.

Looking at what has been achieved in the past fifty years in order to judge and evaluate its continuity and vitality (which is the secret of the survival and vigor of the old noble cities and their architecture) it is troubling to discover that we are living in cities built like temporary fairs to fulfill immediate and materialistic needs. They will quickly fade away, and the place will lose the special character that gave it its identity, negating the importance of time and place in giving man orientation and consciousness of his reality.

Twentieth-century civilization has led to consumer-oriented urban environments that have disturbed the balance of human existence by destroying human values and memories. It therefore becomes necessary to reinforce the connection between the socio-cultural, environmental, and expressive capacities that in reality is what distinguishes Islam from other civilizations. The didactic role of the architect depends on his ability to discover the links between these urban visions and what is of value to all that concerns man and his needs. These links are made through the stabilization of a place by highlighting the particular architectural tools and organizational systems that express the narrative of man and his mental and emotional state in a given place.

We are trying to shed light on an epistemological model of knowledge based on a holistic approach to the Islamic culture, which reflects a certain architectural act generated from metacognitive orders still open for further reinterpretations. By discerning the essence of architectural outputs, we can avoid the trivial historicity and literal copying from the past in creating the semiological images for contemporary architectural expressions.

To exemplify these theoretical assumptions in applicable models, we will use the example of the Saudi desert cities of Riyadh and Kharj. These examples are drawn from a series of projects that established a sequence of development for the local architecture of the region beginning with the Palace of Justice and the Great Mosque (which won the Aga Khan Award for Architecture in 1995) in Riyadh, followed by the mosque at Kharj, and ending with the museum in Darat King Abdul Aziz. Since each successive project became more refined and sensitive, we will concentrate on the two most recent ones. We put a tremendous amount of effort in these projects to highlight the properties of the place, and we consider our solutions to be expressive of these regions and climates.

The first example, al-Kharj Mosque, represents a clarification of the dialectical relation between technology (machine-produced spaces) and craftsmanship (man-made environment) in the spatial order of its main prayer hall. The particularity of this place lies in its plethora of architectural elements that clearly express the functions and dynamic activities that took place in the past and continue to this day. These functions became incentives for the development of adjacent areas for urban development, which is characteristic of Islamic cities, thus shaping a complete system composed of a balance between spirit, mind, and material. This is the secret of the survival of dynamic cities.

Before delving into the specifics of the building's space, it was first necessary to understand some of the social habits, exclusive traditions, and inherited values of the community. The architectural expression was read in terms of resulting form and its connection to the components of the place, namely its social habits and morphological and environmental constraints. An old picture of the Kharj

region taken in the 1940s reinforced and enhanced our reading of the ancient Arab and Islamic city of al-Kharj. It showed the main mosque and the central vegetable market at that time, indicating the great importance of the building and the concentrated movement of people that point to the Muslim's adherence to the act of worship and his awareness of its importance in his daily life. The benches and stores that surround the mosque show that the complex exercised a dynamic attraction. Today, sophisticated citizens display this picture on the walls of their homes and in their offices as cherished evidence of the cultural and spiritual values of the civilization they have inherited.

We were constantly confronted with the following question: What can we do to communicate the message in this photograph to the heart of every citizen of al-Kharj? What can we do to clarify the perception of the past represented by this photograph of an important building that was destroyed and that we were to replace? Only the urban indicators that

Figure 1. Column detail of Al-Kharj mosque

Rasem Badran

are exclusive to Muslims in Saudi Arabia and particularly in al-Kharj can help us comprehend the city. The juxtaposition of the mosque and the market clearly reflects a social vision of life because it expresses its ability to generate an original and unbiased social example through interaction with people.

Behavioral values are therefore contained within an architectural facade that reveals the past and its behavioral contents and encourages man to improve his relationship to and understanding of this building in the present and in the future. However, this will not happen unless man begins to relate to his present and live by its inspiration in the framework of its systems and values. Thus the image is revived through the third eye, which searches for a new architectural understanding of the vital and dynamic contents of the photograph, without literally copying the image. It should also be added, however, that this story would not be complete if we omit the organization between the decision-maker and the creator of the architectural form. In this case, the Riyadh Development Authority assumed the pivotal role of the donor-client.

That we correctly comprehended this spatial

Figure 3. Exterior view of Al-Kharj mosque

Figure 2. Interior view of Al-Kharj mosque

architecture, with its emotional vision of behavioral and environmental parameters, is witnessed by the extent to which the Great Mosque of Riyadh is used as a reference for the design of other mosques in this desert region. This is illustrated by the Great Mosque of Buraida, north of Riyadh in Najd, which was strongly influenced by the spatial values and architectural systems that were implemented in the design of the Great Mosque.

The second case study is the Darat King Abdul Aziz and the *Muraba* (Square) Palace. This complex is one of the components that make up the Saudi History Center, together with the Heritage Museum, designed by Ali Shuaibi and the Human History Museum designed by a Western architect. The *darat* revitalized the value of this traditional space by intensifying the culture of Old Riyadh, which still contains some of its adobe architectural forms. This complex mediates between the values of the past and the values of the present and allows us to comprehend knowledgeable space. It also shows the ability to adjust to the inherited parameters of the site, with the Heritage Museum, on one hand, and the Human History Museum, on the other. The latter

Rasem Badran

presents a contemporary rational example of a structure for displaying historical events (box concept). It follows a traditional idea of a museum, the embalming of inherited values, an idea produced by industrial civilizations and adopted by many global cultural corporations. However, the *darat* attempted to revive, connect, and intensify the relation between the museum and the city, so the concept of a museum becomes that of a living city, which represents the vitality of the values it displays and acts as an extended school or workshop connected to city events. Islamic cultural thought emphasizes the importance of heritage as the connection between past and present and envisions a more transparent and flexible future. Public spaces are kept alive through the cultural values generated by architectural forms, which involve public space in the celebration of the urban and consequently the national culture. This is characteristic of communities in the Islamic world.

The Saudi History Center in Riyadh plays a principle role in enforcing these values; it is an architectural creation in the center of the original fabric of the old city and provides a link that ties the cultural, social, and economic structures together. The idea of a museum in the traditional sense of embalmed knowledge becomes a vital space that is continuously connected with and generated by contemporary events, as seen in historical cities such as Cairo, Baghdad, and Marrakesh which are living museums. This was in the architectural framework of the complex.

The dynamics generated during the planning and organizing process reflected the differences in Western and Eastern attitudes. The Arab architect of the Darat argued continually with the Western architect who designed the adjacent Human History Museum. The Darat and the Human History Museum shared a public space, but the Western architect was unable to relate his architectural solutions to the Darat. He limited himself to his own perception of the master plan for the museum that the architect Ali al-Shuaibi and I had proposed to the Riyadh Development Authority as a guideline for the overall master plan. This forced us, the Arab architects, to adopt the concept of flexibility and fluidity in our proposal. The outcome was fragmented geometry that evokes the memory of an inherited Arab Islamic urban tissue.

It seems that many contemporary architects believe that the dialogue between creativity, implementation, and perception has ended, and that each process is a statement by itself. But it was discus-

Figure 4. Interior view of the Saudi Museum, Riyadh

sion that gave the architecture of this region its ease of human adaptation even in the most intricate details, as is evident in all our old cities. They show the architect's response to this public space and his ability to converse with its users through arcades, corners, gateways, and transitions between alleys. It also shows the balance between light, shadow and darkness, solid and void, and the precise relationship between public, semi-public, and private spaces and the ability of the urban fabric of the city to respect chronological evolution and architectural components. These are cities built on continuously changing additions that accumulate with time and that respect continuity through the organic growth of the fabric rather than the application of a grid that negates any human existence, as seen in the Euclidean model which still influences industrial societies through man-made living spaces.

The objective of these two examples has been to show a response to sociocultural constraints using an ecological model and an architectural expression

Rasem Badran

Figure 5. Exterior view (entrance zone) of the Saudi Museum, Riyadh

that retains continuity with the values and morals of the past and encourages users to remain in harmony with the cultural and moral contents of the place. It is important to emphasize that our interest was the preservation of the moral and social understanding of the culture by developing a dialectic framework upon which we then placed a vague semiological image of the past by reading its underlying values, turning it into an urban statement with a distinguished presence, whose influence reaches beyond its context to the city and the nation.

Islam enhances the innovative process of creation because it is by its nature imbued with human values and ethical considerations. It is a religion that is socially aware and interested in the community without neglecting the individual, caring for the whole without denying the particular. As a result it maintains a balance between the spiritual, intellectual, and physical demands of mankind.

• • • • • • • • • • • • •

Rasem Badran

Comments
Nadia M. Alhasani

It is an indisputable fact that mosques in Islamic cities are the focal point for both the religious and the communal life of its dwellers, bringing together the cultural, economic, political, and social aspects of its society. It is also evident that regional architectural languages are reflected in a mosque through building form, color, texture, and ornamentation, signifying its locale, whether Cairo, Isfahan, or Kuala Lumpur. Thus one must search for the architectural vocabulary that identifies the Saudi mosque rather than the essence of "mosque" when searching for a "poetics of place." How can one distinguish a mosque in the desert from one in the city, one built in Amman from one in Riyadh? What are the models to consider? What is the essence of its "architectural image"? The author seems to imply that there is a universal solution to a very regional issue.

The existence of new building types, of which a museum is one example, raises questions regarding architectural evolution, inheritance, and development. The lack of such models in the original fabric of an Islamic city forces architects either to search for inspiration beyond Islamic artifacts and fabric when available (e.g., it is common practice to refer to the architecture of the Babylonians rather than the Abbasids when designing in Baghdad), or copy blindly the existing building fabric surrounding the site. It is naive to assume that the mosque is the model for the design of any building in the Muslim world. How can issues of scale and proportion, hierarchy and geometry of space be expressed? What is communicated to the viewer and how is it identified?

Response

The relationship between architectural expression and the environment in which it evolves, can be seen in a number of my mosque projects in the region. For example the Grand Mosque in Riyadh (the city), and the mosque in al-Kharj (agricultural)—both belonging to desert environment, the mosque of Ali Bin Abi Talib in Doha, Qatar, (coastal location), and the Grand State Mosque in Baghdad, (religious diversity, rich history, agricultural and urban environment). Here, the formal symbols are expressed together with the ecological treatments of the building and its relationship to the fertility of the land.

The principles of Islamic heritage—*turath*; give the mosque a contextual framework in the architectural contexts. Such buildings become human rather than monumental or symbolic, tying the mosque back to its vital cultural context with an expression that varies with its specific environment being urban, agricultural, or even geographic or topographic. This is in contrast to the modern western approach to design that has reduced mosques to mere material products and empty symbols—more like monumental temples.

I always avoid in my work such practices of monumentality that tend to be authoritarian and overwhelming. Instead, I aim at providing a human message addressed to man in all contexts, whether desert, rural, agricultural, or urban. This approach can be experienced in the mosques I have designed. In this approach, the mosque becomes the focus of human life, spiritually and culturally. The material aspect is related to the degree of proximity of the mosque, and its role in activating other institutions that satisfy these material requirements.

Similarly, I see that the museum according to the western perspective is more of a documentation of obsolete knowledge. This perception differs substantially from the Islamic perspective, in which the contents of memory are vital for the Muslim, because Islamic arts are still alive in the mosque or the house or the palace. Such expressions are seen within their specific locations and their relationship to their environments.

My recent museum projects contemplate an opposite approach to the conventional concept of the museum, by composing a city that is capable of holding the achievements of Islamic arts within a functional framework stressing their vitality and continued material, psychological and spiritual roles.

I started this concept in the museum in Saudi Arabia, and became especially clear in the museum of Islamic Arts in Qatar. This approach contrasts with the concept of museum as "container," or "black box" and the architectural concept of mummified knowledge as it is commonly adopted in the contemporary museum. The space of the museum of Qatar which includes all the tools and aspects of the Muslim way of life may be compared to the khan which used to be the place where the interaction with these achievements took place; where the different cultures met, and where learning took place, this is the museum in my opinion.

Rasem Badran

Project and Tradition

Eugenio Galdieri

The relationship between the Islamic world and modernity in architecture is a topic of debate in which, with varying degrees of success, architects, designers, and historians of art and architecture have been involved for more than two decades. For some time now the Aga Khan Award for Islamic Architecture, and more recently, the Aga Khan Program at M.I.T., have been a source of inspiration and have provided a venue for this debate. In my opinion, however, the premises underlying the debate have not been expressed completely: the debate does not take into account the profound crisis that has affected the entire design process over the past twenty years.

As Seyyed Hossein Nasr has remarked, "The urban crisis is of course worldwide. Much that is taking place in the Islamic world is related to, and is a consequence of, this worldwide crisis."[1] It follows that, before deciding whether there is (or can be) a "modern way to the architecture of the Islamic countries" and before expressing regret over the current obvious lack of interest by architects in this topic, we must attempt to understand the reasons for the crisis in the project as such.

The General Crisis in Architecture

Lack of imagination, absence of clear ideas, increasingly heavy, (although perhaps necessary) interference from the law, widespread desire for standardization (fear of becoming isolated), globalization (and therefore leveling) of popular taste, the elimination of the educational and representative role of public architecture, excessive dependence on technology, the abandonment of any relationship with the environment in which one is operating and thus with local materials and resources are some of the problems. But that feeling, that indefinable something, that each place possesses and can itself transmit—in other words, what the ancient Romans called the *genius loci*—remains.

These are only a few of the many causes of crisis, to which, paradoxically, may be added even a few of the attempts to combat them: for example, the impulse to turn every new building into an "event" and thus to engage increasingly in architecture as spectacle, an architecture intended not to perform its function and serve the city and its inhabitants, but to be written up in architectural journals or to be a symbol of power. The cities where it is possible to create new architecture are filling up with constructions that are bolder and taller (is it possible that Manhattan Island will be reduplicated throughout the world, even in the middle of the desert?) and ever more technological, but increasingly hostile to the people who are supposed to use them.

The guilt experienced on rare occasions even by an architect or a designer or a town administrator sometimes leads to the salvation from destruction of some modest building inherited from the past (whether ancient, old, or only from yesterday is of no importance) but only to exploit it as a counterfoil for some new, immobile giant, almost as though a qualitative comparison were being made, in which of course the older one is bound to be the loser.

All cities are comprised of layers of slow stratification that is made up of history, taste, social and economic upheaval, abandonment, and return. It is precisely this stratification (and the random modifications and juxtapositions accompanying it from different eras, social strata, and styles) that make our urban areas beautiful, harmonious and alive.

The Peculiarity of Islamic Architecture

The cities of the Islamic world have not escaped the process of growth and stratification over time, but they have had an extraordinary advantage. Whatever the changes in the style, differences in the financial resources of those commissioning the work, or the functions of buildings, they have always been linked by a single connective element—the absolute preeminence of the religious component even in civic buildings that is manifested in the form of common, tangible signs of great psychological and visual impact. One example of this is monumental epigraphy (*katiba*): another language that is superimposed on buildings made of stone, brick, mud, or marble, giving a tangible continuity to twelve centuries of building history.

It is thus the written word—and very often the word of the sacred Koran—that forms one of the most important connective elements of Islamic architecture. It is this word, for instance, that allows a *samsara* in San'a', a Koranic school in Katmandu, the Qutb Minar in Delhi, the ramparts of Diyarbakir, the *khanaqah* in Natanz, the Ince Minare Medrese in Konya to be recognized immediately, despite substantial typological, decorative, geographic, and temporal differences between them, as belonging to one and the same culture—the *dar al-islam*. Writes Oleg Grabar, "[For architectonic epigraphy, Muslims] mostly use religious passages and in particular verses from the Koran, although in Iran or in Spain it may also be poetry; by means of the art of calligraphy the Word enters the building."[2] A unifying element such as epigraphy in the common language of the faith is certainly more immediately perceived than other architectonic devices, however common or similar, which are necessarily affected by specific local artistic and cultural features. Examples are geometric decoration, *muharragh* (ceramic mosaics), *muqarnas*, domes, and four-centered arches—in other words, that formal baggage by means of which the West identifies (superficially and often affectedly) the whole of Islamic architecture.

There is no other architecture in the world (including even Christian religious buildings, although they make extensive use of it) in which the word is materialized on such a large scale, with such richness and expressive variety; architectonic epigraphy often succeeds in embracing the whole building, until the material weight of the masonry envelope is dissolved. It thus represents yet another architectonic tool. In this light, it appears as an oversimplification to justify the epigraphic or decorative presence with the usual assumption (which is far from being historically acceptable *in toto*) that inscriptions are merely the necessary substitutes for the forbidden human image.

Where else could this take place if not in the *dar al-islam*—that is, in the place where theoretically the perfect fusion, the absolute identity, between lay and religious power is attained? Geometric decoration, often implemented using *hezar baft* (thousand nodes or traceries) tends to fill that *horror vacui* so deeply rooted in the Eastern world. However, it tends also to represent the perfect harmony, the mathematical perfection that only God can achieve and in which He is able to move. Such an homage to divine harmony can be expressed, and perhaps even more satisfactorily, by the written word: the latter is in fact harmony by virtue of its elegant and refined forms but is also the expression, indirect but tangible, of the truth revealed to Muhammad.

Another, perhaps less perceptible, connective element is the skillful domination of space, exercised for nearly one thousand years by Muslim architects to a degree unknown in other cultures, even though it has been stressed on many occasions that different cultures coexist in the formation and expression of Islamic art. Writes Grabar, "Islamic art is therefore that produced by Jews, Christians or followers of other religions, and addressed to them at the moment it is created within the boundaries of the world of Islam."[3]

As far as we know, the first models, used for at least a century, are to be sought in the Christian architecture of Syria, as in the seventh-century Hijaz even the memory of that which was geographically closer, namely the southern Arabian form (Minea, Sabaea, etc.) had been completely forgotten.

However, above and beyond the formal and exterior references (for example, the construction of the Qubbat al-Sakhra, the Dome of the Rock, in clear opposition to the Anastasis, the Church of the Holy Sepulcher), it is obvious that the Islamic builders learned quickly and well the lesson from the past concerning the creation of the "inner space". The palaces of the powerful, the large and small places of worship, the public buildings, modest dwellings, and the pretentious and complex country villas, starting from the early Umayyad manifestations and ending with the magnificent Ottoman architecture, are all characterized by this imperceptible but secure domination of space, and always in a human dimension. Since architecture consists of the organization of space (to the interior space in which one lives, as

Eugenio Galdieri

112

opposed to the exterior space which is to be looked at), it may be inferred that Islamic architects, or rather those who worked on the construction of the Islamic city, whatever their religious beliefs, always possessed this undeniable ability.

"Arab architecture," wrote Hassan Fathy, "begins with the interior and goes to the exterior. The function of space is primary. The outer form must express the forces on the inside. Every room is respected. You don't start with the exterior shell as with modern sky-scrapers."[4]

Ability, instinct, and sense of proportion in creating the constructed space are all the more admirable in that they are exercised in a context profoundly saturated with mathematics and geometry, but which ignored the handbook theorization of proportions, just as it ignored the architectural orders, the foundations of Western architecture from the Greeks to the late Renaissance.

> [In Islamic architecture] . . . there is also a substantial poverty of architectonic lexicon, which is often buried and concealed beneath a conspicuous and imaginative decorative mantle. . . ; emphasis should thus be given to the ability to use the scanty compositive instruments in a constantly varied way.[5]

The paucity of the compositive lexicon ended up by concentrating and heightening the unifying characteristics, at the same time allowing a high degree of "flexibility" and "adaptability" to be achieved by the architectonic organisms. "Closely related to the concept of a 'hidden architecture' is the striking and almost total absence of a specific architectural form for a specific function."[6]

Oil and Architecture

Between 1970 and 1980, coinciding almost exactly with the most serious energy crisis ever faced by the industrialized West, the basic premises were laid for the growth and adaptation of the architecture of the Islamic world. Western architects were invited to collaborate with the Islamic countries in the *ex novo* creation or the expansion of cities, while young architects from Muslim countries, some of whom were graduates of Western universities, finally came out into the open and engaged in an exciting contest with their foreign, usually older and more experienced colleagues. This contest was also inspired by the memory and the works of those solitary masters of the past who came from the West or had acquired their experience there, and in their turn were coming to grips with a totally different cultural reality.

At the same time the West became aware of—and was thus able to reappraise—architectural works by top Muslim architects who had worked practically in obscurity in their countries and who were not always appreciated even there as much as they deserved.

Supporting all this architectural fervor were the great and virtually unexpected economic resources flowing into many countries in northern and central Africa and the Arabian Peninsula, and in the Middle East in general, from oil revenues. "The economic resources stemming from exploitation of oil fields, the crisis of western colonialism, the renewed political fervor, created the conditions for the development of a new building civilization of a depth and interest that are still largely unknown."[7]

Unfortunately not all the expectations were fulfilled: apart from a few isolated examples of truly modern projects that nevertheless respected the spirit of Islam, the majority of architects, divided equally into "local" and "foreign", designed (and unfortunately also built) works that appeared from the outside to be close to the International Style, but were almost always masked, in a purely cosmetic operation, by all the paraphernalia of grilles, eight-pointed stars, domes, arches, fountains, and stalactites thought to provide local color.

Nor could things have been different: the only "Islamic" experience many of the Western architects had was a trip or two to Egypt or Morocco, in addition to a few ancient prejudices they had concerning the *harem,* the bazaar, or the "dark and dangerous *kasbah.*" They unconsciously retrod the path followed a hundred years before by the European Orientalists, who were fascinated more by odalisques and sumptuous interiors than by the spirit which animated a Muslim's life.

On the other side, Muslim architects were legitimately looking for opportunities to measure their work against the output of international architecture; to do this they were prepared to forget everything their ancestors had created over a period of more than a thousand years in order to approach and refer to the celebrated models of contemporary design.

In 1982, the international exhibition, "Architecture in the Islamic Countries," was set up as part of the Venice Biennale, and provided a fairly complete overview of the building achievements of the preceding years. In a review, Galasso wrote:

> [On view are] ... models, drawings and audio-visual material, and works by some eighty or so

Eugenio Galdieri

architects, both Islamic and of western origin. It is a varied and complex, and often disconcerting, review of the most significant aspects of the 'new building civilization' of Islam. The results are extremely varied, ranging from great works to cheap speculation, from ideas worth remembering to banally obvious stylistic conformism.[8]

At the opening of the exhibition, Bruno Zevi described it as "the petro-dollar building exhibition," while Vittorio Gregotti actually denied that an Islamic architectural culture existed, an idea that had already been expressed in connection with the presentation of the first Aga Khan Award for Architecture (Lahore, 1980).

The section of the Venice show dedicated to exhibitions of individual masters such as Sinan, Ferdinand Pouillon, Le Corbusier, Louis Kahn, and Hassan Fathy confirmed in practice, through the excellence of their works, a concept that I consider important: the history of architecture does not consist solely of project "peaks" but must also take into account everyday buildings of the middle classes and even the poor. It is here that it becomes possible to measure the validity of what Rudofski calls "non-pedigreed architecture,"[9] also the true architectural culture of a people, and thus its degree of ideological and aesthetic adhesion to "cultivated models", quite apart from their economic possibilities and the presence or absence of professional designers.

Imitation and Innovation

If it were true that architectonic culture is reflected above all in spontaneous building, we would have to conclude that there is no hope, that there is no future for the architecture of our cities. If we look at what ordinary people are building today, in the absence of any valid models or perhaps precisely because they hate those models, a shiver of fear runs through us: lack of precision, absence of taste, and of any kind of rules, improper use of materials, ignorance of building techniques, the idle acceptance of half understood passing fashions have gradually crept in from the dismal urban periphery to the city center. The invasion of this pretentious jerrybuilding (often as expensive as its more rational equivalent) has ended up by suffocating the historic centers and often hiding their artistic treasures. Here once again the need is felt for a human dimension, not necessarily monumental architecture, but of a high cultural level, and why not also traditional (in the sense of possessing an intrinsic and recognizable continuity);

a strong architecture that also has a corrective, educative, and stimulating function in present-day Islamic society and not merely a backward-looking or vainglorious appearance.

This brings us back to the original questions: is it still possible to find a modern path to the architecture of the Islamic countries? If so, what could this path be? From what has emerged so far, it seems that only two paths are open to architects wishing to work in countries with a strong Islamic tradition but which are legitimately looking towards the future.

Imitation

They can continue to use the increasingly hackneyed and superficial repetition of past models which are lacking in those contents and values that made Islamic architecture famous and that yield an architecture that has congealed and been reduced to a stylistic container for largely superseded functions. If this path is followed, it is recommended that this false continuity at least be entrusted exclusively to local designers who are better placed than their Western colleagues to know or study their own past artistic manifestations. To this end it is to be hoped that there will be an ever increasing spread, particularly at the university level, of historical, artistic, and building history studies related to local architecture; I insist on the term "local" because, in my opinion, even in the near future the regional features that have always characterized Islamic architecture will have to be reappraised.

To decide to imitate is certainly not a courageous choice; it is without much future and in a sense the easiest way out. It also brings with it the danger of a constant, rapid drop in quality, since not much talent is needed to copy. However, in the absence of anything better, it could ensure at least the external survival of certain forms and certain peculiar structures that are gradually disappearing and that soon no one will any longer be capable of reproducing. I certainly do not consider this to be the best solution, but it is always a possible path to follow.

Innovation

There is no doubt that this is the most difficult path. It calls for great talent and a profound knowledge of the history and techniques of other architectonic cultures. Moreover, it requires dedication to the authentic faith and traditions of the Islamic way of life and thus of its specific temporal and regional features. It cannot be an architecture which breaks with its past

Eugenio Galdieri

but a natural and rational evolution of forms and functions in which Western architectural language can be seen as a possible tool of communication and not as a purely aesthetic, or worse ideological, model. From the orthodox point of view, the sumptuousness of the great mosques of the past can and must be considered as a limit to the moral and social legitimacy and justifiable solely as a sign of power. But this same sumptuousness would never be serenely accepted today as a representation of modern Islam if it were applied to new social buildings such as schools, hospitals, hotels, and public offices. The time for competing to see who can spend more and thus demonstrate his power and wealth is long since over, even in those Western countries that made consumerism and the ostentatious display of the superfluous their ideological banner.

In any case, if there exist today designers (not necessarily Muslims) who are capable of suggesting new forms that are also respectful of the context and of an almost uninterrupted tradition, they are welcome and should be allowed complete freedom to measure themselves within that context and that tradition. There is only one thing that must be avoided at all costs in a possible new architecture, and that is contamination, easy compromise, scholarly quotations—in other words a kind of post-modern *a la moresque*. We already see with horror that it is spreading in the desolate peripheral quarters of the Jordanian, Moroccan, and Uzbek cities, borrowed from the costly and absurd high-class buildings scattered from Tehran to Samarqand, from Lahore to Jedda. But a glance must also be cast over the recent proposals for Mecca or Mashhad. Writes Nasr: "Islamic architecture has been eclipsed by a conglomeration of often hideous styles or at best bland ones, in both cases imitated from foreign models with the pretense of universality and world-wide applicability."[10]

A discussion of the search for a modern way to Islamic architecture, a problem raised on a number of occasions in the past, found a favorable opportunity in 1970 when the International Congress, "Interaction of Tradition and Technology," was held in Isfahan. Although limited to Iranian architecture (if this can be called a "limitation"), a number of well-known architects agreed upon the principle to guarantee a more rigorous continuity for new social, aesthetic, and urban needs. In practice, however, twenty-five years have passed with little action, and today we are still asking architects, over and above any theoretical considerations, to pay greater atten-

tion to specific problems and to show a greater operational involvement in the development of architecture in Islamic countries. What is to be done?

It is no easy matter to draw any conclusions or practical advice from what has been said so far: the examples of architecture implemented in the Islamic countries over the past fifty years are certainly of little help in pointing the way. However, several observations can be made for the benefit of future designers and administrators responsible for the development of cities.

We are all aware that the crisis in modern architecture has continued to degrade the character of ancient cities, whether Paris or Damascus. The negative effects of the crisis in architecture are obviously least conspicuous and serious in those cities in which the urban fabric has been maintained almost undisturbed and where the volumes and spatial and exterior relations among buildings from different eras are more homogeneous: Assisi, Isfahan, Avignon, and Fez al-Bali are to some extent "doomed" (to their good fortune) to have little in the way of modern development.

The problem arises where the cities have been extensively modified and adapted to cope with constantly changing circumstances; in other words, where it is not possible to deny the right to progress, expansion, improvement of living conditions and thus to the replacement of the ancient peculiarities with new and more tangible "values". In this case, a number of recommendations must be made. First and foremost is that of measure: a correct and natural size ratio must be maintained between man and the environment in which he operates. Another is to try to reestablish that fertile relation that, in all architecture of the past (in particular Islamic architecture), linked together the designer with master builders and craftsmen, allowing the second group a wide margin of creative freedom, albeit within the most rigorous confines of the building program: in this way every trace of industrial product would be removed from new buildings, which could thus be constructed always and anywhere.

...the forms of eastern architecture are all the result of a close collaboration, almost a symbiosis, between the "sophisticated" work of the architect—whose social origin we do not know and which does not interest us—and that of the innumerable craftsmen. . . .[11]

Next is to have the courage of their convictions about design, once all the historical, artistic and so-

Eugenio Galdieri

115

cial data concerning the context have been acquired. Then to remain humble (which is not inconsistent with courage!) so that the confrontation does not turn into a breach of trust. To use as far as possible all the techniques and materials that have characterized Islamic architecture, but with boldness and freshness of invention; and to avoid the use of such techniques and materials as a "quotation" or, worse, a mere copy of the past.

To construct functionally modern buildings does not mean necessarily copying from models that are alien to one's culture: only those elements deemed useful or necessary to one's own way of life should be borrowed from the West. An example: what is the sense in designing a dwelling with those large expanses of glass that are doomed immediately to be covered with curtains, venetian blinds, or even sheets of newspaper for reasons of climate or privacy? Is this "modern" behavior? Once upon a time the *maristan*, caravanserais, *samasir, bad-gir*, aqueducts, and cisterns were "modern" because they contributed to the rationalization of social functions and primary needs.

The validity of these recommendations is naturally dependent on the assumption that the designer (and also the client) is genuinely determined not to betray his own "Islamicity," quite independent of the strictly religious connotations of this term. If this assumption is correct, it will be enough to have received serious professional training and to have knowledge of one's own history, humility, and the design courage needed to ensure the continuity of the architecture of the Islamic countries.

I shall conclude by relating an experience that will perhaps explain more clearly what I mean by "design courage". In 1968 I was invited together with Eugene Beaudouin—we were the only two foreigners—to sit on the adjudicating commission for a national competition (i.e., limited to local architects) for the National Theater at Isfahan. Some thirty competing projects were divided into three groups, on the basis of their "inspirational models": the first group represented projects that in some way referred to the influence of the French architects working in Iran in the 1930s and thus to a style fluctuating between the neo-Achaemenian and the neo-Sasanian, of the type represented by the Iran Bastan Museum in Tehran. The second group of projects were related to the same models, but unfortunately in a structuristic re-elaboration: there was therefore an abundance of hypostyle halls of the Achaemenian type (the Apadana of Persepolis or Susa), but built

of steel. The third, and smallest, group had chosen as its source of inspiration the grandiose complex of the Sydney Opera House, still uncompleted at the time.

In the face of the scandalized reaction of numerous members of the commission, I and a small number of Iranian colleagues indicated this last group as containing a possible winner: in the ingenious and spectacular overlapping of the great sails we had glimpsed a metaphor of the great domes of Islamic Iran, fragmented and disassembled, just as Islamic art had geometrically broken down the spherical pendentive of late Roman and Byzantine architecture into the *muqarnas*.

I do not know (nor did I bother to find out) whether any of those designers were aware of the significance of that choice; however, if they were, perhaps without realizing it they had opened up a new path, thus providing a partial but workable answer to our question.

Notes

1. Seyyed Hossein Nasr, "Toward an Understanding of Architectural Symbolism", *Toward an architecture in the Spirit of Islam*, proceedings of Seminar One by Aga Khan Award for Architecture, France 1978, p.5.

2. Oleg Grabar, "Le tradizioni architettoniche e urbane nel mondo islamico", *Architettura nei Paesi islamici*, seconda mostra internazionale di architettura, la biennale, Venezia 1982 p.17 (Original text in Italian).

3. Oleg Grabar, *Enciclopedia dell'Arte Medievale*, Istituto della Enciclopedia italiana, ad vocem Islamica, Arte. Vol;VII, Roma 1996, p.432 (Original text in Italian).

4. Hassan Fathy, as quoted in: *Domus*. Monthly magazine of Architecture, Design, Art. Milano. Dec. 1980, no. 216, p. 9.

5. E. Galdieri, "Considerazioni sull'architettura dell'Islam", AA.VV. *Architettura islamica e orientale*, Accademia delle Arti del Disegno, Alinea, Firenze 1986, p.12 (Original text in Italian).

6. Ernst Grube. "What is Islamic Architecture?" In George Michell, ed. *Architecture of the Islamic World*, Thames and Hudson, London. 1978, p.12

7. Paolo Portoghesi. Introduzione. la Biennale (see

Eugenio Galdieri

n.2), Venezia 1982, p.5 (Original text in Italian)

8. Giuseppe Galasso. Forward. la Biennale (see n.2), Venezia 1982, p.5. (Original text in Italian).

9. Bernard Rudofski. *Architecture without architects.* Doubleday & Company, New York. 1964, pp. 1.

10. Seyyed Hossein Nasr, "Toward an Understanding of Architectural Symbolism", *Toward an architecture in the Spirit of Islam*, proceedings of Seminar One by Aga Khan Award for Architecture, France 1978, p.1.

11. Ludovico Quaroni. "Le mille e una citta, piacere d'Oriente". la Biennale (see n.2). Venezia 1982, p.22 (Original text in Italian).

• • • • • • • • • • • • •

Comments
Ronald Lewcock

If we define the word "architecture" as most architects and critics do, in Vitruvius's terms, viz., a building which intends to and succeeds in giving delight, then we have to accept that the great bulk of building is not today—and was not in the past—"architecture." But this is not a new state of affairs and certainly not one that is limited to the Islamic world.

Issues that serious architects elsewhere are attempting to grapple with in the late twentieth century also need to be addressed there, e.g., how to center delight in architecture on appropriateness. More architects in these transitional times must focus on replacing established Western solutions with alternative ones that are responsive to local societies and their values. They must be willing to relativize engagement with, rather than to reinforce, the contrast between mass production and craft building. And they must oppose the concept of individual buildings sufficient unto themselves, designing instead for the positive pleasures of interaction in a society of different communities living together - an architecture diverse yet responsive to the collective future.

Response
I agree with Professor Lewcock on the necessity of a "relativization" of the contrast between mass production and the art of building. Nevertheless I think that cultured buildings—often objects of direct patronage by sultans, shahs, or pontiffs—represented an acceptable model to the poorest classes too through a very complicated psychological process involving imitation and envy in equal measure.

Today this thin thread of an ambiguous continuity has disappeared all over the world: everywhere slums are similar and the sole difference—if there is one—consists in the kind of building materials available to build them. For this reason I speak of a "sub-building issue" made of bad taste, even if there is a magnificent patron. This phenomenon is now almost global. What I fear—even more for the Islamic world—is a total loss of any cultural (both historical and artistic) identity after centuries of well-known excellence and therefore a higher fragility with regard to more aggressive cultures (or pseudo-cultures).

Eugenio Galdieri

117

What Islamic Architecture Is Not

Kamran T. Diba

Architecture is always a response to the culture of its time. The role of the architect is to accommodate and enrich his culture by innovation and the introduction of challenging ideas. After all, architects and artists register and document their era for future generations.

The twilight of the twentieth century in which we live is an important and pivotal era in the history of mankind. The West, master and maker of the twentieth century, has imposed its values and forced its superior methods of science, technology, and production onto less-developed societies. Loss of independence and perhaps a perceived humiliating subjugation to Western ideas and values has brought about an identity crisis in Islamic societies. Having been bypassed by the processes of material and human advancement, these societies have had no choice but to look inward and to their past.

Iran is a pioneer in this endeavor. In spite of its material prosperity, rapid progress, and Western-oriented technocracy, it chose the way of defiance and independence from the West. Although Iran has never been colonized, its adherence to the Western model of development has nevertheless created around it an aura of surrender and subordination. In reaction, in 1979 Iranians took to the streets, toppled their government, acted as the liberator from the colonial regime, even going so far as to create a Western culprit as enemy. It is obvious to me that the roots of the so-called politicization of Islam stem from this cultural conflict that is far beyond the control of politicians and political parties; this is a wave to ride out, not to resist.

It is of paramount importance to understand the cultural schism that exists between the West and the Islamic societies, and it is therefore necessary to look at the contemporary architecture in those countries from this vantage point. One of the contradictions of our time is that as Muslims we are searching superficially for our identity, while at the same time Islamic societies, whether on the left or the right side of the ideological spectrum, are all building Western-style metropolitan life on different scales—high rises, slums, divisive social classes, megatransportation systems generating everything from pollution to social incoherence.

The question is: do we lack thinkers or informed leaders? Or have we simply failed to engage our intellectual and professional resources to tackle this problem? No doubt we have debated and put into practice Islamic economic models, acceptable social behavior, and eventually political structure, but have we recognized the importance of an Islamic urban environment and mobilized our efforts to achieve certain model communities? I am sure we have made attempts in that direction, but I wonder if any Islamic nation has ever communicated such ideas across transnational boundaries or rewarded such attempts by attending to them. I cannot ignore the fact that Islamic countries do not have any cultural interrelation, and probably had it not been for the Aga Khan Award for Architecture, our profession would not even have been aware that some architects of the contemporary Islamic world existed. I often wonder how it can be that historically one could note an inspiration of Persian gardens and Middle Eastern architecture in its finest form duplicated in southern Spain; this has to do with cultural inter-relation and exchange of ideas among architects, craftsmen, and artists. No doubt this was the result of a deliberate policy and not a historical accident.

Kamran T. Diba

119

Figure 1 through 5. Images of a project showing that it is possible to achieve high-density communities without high-rise buildings. The design provides small and large houses with gardens for diverse social classes. These gardens create green vistas for the community but are cared for by the owners.

If we look at Stonehenge in England, the Renaissance, or the architecture of bazaars and mosques of the historic Middle East, they all tell us the story of a culture and a proud and creative people. It is not important how many times they prayed and fasted or how much of their body was covered. It is important how they led their lives, and by looking at their architecture we get to know them and even thank and respect them. But a glance at our contemporary urban environment speaks of a confused and disoriented culture that occupies itself with short-lived debates. Unfortunately, while Islamic societies are arguing over the design of the buttons, the suit itself is being produced according to the Occidental model. Only poverty and lack of means saves us from this self-destruction and subjugation to irrelevant Western models.

We live in the age of progress. We cannot

Kamran T. Diba

blindly copy past styles and architectural features; but we should certainly learn about their scale, environmental sensibility, and communal life. We should be involved in creating communities of social relevance, not apartments, streets, and highways. A few pretty buildings in the chaotic jungle of disorder, greed, and one-upmanship are irrelevant.

On my blacklist I identify two basic enemies of Islamic or any other traditional and humane environment: high-rise buildings and uncontrolled vehicular traffic. We Muslims should avoid high-rises and create density horizontally. We can do without left-over open spaces around towers that are unwanted and unloved. This type of public space is unknown in traditional societies. On the other hand, we need and should provide well-defined, well-kept, sustainable public gardens in each community, but not a no-man's land or clubby, manicured gardens for high-income apartment residences.

Eventually, we could have horizontal high density and separate the vehicular transport system from pedestrians. Often when we design a middle-class housing project, we think of giving private-car access to every unit. As a result, we sacrifice the quality and scale of our environment, making the community subservient to cars, and we give in to indi-

Figure 2. (Photo: Kamran Adle/AKTC)

Figure 3. (Photo: Kamran Adle/AKTC)

Kamran T. Diba

121

vidual modes of transportation. At the same time, when we make a tower block, we know that it is not possible for everybody to drive their car to their apartment unit and park in the hallway, so we store them in public garages.

We have all heard the argument: what about access for fire engines and ambulances in narrow pedestrian spaces and streets? I do not suppose that in the labyrinthine corridors of high-rises these vehicles are driven to the 11th floor and parked in front of apartment 1125 for the rapid delivery of fire and health services! We often ignore the fact that people go crazy in stacked-up crowded conditions, homes burn to ashes, and people die, while the twentieth-century contraptions designed to rescue them are stuck in traffic, unable to reach their destination.

I am neither a romantic nor an advocate of total segregation of pedestrian and vehicular traffic. But I recommend that every time we think of creating socially coherent and harmonious communities, we should distinguish our priorities rather than copy Western models.

We spend enormous sums in construction and maintenance in both poor and rich nations to recreate a life patterned after that in the West. As Muslims we are willing to kill for superficial and symbolic aspects of our traditions, but we ignore the essentials. We reject the necktie, but go right on recreating bad versions of the Western metropolis for future Muslim generations to live in.

• • • • • • • • • • • • •

Figure 4. (Photo: Kamran Adle/AKTC)

Kamran T. Diba

122

Figure 5. (Photo: Kamran Adle/ AKTC)

Comments
Khalil K. Pirani

I agree with the fact that Islamic societies have been influenced by western ideas, that Muslim societies should not imitate historical architectural styles and features blindly and that high-rise residential towers have tendencies to be a failure—both for the end-users and for local environment. But I disagree with the notion that certain building types such as high rises should be completely eliminated from Muslim societies. Reasons being that high rise cater to socio-economic and developmental needs of a society and eliminating them may not be practical. Secondly, has enough research and analysis been done to de-

termine why high-rise residential models fail?

How do you suggest Muslim societies will gain world leadership in discovering innovative solutions to complex problems? This becomes more pressing when Islam requires using the intellect to the utmost and analyzing and reasoning thoroughly in determining solution to any societal problem.

Response
My anti-high rise attitude is not to be taken as absolute dogma or as an unconditional commitment. High-rise structures, if necessary, could be advisable in case of scarce land resources or in technologically developed societies with relevant social values, appropriate urban life style and behavior. The two out-

Kamran T. Diba

123

standing examples of concentration of high-rise living are Manhattan and Hong Kong—two memorable examples of exciting and charged urban landscapes. This concentration no doubt generates power, wealth, and in the case of New York exceptional artistic and cultural energy unique in the world. But let us not ignore the inferior living conditions, crime and social anomaly often associated with these centers.

In response to your comments I have my reservations about "socio-economic and developmental needs" attributed to high-rise living and its relevance toward the majority of Muslim nations with their present economical conditions, anticipated social behavior and their overall attitude toward collective life. High-rise concentration of population fails in most metropolitan areas in prosperous western countries, and Muslim communities living in the suburbs of Paris in high-rise apartments are also a model of failure. Why they fail could be the subject of another essay.

In response to your last comment about Muslim societies gaining leadership, I should admit that Muslim nations are generally isolated societies, which pay more attention to politics than culture. They are more interested in the pursuit of the material world than intellectual and cultural dialog among themselves.

It is accidental that we sometimes have a dialog and forum. If it were not for the interest of one man, Prince Aga Khan and his generous endowment, we would not even know about each other. Intellectual and cultural apathy and lack of interaction amongst Muslim nations speaks of underdevelopment, or perhaps failure of our socio-political and cultural institutions.

When we review the events of the last twenty years, the aggression of Iraq toward Iran and subsequent war, the invasion of Kuwait by Iraq, the massacre of the Kurds, the recent confrontation of Iranians with Afghani Taleban, and the weekly massacre of civilians in Algeria. If we withhold the names of players, countries and dates, one may no doubt think of a story about a cruel world in Dark Ages.

Kamran T. Diba

Architecture in Islamic Societies and the New Development Paradigm

Arif Hasan

Almost the entire Islamic world was colonized by the European powers in the nineteenth and early twentieth century. Even those Islamic societies that were not colonized were forced to adopt European political, legal, educational, and financial systems and developed a small Westernized elite that in most cases struggled for independence and progressive reform.

For most Islamic societies (except in Central Asia) freedom from colonialism came at the end of the Second World War. The societies that had not been colonized also took up nationalism in the post-war period inspired by the changed global political environment and by the small independent neighbors they acquired with whom they shared a common history and culture.

After independence, the new Islamic states quickly adopted models for development—either a "welfare state" or a regime based on the socialist pattern of the Soviet Union. In both these models the state was paramount, responsible for producing housing, building and managing transport systems, providing education and health facilities at subsidized rates or free of cost, and either developing industry or exercising often rigid controls on its development.

In such a situation, the architect, when he was not working on residences for the rich, invariably found himself working on state-sponsored projects. Almost all architects in the newly independent states were either educated in the West or in local institutions whose curriculum and manner of teaching were derived from a Western or Soviet academic tradition, which was in turn closely related to the political and institutional framework that had been developed to support the respective models. Thus, most architecture of the period was in the International Style, a style that not only popularized new technologies and materials of construction in Islamic societies, but created powerful academic and bureaucratic interests that wished to see its perpetuation.

Major changes also took place in the country-side as a result of the development models. Green-revolution technologies were introduced in the "democratic" societies and radical land reforms in the "socialist" ones. In both cases, well-established relationships between different segments of the rural population underwent a change, making old institutions and production processes redundant. In architecture, the traditional inter-dependence between the house builder, the local artisan, and the supplier of building materials was destroyed with disastrous effects on the built environment in the rural areas. These changes, coupled with the introduction of capitalist farming and ill-conceived and badly implemented land reforms, impoverished the people, forcing them to move to the urban centers.

One can safely say that neither the welfare state nor the socialist model worked. The major reason for this is that they were incompatible with the sociology and economics of the societies that they were forced upon and given financial, political, and human resource constraints, they could not cater to the needs that were created as a result of attempts to implement them. Unforeseen rural-urban migration added fuel to the fire and made a mockery of the entire planning process. Among the side effects of this failure were the development of large unserviced informal settlements in most Islamic cities; the ad hoc evolution of unregulated transport systems; a lack of adequate health and education facilities; and the large-scale overpopulation and degradation of the inner cities due to the failure to develop basic urban infrastructure. Meanwhile, the formal private sector expanded cautiously to provide housing to the upper and middle classes, but it remained firmly subservient to procedures and processes laid down by relevant state agencies. In such a situation, development took place before planning in most cases, and it continues to do so. By the mid seventies, many Islamic states had accepted this de facto situation. In the eighties attempts were made to regularize and regulate "development before planning." Upgrading informal settlements, planning bypasses and transport terminals, rehabilitating and gentrifying the inner city were all attempted. However, at the level of policy and larger conceptual issues, the architectural profession and its associated institutions played no significant role in these attempts. The architecture schools continued to teach as before and the architect remained wedded to the concepts and processes imposed on him by the post-independence development models borrowed from the West or the socialist bloc.

All this is fast becoming history, and today we are facing a new and completely different situation. In the nineties, a dominating neo-classical economics has led to the liberalization of the economies of almost all Islamic societies. In addition, the Soviet Union has collapsed, and with it, the socialist model of development. In almost all Islamic countries at least one major city dominates trends and directions in society as a whole and has close links with international trade and finance. The absence of urban facilities in these major cities and the presence of an increasingly aware and deprived population are helping to promote extremist political views leading to strife and conflict. The combination of these realities is having a marked effect on the development of the built environment, and the architectural profession as a whole can play an important role in helping to develop and manage it better.

With neoclassical economic theory dominating the planning process, land has at last and unashamedly become a commodity. Subsidy on land is out, and the market increasingly determines land use. This has already led to powerful developers' lobbies, which increasingly control the urban-development process. In many cities, citizens and the press complain that the city authorities and the politicians are subservient to the developers' lobby and that this subservience is a major cause of environmental degradation and ecological distortion. In such a situation the architectural establishment has to support the citizens and help to create conditions where all

land transactions are transparent and where all major land-use changes or projects are approved by committees, to which citizens and interest groups (architects included) belong and have executive powers. The institutional links and professional skills of the architectural profession are crucial to the success of such initiatives. And without such initiatives, the rapid deterioration of the built environment in Islamic cities cannot be prevented.

Treating land as a commodity has particularly serious repercussions for housing. State-built housing and plot development with subsidies is already on the decrease. In addition, land for squatting or for informal development catering to low-income communities is becoming increasingly difficult and expensive to acquire. Government policies in the future will have to focus mainly on providing individuals or groups access to loans so that they can control the land and housing market. This trend has already led to the large-scale development of developer-built middle- and high-rise apartment construction—what one might call the "vernacular architecture" of our times. It is slowly dominating the skyline of most Islamic cities. This vernacular is profit-oriented, and its promoters have little or no interest in larger environmental issues. This reality has to be recognized, and the architectural profession must try to develop some practices that can improve the quality of this vernacular and at the same time reduce its costs and make it affordable to poor families. Relevant bylaws and zoning regulations need to be developed to guide this vernacular, and the profession must press for their implementation. It also poses problems. The architectural profession ought to establish links with the numerous owners' cooperatives that have sprung up to facilitate maintenance and modification of their residential complexes.

Contemporary Islamic cities, especially the larger ones, require mass transit systems, bypasses, and transport and cargo terminals if they are to function efficiently. Most of these facilities exist to some degree, but they are often located in the densely populated inner cities. Many Islamic cities are building, or planning to build, new facilities. However, there is a big difference between the way they will be built today or in the near future and the way they would have been built in the seventies and eighties. Today they are invariably being put up by contractors on a build-operate-transfer (BOT) basis. The contractors building them have a major say in how they are built, their location, and their subsequent operation and maintenance. In addition, they are

Arif Hasan

built to cater to the period—never more than thirty years—when the contractors will run and operate them. The interest of the contractors and those of the city conflict, and they must be reconciled equitably in the larger interest of the city and its inhabitants.

Similarly, economic liberalization has opened the way for large-scale foreign investment in industry, tourism, and energy in many Islamic countries. Here again, issues related to ecology, environment, and the larger operation and maintenance of industrial and power-producing infrastructure become important. In most Islamic countries, these problems are not being addressed, and the institutional framework required to address them is not yet in place.

It is important that the architectural profession involve itself in these ecological and environment-related issues and link up with lobbies and groups that have taken them up as concerns. In addition, the transport and cargo-related facilities require sensitive designing not only of the buildings but also of signage, street furniture, and fixtures. Here links with graphic and industrial designers become important, and if they do not exist, then steps to build up these disciplines have to be taken. The construction of cargo and transport-related facilities, if done at the right locations and in an appropriate manner, can release pressure on the inner cities and make their rehabilitation a far easier task than what it seems today. Again, in a market-dominated economy, the rehabilitation process will be a very different affair from what it was a decade ago. An understanding of the new forces at work in the inner cities and their perceptions and interests becomes imperative.

The most crucial issue facing the urban Islamic world, however, is that the second generation of deprived city dwellers has come or is about to come of age. These people, unlike their parents or grandparents, are not pioneers, and have few, if any, links to the clan, tribe, and village-based institutions their parents left behind. They need to be integrated physically, culturally, and politically into the rest of the city. Liberalization, especially in the manner in which it affects land and housing, only increases their alienation.

The recent spate of private-university formation also increases the rich-poor divide, as does the privatization of the health sector. In such a situation, the development of common physical and social space and a better work and living environment become essential. Here, the profession, as a creator and an enabler of the built environment, has an important role to play. Its first loyalty has to be to the social and physical environment and not to its clients. How the profession can achieve this goal needs to be explored. But before such an exploration occurs a consensus has to be reached within the profession as to what the needs of the evolving social and physical environment are and how best they can be served within existing social, political and economic constraints.

The new development paradigm will continue to have a major impact on the built environment in the Islamic world for the foreseeable future. The architectural profession has to understand this paradigm and its repercussions. It has to develop the awareness and the tools to regulate the negative aspects of these repercussions and subsequently help to institutionalize this process of regulation. To do this it will have to forge links with both the beneficiaries and the victims of these processes. But above all, it will have to bring about realistic changes in the theory and process of architectural education. If this does not happen, then the new development paradigm will devastate the built environment just as the post-independence development models of the newly independent Islamic states did.

• • • • • • • • • • • • •

Comments
William A. Doebele

Mr. Hasan has written a succinct, insightful and challenging summary of the changing role of the architect in Islamic cities. He is correct in suggesting that a radically broader professional education is essential if architects are to influence the built environment effectively. Courses in such subjects as development finance and the political economics of contemporary urbanization have become indispensable.

With respect to the poor, who comprise such a large percentage of the population of many Islamic

Arif Hasan

127

cities, it must be recognized that the role of the architect, as architect, is a very limited one. The amelioration of the conditions of the poor calls for a restructuring of the institutions of land tenure, credit, and building materials; the creation of informal employment opportunities; and the establishment of a planning process oriented toward channeling the powerful market forces that mold the contemporary city. These are fundamentally political, not architectural, issues.

Response

I agree with Professor Doebele that the amelioration of the conditions of the poor calls for a restructuring of institutions related to tenure, credit, and building materials and also for establishing a planning process oriented towards channeling market forces. However, for the improvement of housing and environmental conditions in low-income settlements, the architect has a very important role to play. I will elaborate.

Most Third World governments have fairly large program related to low-income housing, squatter-settlement upgrading and regularization, rehabilitation, and/or redevelopment of the inner-city slums. Architects are invariably involved in these government programs. In the vast majority of cases, they fail to benefit the target groups and end up serving the interests of developers and property speculators. This is because of the poor understanding on the part of architects and planners of the realities of sociological and economic conditions.

In almost all Third World cities, informal housing and land-delivery processes that cater to the needs of the urban poor are in place and in a number of cases are also recognized by government policies. The actors involved in these processes require technical advice that is compatible with the economics and sociology of the process, design support, and the development of construction skills. In addition, the development of appropriate building bylaws and zoning regulations are also required for those settlements that are upgraded. In almost all cases existing bylaws and zoning regulations are incompatible with the manner in which people incrementally build their homes and subsequently bring about changes in community-related open spaces.

It is my contention that only architects can play the role that is required to solve these problems since they are perhaps the only professionals dealing with the built environment who have an understanding of design, technology, and sociology at the same time. Where architects have played this role, housing and environmental conditions in low-income settlements have improved considerably.

Professional and academic institutions also have an important role to play. If they have an understanding of the larger issues of the built environment, then they can provide support to those citizens' groups and organizations that constantly lobby in Third World cities against projects that destroy or damage the physical and social environment. Such an understanding will also help professional and academic institutions in taking a stand on such issues. What we need to decide is whether the purpose of an architect is to build a building or cater to the built environment as a whole.

Arif Hasan

An Overview of Architecture Education in the Contemporary Muslim World

Kausar Bashir Ahmad

Islam is more than a faith; it is a complete way of life. Its architecture is the embodiment of the precepts of the faith of the Muslim Ummah (polity of believers) and of the perspectives of its historical ethos in the lands where Islam flourished. The *mimar* in Muslim communities practiced his art in the tradition of the universal man and not merely as a constructor of buildings. His education, relying on the growth of knowledge of matters both mundane and metaphysical, created personages such as Sinan, Omar Khayyam, Ustad Issa, and many others. Educating architects in this tradition on the threshold of the twenty-first century requires reappraisal and a true renaissance.

One question is how the Muslim art and architecture of the post-colonial era should draw on its roots and traditions, and still survive as a discernable and distinctive entity. Another is how architectural education in Muslim communities can find the right meaning, true perspective, and proper personality to fulfill its destined purpose. In this essay I will try to establish the parameters within which architectural education can find the sensibility to deal with the way Muslims live, from Morocco to Indonesia, from Kashgar to Kumasi.

My observations are based on the data collected from more than 26 countries and over 100 schools of architecture in 7 regions comprising Muslim nations mainly in Asia and Africa. The problems to be considered related to the pursuits that form the context for building activity are (1) meaning and truth ordained through faith; (2) regional manifestations in transformation; (3) implications in education and training; and (4) reformation strategies. The basic premise is that the role of the architect in Islamic societies involves more than just building in its most mundane and literal sense. The art of architecture cannot be just another discipline developed from a framework borrowed from the educational models of the developed nations who happen to have attained that status as a consequence of history. Earlier models were logical for Muslim communities until alien influences drove wedges between them. The links with tradition must be restored to achieve continuity in thought.

The present-day models for training architects in Muslim traditions need to have both a symbiotic relationship with the essence of what architecture has been about in its historical context and a global perspective on architecture as a living phenomenon in the world today. Objective study should then result in an entirely distinct framework for the training of architects in Muslim societies as a whole while still retaining regard for their regional differences.

With respect to history, tradition, language, ethnicity, social and cultural imprint and geographical similarities the Muslim world can be divided into two distinct zones: those regions west of Iran (except for Turkey and some African countries), which have the Arabic language in common, and the central, south, and southeast Asian area. There are three sub regions—North Africa, the Middle East (including Turkey and Iran), East and West Africa. In addition, there are several countries outside this regional classification where influence of Islam has been appreciable and the impact of Muslim population is obvious. They are China, the Philippines, Spain, and some of the Balkan states, which remain essentially on the periphery of Islam both geographically and in terms of actual impact.

The dilemma for the so-called developing world, including the Islamic lands, is that in the name of progress they have been compelled to adopt processes and methodologies without regard to their own historical past at the point where each has been awakened from the enforced slumber of the past couple of centuries. The logistics developed at the Beaux-Arts or Bauhaus, the theories ascribed to Corbusier or Kahn, the sweeping movements of post-modernist connotations, and even the humanistic approach of architecture for the masses are all trends that grew out of conditions prevalent in specific times and places. Some of them have been copied blindly out of context and with no relevance to local conditions. It is only with the proper understanding of the ten centuries of intellectual activity and scholarship preceding the fall of these countries into colonial servitude that the rightful and practical approach to the understanding of building as an act of faith can be properly conceived.

In most Muslim nations, architectural education is a public activity under the direct control of the state; occasionally it is autonomous or semi-autonomous. Bureaucratic and state interference by non-professionals and unnecessary procedural restrictions and constraints prevent institutions from developing a distinct identity, a teaching philosophy, or a personality and image of their own.

Higher education generally remains neglected and aimless and this is true of architectural education as well. Events and programs such as the Aga Khan Award, Union of International Architects (UIA), Architects Regional Council for Asia (ARCASIA), SAARC, etc., have contributed to the development of the discipline, but decline in the quality and content of education, which tends to become goal and project oriented, continues. The key factor affecting the quality of education is the system of admission, which needs drastic reform in most cases. Criteria for admission should be strictly enforced through entrance examinations and aptitude tests.

Architectural education in Muslim societies has generally remained influenced by foreign and alien points of view. There has been a total failure to adapt to local culture, socio-economic realities, and even climatic factors in a particular area. Some schools have tried to introduce courses with some relevance to local conditions, but other areas remain neglected. For most schools the starting point and basic reference of architectural design remains the four pioneers of modern architecture, Gropius, Mies, Corbu and Wright. The admission criteria and the manner of teaching have only served to produce elite architects who serve the few; the urban poor and rural masses remain unaffected by their work and training. The emphasis is either on luxury projects and aesthetic-based exercises or on project methodology detached from the virtues and spirit of the traditional habitat and the socioeconomic parameters and realities of today.

The education of future generations of architects has to embody various concepts and movements from foreign countries, but it needs to rediscover the spirit of its own past and historic architecture as well. In the recent past modern architecture has remained entangled in concepts such as utilitarian architecture, functionalism, speculation, and site economy. There is growing interest in one or two areas of historic Muslim architecture reflected through teaching modules and practice, but these are limited mainly to documentation of old buildings and interest in the metaphysical aspects of building plans and craftsmanship. The approach lacks any serious effort to overhaul the curriculum and teaching methodology into an integrated whole. It remains mostly theoretical and under the influence of "modern architecture" through the local breed of academicians trained in the West. Whatever change that is occurring is ironically creeping in again through the foreign-educated local architects who encounter it in many Western schools where interest in finding the roots and relevance of architecture of past cultures and modern sub-cultures is increasing. This can often spark a spirit of inquiry, nostalgia, and even pride in the achievements of the historic past, and some of the younger professionals returning from the West are becoming a sort of nucleus for this thought. Their efforts and endeavors should be supported, for they can launch the formidable task of shaking up the whole system that has remained so long in a state of blissful slumber.

It would be naive to consider architecture in isolation from the fundamental conditions of production, that is, land, finance, and infrastructure. The profession of architecture will be handicapped so long as property rights are not secured and tenure and savings are not guaranteed. The increased investment opportunities in building construction will in turn create more opportunities for architectural practice.

The education of architects should include a multidisciplinary approach suitable for each region and state. In old towns where new building bylaws are applied, traditional and conventional building practices become difficult to follow because the bylaws are based on contemporary practice by planners educated to have little understanding of local building practice and socioeconomic conditions. Traditional introverted building plans with courtyards, multitiered structures with protruding balconies, and buildings on winding streets are forced to give way to straight streets on grids for the convenience of vehicular traffic and the provision of utilities and services. Thus there is a conflict between the provision of necessities and the physical manifestations of traditional buildings.

Selection criteria are deficient in many schools. Selection is primarily grade-based with little emphasis on knowledge of aesthetics, culture, and the humanities, or evidence of sensitivity towards architecture. Younger faculty lack motivation or incentives to change. Schools are largely concentrated in urban centers and do not serve the needs of rural areas or regional interests. There is a tendency to establish private schools to achieve independence from bureaucratic controls and financial constraints. Architects are preoccupied with asserting their professional status vis-a-vis engineering, law, medicine, and other professions. Affiliation with engineering schools limits and restricts their academic freedom.

The curriculum shows little emphasis on practice. Intellectual stimulation through mobilization of external resources and media facilities on the interregional and international level is lacking. Professional organizations are either nonexistent, dormant, or bureaucratic. Definite teaching goals and a clear philosophy of education are lacking. Shortages of funds and resources hinder proper teaching and education and encourage dependence on Western books, journals, reports, and other media. There is little attention to developing original reference tools and research. Studies and activities of NGO's have not been made part of the architectural curriculum.

Architects should be working in less developed parts of the country, not just in urban areas, and schools should be giving attention to helping education in rural areas as well. Government officials should recognize architecture as a profession equal in status to law, medicine, and engineering. The individual architect should be trained as a professional competent to deal with technical and managerial problems as well as the understanding of human needs, behavior, and motivation. Architects should be involved in formulating policies for housing and building.

Architectural schools and professionals ought to be documenting and maintaining the legacies of regions that used to be populated by Muslims, such as Spain and the Philippines. Frequent exchange of faculties and students between regions and schools would be useful. The public should be made aware of the role the architect and the architectural heritage should play. Frequent field trips for serious research should be organized between Muslim countries.

For Muslims struggling to find the proper direction for the teaching and practice of architecture, a series of important questions needs to be answered. Is it really a matter of adhering to the culture and maintaining discipline, or are we in fact in need of a completely new vision? Does the need to serve the masses that has so far remained neglected involve redefining the role of architect? Is it the role of the Union of Architects to generate in their professionals an attitude of social responsibility and professional obligation? How can the Aga Khan Program, the Aga Khan Award, and the Trust for Culture affect the recipients and those around them in their response and their role as catalyst? Does the professional need to assume the role of "bare-foot" practitioner? Do we really need the "de-schooling" of formal education? Should we shun all alien ideologies in an effort to rediscover the spirit of the faith as applied to the physical environment? Is architecture gradually becoming a social science or a liberal art? What, if any, far-reaching changes are in store for Muslims in general, or is the question of transition and transformation of architecture and planning common to all developing countries? Do architects and academicians in the Muslim countries need to respond to problems in ways any different from those in non-Muslim nations?

The aim remains to reformulate architectural education and architectural parameters for Muslims living in specific regions and countries with regard to the precepts and norms of tradition as well as the perspectives of the contemporary Muslim world and its international context.

• • • • • • • • • • • •

Kausar Bashir Ahmad

Comments
Abdul Rehman

The paper is quite comprehensive and gives a fair idea of the state of architectural education in Islamic countries. The following are some additional comments for consideration:

A "future without the past" is a basic idea on which most of the architectural schools in Islamic countries are working. A lot of emphasis is given to Western, Modern, and Post-Modern architecture, but very limited attention is paid to their own heritage.

No serious research work is being carried out and published for students, architects, historians, and concerned professionals. This is due to lack of incentive and the scarcity of funds. A number of manuscripts are lying unnoticed or not explored comprehensively. A multidisciplinary approach in understanding built environments is required.

There is a lack of coordination between schools located within the same cities and countries. The sharing of ideas between schools is important to update curriculums and course readings.

There is a large gap between theory and practice, particularly in Pakistan. The graduates are not well versed in traditional vocabulary and construction techniques. It is important that knowledge of traditional building arts and crafts be acquired from master builders/craftsmen. Seminars and conferences on various aspects of the profession are rarely held. Visual resources and archives are almost non-existent in most schools. History is taught without visual resources or with insufficient material.

Response
The author has opted not to respond to these comments as these comments do not contradict the contents of the essay.

Kausar Bashir Ahmad

Biographies

1. Kausar Bashir Ahmad has studied and worked in Karachi, Ankara, Stuttgart and London (1956-78). He is the dean of Faculty of Architecture and Planning at Dawood College of Engineering and Technology, Karachi. He has helped NGOs and initiatives like Dawood College-Aga Khan Program for Architecture and Urban Design, Karachi Mega City Institute, Architecture and Planning Education Forum and Illumination Society of Pakistan.

2. Mahvash Alemi, born in Iran, is an architect trained in Italy where she lives and works today. She is a scholar of Persian gardens and has taught architectural courses in Iran, Italy and the USA

3. Nader Ardalan is an award winning and critically acclaimed international architect. He is an expert with over 30 years of experience in the case of advanced technology to achieve sustainable, environmentally adaptive and culturally sensitive planning and designs related to various types of public and private projects. He is an author, teacher and was on of the founding members of the steering committee for the Aga Khan Award for Architecture. Currently, he is the senior Vice president of Design for KEO International Consultant with offices in the Middle East and the USA.

4. Mohammad Arkoun is a Professor of History of Islamic Thought at the Sorbonne (Paris III) and visiting professor at universities in the United States, Europe and the Muslim World. He has served as a member of the Aga Khan Award Steering Committee from 1983 to 1992.

5. Rasem Badran received his formal architectural education in Germany and has been a practicing architect in Jordan. He has received numerous awards including the Aga Khan Award for the design of the Grand Mosque of Riyadh and redevelopment of Riyadh Old City Center.

6. Tulus Setyo Budhi is an Indonesian architect and writer.

7. Kamran T. Diba, an architect, planner and Aga Khan Award winner for Shushtar New Town in 1986, was born in Iran. His work represents a synthesis of modernism, traditional Islamic and vernacular architecture. His Shushtar New Town project, a high density, low-rise, low-income housing project is included in the exhibition: "At The End of the Century: One Hundred Years of Architecture", a survey of 20th century architecture curated by the Los Angeles Museum of Contemporary Art. Mr. Diba was founder, architect and director of the Tehran Museum of Contemporary Art, inaugurated in 1977. He now lives and works in southern Spain.

8. Jale Nejdet Erzen is a painter and art historian. She earned her Ph.D. from Istanbul Technical University with a thesis on Mimar Sinan and has written several books on the same subject. She now teaches art and aesthetics at the Middle East Technical University, Faculty of Architecture, in Ankara.

9. Achmad Fanani, is an architect concerned with Islamic issues in Indonesian society.

10. Eugenio Galdieri born in Napoli Italy 1925. Since 1950 he is interested in history of Islamic Architecture. He has carried out conservation work and historical research in the Middle East and Central Asia. More than 100 works published. He received an Aga Khan Award in 1980 for his work in Isfahan.

11. S. Gulzar Haider is Professor and past Director of the School of Architecture at Carleton University, Ottawa, Canada. He is also the designer of four built Islamic centers in the USA and Canada and has written extensively on architecture and culture. He has been a member of the International Commission for Islamic Cultural Heritage based in Istanbul, Turkey.

12. Arif Hasan is a Pakistani architect, planner, social researcher and writer. He has been a consultant to the World Bank, the Asian Development Bank, various United Nations Agencies and the Aga Khan Foundation.

In 1990 the Japanese government awarded him with the Shelterless Memorial Award.

13. Ronald Lewcock has been engaged in urban conservation in the Islamic world for UNESCO since 1978, focusing on the study and protection of old cities including Fez, Cairo, San'a' and other cities in the Yemen, as well as many in the Gulf, together with Samarqand and Bukhara in Central Asia. He was Aga Khan Professor of Islamic Architecture at MIT from 1984 to 1991, and is now professor in doctoral studies at the Georgia Institute of Technology.

14. Ludovico Micara 1942, is an architect based in Rome, Italy. He teaches design at "Gabriele D'Annunzie" University, Faculty of Architecture, Pescara, Italy. He is particularly interested in architectural and urban issues of Islamic countries. At present he is the director of the Italian Mission for the Study of the Architectural Heritage of the Islamic Period in Libya.

15. Adhi Moersid is a prominent Indonesian architect and now a member of the Steering Committee of the Aga Khan Award for Architecture

16. Dr. Suha Özkan (B.Arch. M.Arch. AADipl. Hons. PhD.) is an architect, historian, theorist, and administrator. He was associated with the Middle East Technical University as a professor and associate dean of architecture, and then as vice president of the university, until moving in 1983 to Geneva, where he is now Secretary General of the Aga Khan Award for Architecture.

17. Khalil K. Pirani is a registered architect working for a local firm in Cambridge, MA. He was a Visiting Scholar (1995-97) at the Aga Khan Program for Islamic Architecture, MIT. Recently completed a study on the Mosques in the USA that was funded by the American Institute of Architects.

18. Abdul Rehman is an associate professor at the Department of Architecture, University of Engineering and Technology, Lahore, Pakistan. He holds a Ph.D. from Ion Mincu Institute of Architecture, Bucharest, Romania. Has worked as a consultant for the Lahore Walled City Conservation and Upgrading Project and co-authored, with James L. Wescoat, Jr., the award-winning book, *Pivot of the Punjab: The Historical Geography of Medieval Gujrat* 1993. He is also a Fullbright scholar and a Fellow of Harvard University.

19. Ali Shuaibi (MIT '75) is a partner of Beeah, Riyadh and occasionally teaches architecture. His awards include the Aga Khan Award for Architecture in 1989 for Al-Kindi Plaza project. He was a member of the Aga Khan Award Master Jury 1989-92 cycle and has been a member of the Aga Khan Award Steering Committee 1992-98.

Editors

Attilio Petruccioli, born in 1945, currently is a Professor of Design at the Polytechnic of Bari, Italy. He has been the Aga Khan Professor at MIT until 1998. He has written extensively on the subject of Islamic Architecture and Landscape design such as Dar al Islam, Rome, 1985; Fathepur Sikri, Rome, 1988; and Il Giardino Islamico, Milan, 1994. Since 1984 he is the director of the magazine Environmental Design, Journal of the Islamic Environmental Design Research Center.

Khalil K. Pirani is a registered architect working for a local firm in Cambridge, MA. He was a Visiting Scholar (1995-97) at the Aga Khan Program for Islamic Architecture, MIT. Recently completed a study on the Mosques in the USA that was funded by the American Institute of Architects.

Oleg Grabar, Professor emeritus at the Institute for Advanced Study, Princeton, New Jersey, was the first Aga Khan Professor of Islamic Art and Architecture at Harvard University. His most recent publication is La Peinture Persane, une Introduction, Paris 1999.